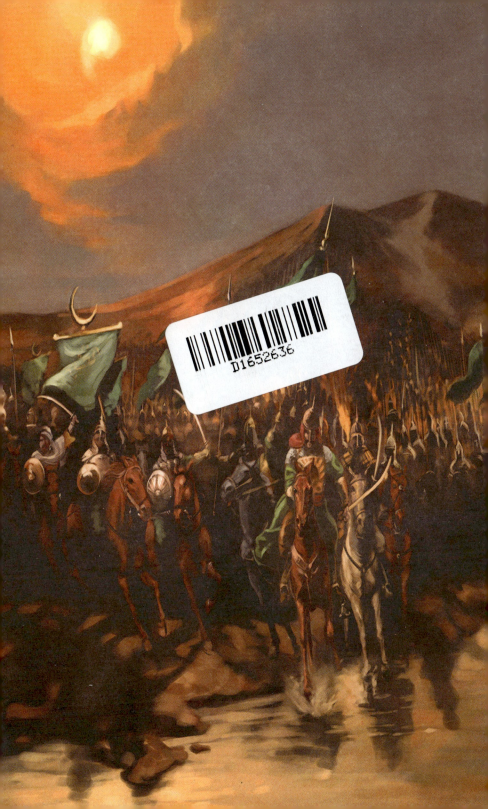

First Raj of the
SIKHS

Other titles by the same author

The Wayside Tree – a novel

The Lives and Teachings of the Sikh Gurus

Love Stories of Punjab

After the Storm – short stories

The Living Saint

The Song of Silence

Nanak

More than Everest

Shaheed Bhagat Singh

Lala Lajpat Rai – The Unsung Hero

First Raj of the SIKHS
The Life and Times of Banda Singh Bahadur

Harish Dhillon

HAY HOUSE INDIA
Australia • Canada • Hong Kong • India
South Africa • United Kingdom • United States

Hay House Publishers (India) Pvt. Ltd.
Muskaan Complex, Plot No.3, B-2 Vasant Kunj, New Delhi-110 070, India
Hay House Inc., PO Box 5100, Carlsbad, CA 92018-5100, USA
Hay House UK, Ltd., Astley House, 33 Notting Hill Gate, London W11 3JQ, UK
Hay House Australia Pty Ltd., 18/36 Ralph St., Alexandria NSW 2015, Australia
Hay House SA (Pty) Ltd., PO Box 990, Witkoppen 2068, South Africa
Hay House Publishing, Ltd., 17/F, One Hysan Ave., Causeway Bay, Hong Kong
Raincoast, 9050 Shaughnessy St., Vancouver, BC V6P 6E5, Canada

Email: contact@hayhouse.co.in
www.hayhouse.co.in

Copyright © Harish Dhillon 2013

Cover artwork: Kanwar Singh Dhillon
Photographs: Malkiat Singh
The Banda Bahadur Coin: Saran Singh
The Shah Alam Bahadur Coin: Jyoti M. Rai

The moral right of the author has been asserted.

The views and opinions expressed in this book are the author's own and the facts are as reported by him, which have been verified to the extent possible, and the publishers are not in any way liable for the same.

All rights reserved. No part of this book may be reproduced by any mechanical, photographic, or electronic process, or in the form of a phonographic recording; nor may it be stored in a retrieval system, transmitted or otherwise be copied for public or private use – other than for 'fair use' as brief quotations embodied in articles and reviews, without prior written permission of the publisher.

This is a completely updated and revised edition of
The Legend of Banda Bahadur, published in 2004.

ISBN 978-93-81431-89-4

Designed and typeset at
Hay House India

Printed and bound at
Thomson Press (India) Ltd., Faridabad, Haryana (India)

To
my granddaughter, Mannat,
who reflects, to a remarkable extent,
Banda Bahadur's indomitable courage and
invincible spirit even when faced with
powerful and ruthless adversaries.

BANDI BIR
(THE VALIANT PRISONER)

by Rabindranath Tagore

The Nobel Laureate Rabindranath Tagore gave a befitting tribute to Banda Singh Bahadur in his much celebrated poem *Bandi Bir* (The Valiant Prisoner) by outlining the heroic Sikh rebellion and resistance of Mughal atrocities. Extracts of the first and last parts of this phenomenal poem (in Bengali, written phonetically here):

Pancha nadir tirey
Beni pakaiya shirey
Dekhite dekhite Gurur mantre
Jagiya uthhechhe Sikh
Nirmam, nirbhik.
Hajar konthe Gurujir Joy
Dhoniya tulechhey dik
Nutan jagiya Sikh
Nutan ushaar Surjer paane
Chahilo nirnimikh ...

Sabha holo nistabdha
Banda'r deho chhinrilo ghaatak
Shanraashi koriya dagdha
Sthir hoye Bir morilo
Na kori ekti katar shabda.
Darshak-jan mudilo nayan
Sabha holo nistabdha.

(An approximate translation)

The Mughals and Sikhs together kicked up
the dust of Delhi thoroughfares;
Who will offer his life first?
There was a rush to settle this;
In the morning hundreds of heroes
offered heads to the executioner,
calling "Glory be to Guruji";

The Kazi put into Banda's lap one of his sons;
Said... must kill him with own hands;
Without hesitation, saying nothing,
slowly Banda pulled the child on his breast;
Then slowly drawing the knife from the belt, looking at the boy's face, whispered
"Glory be to Guruji", in the boy's ears.
The young face beamed;
The court room shook as the boy sang,
"Glory be to Guruji";
Banda then threw the left arm around his neck
and with the right plunged the knife into the boy's breast;
The boy dropped on the ground,
smiling, saying "Glory be to Guruji".
The court was dead silent.
The executioner tore apart Banda's body
with a pair of red-hot tongs;
Standing still the hero died,
not uttering a sound of agony;
The audience closed their eyes;
The court was dead silent.

(*Source*: Wikipedia)

CONTENTS

Introduction 13

Acknowledgements 19

Chapter 1   21
Chapter 2   53
Chapter 3   83
Chapter 4   105
Chapter 5   131
Chapter 6   171
Chapter 7   203
Chapter 8   235
Chapter 9   259

Contents

Epilogue	291
Notes and References	297
Further Readings	299
Glossary	303
Index	309

If Bahadur Shah had not quitted the Deccan, which he did in A.D. *1710, and marched towards Punjab with all his imperial forces, there is every reason to think the whole of Hindustan would have been subdued by these invaders (Sikhs).*

– Lt. Col. M. Malcolm

INTRODUCTION

THE FASCINATING, COLOURFUL AND LARGER THAN LIFE personality of Banda Singh Bahadur has spewed dozens of books – some well-researched, some indifferent. They bring us details of his remarkable career and seek, with varying success to explain his enigmatic persona. Here was a man who had lived life in reverse. He had become an ascetic when he was in his teens and had perforce to return to the material world in his later years; a man who turned from a scholar of Hindu religious and spiritual texts into a great warrior and a remarkably efficient leader. According to Harinder Singh, co-founder of the Sikh Research Institute, Texas: 'His [Banda's] was a life defined by two extreme identities by the age of 38 when he met Guru Gobind Singh…. Before that fateful meeting, his allegiance had been to Vaishnavite and Shavite traditions. He was a natural fighter and hunter and… had studied religious texts, spirituality, and Tantra…. He attempted an ardous and punishing journey of some 2,500 kilometres, with no training, no weapons, no army.... Yet, in 20 months, Banda Singh Bahadur captured Sirhind and established the Khalsa Raj.... His deeds were that of a mortal, legendary accomplishments not rhetorical or magical. He prepared the coming generations of Sikhs for future conflicts: Sikhs warring with Afghans, Persians and the Mughal empire.'

And yet, he remains a distant figure in history. This book seeks to present Banda Singh Bahadur as a flesh-and-blood character, a character, who, it is hoped, will stay with the reader long after he has finished reading the book.

I knew I could not hope to achieve this if I adopted the guise of a historian. My style would be precise, clear and crisp and my depiction of Banda Singh Bahadur would be accurate and historically correct. But there would be no flesh and blood, no life, no passion, no pain. My Banda had to be pictured as a living, breathing man and for this I would have to take on the role of a narrator, telling a story with all the trappings that go with it. Hence, I have used real life incidents while creating others to support the bald statements of the history books. Periods of Banda's life on which the history books are silent or where both legend and accounts have offered what is plainly implausible, I have taken liberties with, for which I offer no apologies.

First and foremost is the nature of Banda's mission. Common perception would have us believe that his mission was to wreak vengeance on those who had been cruel to the family of Gobind Singh, the tenth guru. Like Dr Ganda Singh and Harbans Kaur Sagoo, I too would like to believe that neither the guru nor Banda Singh Bahadur would involve themselves in something as petty as personal revenge. There is also a commonly held belief that the reason for Guru Gobind Singh's visit to Madho

INTRODUCTION

Ram's ashram, on the banks of the Godavari, was that the latter in his arrogance used a magical cot to cause discomfort to many of the holy men who came to visit him. The guru wanted to put the ascetic in his place. However, I find myself subscribing to Dr Hari Ram Gupta's hypothesis that the guru had probably met Madho Ram earlier and learning that he was at Nanded had come to see how he was doing. It is around this hypothesis that I have built the opening scene of my story. In any case the gurus were firm in their rejection of miracles and magic.

Here, I must mention about the battle at Chappar Chiri (see Chapter 4). According to Dr Sukhdial Singh, 'right from the invasions of Mahmud of Ghazni in the eleventh century to the beginning of the eighteenth century, there have been many battles fought throughout Indian history but in all of them the people of India were defeated and their culture sought to be destroyed. Till the battle of Chappar Chiri that is, fought between the Sikhs and the Mughal forces in May 1710, under the leadership of Banda Singh Bahadur. The Mughal forces were defeated and for the first time in Indian history, an indigenous Republic was established on the land of the five rivers.' The date of the battle is given in the *Akhbar-i-Darbar-i-Mualla* as 22 May 1710 (24th Rabi-ul-Awwal, 1122 Hizri). This date is also supported by various historians and researchers of the period including Rattan Singh Bhangu, Sohan Singh and Dr Ganda Singh in the original edition of *Banda Singh Bahadur*; as also William Irvine (see his *The Later Mughals*, wherein he refers to the fragment of a Farrukkhsiyarnama, which supports that the battle was fought in Chappar Chiri). I have used accounts by all these writers as also those of contemporary Muslim writers, like Muhammad Qasim, to create the battle of Chappar Chiri. The end of the battle and the death of Wazir Khan has also been described differently in various accounts.

'Ibratnama'
Mohammad Qasim's Account Of the Battle Of Chapar Chiri In 'Ibratnama'

When the news reached His Highness Wazir Khan, Faujdar of Chakla Sarhind, he rode out with the troops he had with him, to punish this evil rebel force. A great battle occurred twelve kurohs from Sarhind. The young men of the army of Islam, showing exemplary bravery, tasted martyrdom after obtaining repute in the field of valour. Especially was heroism displayed in this battle by Sher Muhammad and Khwaja Ali, Afghans of Kotla Maler, who in this sarkar were masters of a host and commanded trust. After much fighting, they stood firm like the Pole Star within that very circle and surrendered their lives to the Creator. When the chiefs of the army, by the will of God, were sent to their death, Wazir Khan, despite his old age, weakness of hand and foot, and the decline of the strength of the body, strove to shoot arrows and encourage his companions. But once the boat of hope is destroyed by an accident, it cannot thereafter be set to sail by the strength of any of the professional captains of the world of stratagem. At last, the wicked Infidels extended their victorious hand for the plunder of the (Mughal) army and (the seizure) of the commander's elephant. Treating the corpse of that martyred Saiyid (Wazir Khan) with every visible indignity they could devise, they had it suspended from a tree.

With such malevolence, they marched on the city of Sarhind. When the news of this calamity reached the city, all alertness and action deserted the luckless officials and the helpless citizens (*ri'aya*). Wazir Khan's own eldest son did not bother about (his father's) treasure and hoard, but, taking the young and old of his household with him, took the road to Shahjahanabad (Delhi). Everyone who within that short time abandoned goods and property and took to exile, with every humiliation and dishonour, at least saved his own life. Anyone who got involved in thoughts of gathering his goods, or searching for mounts for carriages), or (other) various designs, fell prisoners at the cruel hands of those wicked Infidels. Troop after troop of unfeeling sweepers surrounded the city, in the manner of a thorn-bush enclosing a flower garden and laid their insolent hands on people's possessions and proceeded to dishonour both the small and the big.

They specially plundered the goods and houses of Suchadanand (Sucha Nand), Chief Clerk (*Peshkar*) of the late Wazir Khan. You may say, he had gathered and set up these for this day, so that the flower-garden may become the ground for the growth of thorn bushes and Paradise turn into the nursing ground of the vile crow! Praise be to God, in the court of the Divine Avenger, a helpless ant can be the cause of the death of the man-killing snake, and an impotent and powerless gnat can bring about the destruction of a bloodthirsty elephant. What has been heard from trustworthy persons of that area is that this unjust, noxious raw man in the time of government of the martyred Wazir Khan had withheld no cruelties from being inflicted on the poor and had laid every seed of tumult for his own advantage; so he reaped the fruit of it all. Otherwise, persons who were guarded by God's protection, scorned their own large treasures and fled with their honour intact. Some, by changing their clothing, remained concealed in that city and stayed safe from the oppressive hand of that tyrannical crew. The harm that came to persons and places and honour and dignity, without precedent, a feeling of sadness and civility does no permit one to record; it is well known to contemporaries and eyewitnesses. In short, that flood, which overthrew the foundations of the honour of a whole world, left nothing undone in destroying that city and the inhabited places of that neighbourhood. So far as possible, they did not let anyone else retain arms, horses, other goods and chattel of chiefship. They called upon most people to adopt their own disreputable faith; some willingly, and others under compulsion, obeyed. A Jat called Baz Singh, one of the wretches from pargana Haibatpur, belonging to the suba of the Panjab, had the accursed turban-tail of pseudo-chiefship tied on his head to assume the subadari of Sarhind, appoint officers over the parganas, and carry out destructive activities. He waited for the coming of warriors from the void".

Source: *Nishaan*, Issue II/2010, p. 14

INTRODUCTION

For example, the one by Rattan Singh Bhangu says:

At the climax, Banda Singh Bahadur, flanked by Baj Singh and Fateh Singh came in front of Wazir Khan and on seeing him, 'He roared like a lion and sprang upon him like a bolt from the blue.'
'O sinner, thou are the enemy of Guru Gobind Singh, thou has shown Him no respect, but on the contrary hast put to death His innocent children, and thereby committed grievous and unpardonable crime, the punishment for which I am now going to deal thee. Thine army and the country shall be destroyed at my hands.' Banda Singh Bahadur then struck off his head with one blow of the sword.... Khafi Khan writes that not 'a man of the army of Islam escaped with more than his life and the clothes that he stood in. Horsemen and footmen fell under the swords of the infidels (Sikhs), who pursued them as far as Sirhind.' In the words of William Irvine, 'The baggage was plundered, the elephants captured and the body of Wazir Khan dishonoured and hung from a tree.' This jihad tree remains standing in the grounds of the Guru Nanak Public School adjacent to the fields of battle.

However, my research shows that it was Fateh Singh who killed Wazir Khan and I have stuck to that.
The other departures from history are of a minor nature. For example, I have built the character of Sushil Kaur, Banda's first wife and the details of the period of their lives on the banks of the Chenab, as I firmly believe that she was an important influence in his life. Also, there is no evidence in history to support the fact that Bulleh Shah and Banda Singh Bahadur ever met. I admire the two personalities immensely and when, during the course

of my reading, I found that they were contemporaries, and were in close geographical proximity at that time, the temptation to bring them together was too strong for me to resist. All that I can offer by way of justification is that what transpires at their two meetings serves to illustrate essential features of Banda's character and personality, features that, history tells us, he had in ample measure. If such creations seem flawed, I must live with my failure.

– H. D.

Acknowledgements

I would like to express my deepest gratitude to the entire team of Hay House Publishers India for having had the faith and the strength to take up this project. My heartfelt thanks are also due to Ashok Chopra who took upon himself the task of editing this work and has done such a commendable job with it that when I read the edited draft, I couldn't believe that this taut, engrossing narrative was my work. I would also like to convey my immense gratitude to Jyoti Rai (a writer and a renowned numismatist and specialist on coins of the Sikh era) and Pushpinder Singh Chopra (publisher and editor of *Nishaan*).

I owe a debt of gratitude to both Kanwar Singh Dhillon for readily providing me with the artwork for the cover from his famous painting on Banda Singh Bahadur and Malkiat Singh for placing at my disposal his entire collection of photographs for me to choose from. Their valuable inputs have greatly enhanced the book in many ways.

My thanks to Bhim Inder for having, at such great trouble, got me all the source material, to Hema who so patiently typed her way through a manuscript which even I found difficult to decipher. And, finally, to all those who have done such wonderful work on Banda Singh Bahadur before me, especially Dr Ganda Singh and Harbans Kaur Sagoo. Their work not only helped me with my research but also motivated me to try to come up to their high standards in this work.

Chapter One

The baptism ceremony was a simple one. Sugar crystals were added to water in an iron cauldron and the water was stirred with a sword to the reciting of prayers till the sugar dissolved. The guru gave this amrit, nectar, to Madho Das to drink. 'I give you the name of Gurbaksh Singh. It is an apt name because you are indeed, for me, a bakshish, a reward from God. But in my heart I will always think of you with the name that you gave yourself, Banda. May you always be my Banda Singh Bahadur.'

1683

IT WAS A CLEAR CRISP MORNING WITH THE CRISPNESS THAT comes as the first indication of approaching winter. At this early hour as Lachman Dev strode across the open fields towards the forest, he felt the morning chill and hugged himself close against it. He walked gingerly, one cautious footstep at a time, along the narrow embankment, which served both to carry the irrigation channel and to mark the extent of possession. Once the rhythm had been established he was freed from the need to look down at the ground. He lifted his eyes to the approaching forest and what he saw took his breath away and made him stop in his tracks. It was as if some artist had taken a large canvas and divided it into four horizontal sections. The lowermost band had been filled with broad strokes of gold, the gold of the ripening corn. The section above it was a dark swath, the dark of close growing trunks of trees. The third band was the widest and was filled with myriad shades of green and highlighting them were masses of yellow, brown and hectic red. The topmost band was a crystalline blue, flecked here and there with tufts of pure white, cotton wool clouds. For a moment the boy forgot the cold, forgot the purpose for which he was striding towards the forest and stood their marvelling at this tremendous, awe-inspiring beauty. A sudden gust of wind shook the foliage of the treetops and blew across the fields to where he stood, making him shiver with the cold. He was pulled back to the present and resumed his walk towards the trees.

Lachman Dev had come from Buttana, a three-day journey from Haripur, to attend his uncle's funeral. By the time they reached the cremation was over and there was the endless round of tedious rituals and prayers. His relatives, after the first perfunctory greetings, had turned to perform their roles in the ceremonies and his parents too had become deeply involved. The other village boys treated him with the disdain that the young reserve for strangers and carefully and assiduously excluded him from all their games. Lachman did not mind. He was a solitary child by nature, who normally liked being by himself. Even at home, in Buttana, he was close, if it could be called closeness, only to his cousin Mulk Raj. He was content to pursue one of his favourite pastimes, hunting birds and small animals. He had been introduced to the sport two years ago by his cousin and found that he had an intuitive aptitude for it. At first he hunted with the sling and shots but soon graduated to a homemade bow and arrows and earned the respect and admiration of his peers by his skill as a marksman, though his targets were limited to rabbits and squirrels and birds of all kinds. He had reached the point where he was getting a little impatient with his achievements and wished to graduate to bigger game. But for this he needed a more sophisticated bow and training under a teacher more adept than his cousin.

He was new to Haripur and not familiar with the terrain but recognized a fairly well-trodden path winding through the trees, and followed it till he came to a little clearing in the forest. The clearing was smothered in thick, lush grass and myriads of delicate wildflowers in soft pastel colours. The early morning dew beaded the grass and the sunlight fractured the dewdrops into sparkling diamonds so that each blade became the exquisite creation of a master jeweller. Lachman stood, marvelling the beauty of the scene, the irony that the very sun that created this beauty would, in a short time, destroy it. Then a small, tentative movement at the further edge of the clearing caught his eye and he froze where he stood. It was a rabbit. Cautiously, one quick movement at a time, it stepped into the sun-kissed patch of green, followed by three smaller rabbits. The mother rabbit had begun to feed on the tender leaves of a small shrub while the younger rabbits too sniffed and nibbled at the grass.

With a quiet but sweeping movement, Lachman drew his bow from his shoulder and placed an arrow in it. He took careful aim at the dead centre of the rabbit's sleek, well-fed body. As he drew the string he had the uncanny feeling of being watched. He hesitated, then realized he could not afford to wait. He pushed the feeling out of his mind, concentrated on his target once again, steadied his aim and released his arrow. The arrow sang through the air. The rabbit heard it too and stopped in her nibbling. But before she could decide to run, the arrow had found its mark. The baby rabbits fled back into the safety of the forest.

Lachman hurried forward into the clearing to claim his prize. Through the trees to the left emerged a handsome young man with firm, purposeful strides. He was not very tall but something about him made him appear to tower above the two men who had now stepped out from among the trees behind him. He was young, very young, not more than seventeen or eighteen years old, yet he had about him the air of authority that would usually be carried by a much older man. He had a strong, well-built body and this strength showed itself even through his loose-fitting clothes. But it was the sinewy, agile strength of an athlete, not the stocky, stolid strength of a wrestler. Something about the youth compelled attention but it was only years later that Lachman would understand what it was. It was the strange paradox that existed between the youth's body and his face. His body, in its long flowing robes, carried with it an aura of regal distinction, the distinction of a prince leading his army into battle, exuding pride and confidence from every pore of his being. The face, on the other hand, had in it the austerity of an ascetic and the radiance that comes with the long pursuit of spiritual attainment. He smiled as he came within speaking distance of the boy: 'That was a beautiful shot, my friend,' the voice was gentle, almost caressing in its kindness. 'The aim was true and sure. Tell me, how came you to be so perfect a marksman? Who has been your teacher?'

Lachman felt his face flush with embarrassment at such fulsome praise. 'I have been my own teacher,' he said, lowering his eyes to the ground at his feet. 'I learnt from a story that my mother told me – the story of the test that the great Guru Dronacharya imposed upon all his disciples. He asked of each what he saw while taking aim at a bird. One said he saw the foliage of the trees and in the foliage, the bird. Another said he saw the bird. Arjun alone said he saw the bird's eye, only the eye and nothing else.'

'It is a lesson worth learning by all who seek to wield a bow and you have learnt it well. You do not come from Haripur?'

'No. I do not come from Haripur. I live in Buttana, near Sadhaura though I am a Dogra from Rajauri in Jammu. My grandfather, my mother's father, had no sons. I am the son of his eldest daughter. So he wished that his land should come to me. Shortly before his death we moved to Buttana to claim my inheritance.'

'And are you happy in your new home?' the stranger asked.

'Happy enough,' Lachman answered. But there was reservation in his voice and he looked away as he spoke. The stranger said nothing and Lachman was forced to explain: 'I have friends, many friends, and am loved and admired by them. Yet I find myself at odds with them and with their interests. They all seem to be obsessed by trivial things, and when they quarrel it is over such petty matters that I am both amused and irritated. I join in all their games and excel at them, but they seem such childish games. Everything about my life seems unreal, like a dream. I am a part of it, yet not a part of it. When we fly kites I often feel that I am no longer on the ground, holding my string and guiding my kite, higher and ever higher. It is as if I am floating above like a cloud, looking down over the thousands of colourful kites, at the boys who are flying them, and wondering how they can find such great pleasure in so childish a pastime.' He paused, afraid that he had said too much, afraid that the stranger would not understand. But when he looked again into the young man's eyes, he saw a gentle smile of understanding and tolerance.

'But you do find pleasure in hunting.' It was a statement, not a question.

'Yes,' replied Lachman. 'I find pleasure in hunting. Great pleasure in pitting my wits and my intelligence against an adversary who is more intelligent than I, and in overcoming it.'

'Then you deserve a better bow than the one you have.' He glanced at one of his companions, who smiled, unslung his own bow and handed it over to Lachman, who ran his fingers along it. It was so different from his own. It was made of wood and horn glued together in layers, and reinforced with bands of sinew.

'It is different from your bow,' the stranger said, as if sensing Lachman's thoughts. 'It is more strong and flexible. It is also much longer than your bow and is affected more by the diferring conditions of temperature and humidity. So to protect it you must leave it unstrung when it is not in use. You cannot be as quick with this as you were with your bow. Yet, you will get with this the maximum killing power at medium range. You will now be able to hunt the fastest deer and the strongest cats. You will have to work hard not only to build up the physical strength to get this bow to obey your commands but also to develop the skill that will enable you to use it effectively. You will need to find a competent teacher.' He paused, then asked:

'What is your name?'

'Lachman Dev.'

'And your father's name?'

'Ram Dev.'

'Ask him to bring you to Anandpur before you return to Buttana. There is much for you to see there and I would like it much if we were to meet again. Now I must go for I have pressing matters to attend to and you have been so long from home that your parents must be anxious for you.'

Lachman slung both the bows over his shoulder, retrieved the dead rabbit and ran back home. The guru turned to his companions: 'This boy will go far,' he said. 'Even at so young an age he is remarkably focused. There is a restlessness of the soul, a desire to embark upon a special journey, and this desire will lead him to higher planes of being and of achievement. Men such as he are born to be leaders. Mark my words, in the years to come, we will hear much of our young friend.'

1685

It was a late monsoon that year, but that particular day was a gift from the gods. The sky was overcast with thick dark clouds.

Occasionally a soft breeze stirred and brought a balmy comfort to Lachman's restless soul for he longed to escape from Buttana. His continued presence at home was becoming irksome to his father. Ram Dev was disappointed that his son had dropped out of the small village school run by Pundit Dev Dutt. 'It is not that the boy is not bright,' he had overheard the pundit complaining to his father. 'His is a mind that is more alert than the minds of all my other pupils put together. But he just won't work and now he has given up coming to school altogether.'

Lachman on his part, tried to make up to his father by showing a willingness to work with him in the fields and in doing odd jobs for all his relatives and his father's friends. But even here, Ram Dev saw, in spite of the ungrudging work, a lack of interest, a sense of detachment, as if he were holding himself back. There seemed to be a singular lack of ambition. However, Lachman did, of course, continue his athletic pursuits. In spite of his wiry frame, he won many a wrestling bout at the numerous village fairs held in the area and his fame as a marksman with the bow and arrow had spread far and wide.

On this lovely monsoon day, Lachman remembered the encounter in the forest near Haripur and how on his return to Buttana he had looked around for a suitable teacher. He did not have far to seek for in the village of Amuwal, close to the fort of Mukhlispur, lived one Salim Khan. He had been a naib in the Mughal detachment in Sadhaura and had recently returned to lead a life of retirement in his native village. Within a few months of his return, stories of his great prowess as a shikari, hunter, began to circulate in the villages around Mukhlispur and at the village fairs people would turn to look at him with awe and respect and point him out and say: 'There is Salim Khan, the shikari.'

Salim Khan was amused that anyone would want to take

on the learning of hunting in such a dedicated and exclusive manner. But seeing the boy's keenness and single-mindedness of purpose, he accepted the unfamiliar role of a teacher of shikar. The middle-aged soldier and the young boy scoured the hills and forests around Mukhlispur for game and Lachman came to know each ravine, each fold of the mountains, like the back of his hand.

Salim Khan taught him not only the skills of stalking and shooting his bow but also the importance of regular exercise so that his body would retain its flexibility and its ability for swift motion. He taught him how to build up the muscles of his arms and his shoulders so that he had the power to handle the wondrous bow the way it deserved to be handled. When there was nothing more that he could teach him, he bade the lad goodbye and Lachman went his way. He had been a good pupil and it was only a short time before he had earned fame as a shikari in his own right.

On this balmy monsoon morning, Lachman and his cousin moved through the forest with carefully practised stealth. At last, they came to the edge of the tree cover and carefully scanned the stretch of waist-high elephant grass, which covered the gentle slope. Off to the left they saw a herd of at least a hundred cheetals whose spotted coats of reddish-brown made for excellent camouflage. A group of three cheetals grazed some distance away from the main herd, which the boys identified as their possible targets. They moved backwards carefully, one step at a time, till they were sure the breeze would not take their scent to the animals below or their movement arouse any suspicion. There were two males and one female. They all stood about three feet tall at the shoulders and both the males had magnificent branching three-tiered antlers about thirty inches long. The white of their under-bellies shone sleek and glossy.

They were so beautiful, all three of them, that Lachman felt the desire to reach out and caress their coats.

The two youngsters looked at each other and smiled. By tacit consent they had established that the female was to be their target. Lachman put an arrow to his bow, raised it high with his left arm outstretched, then lowered the bow slowly till the arrow was at eye level. Taking careful aim, he drew the string, took a deep breath and released his arrow. It flew through the air and hit its mark. The other deer took off with the speed of lightning while Lachman looked after them, admiring their long, graceful strides. Then he turned his attention to his prey. The deer stumbled a few ungainly steps and fell. She made a brave effort to get to her feet again but without success. The boys hurried to the stricken deer, all need for stealth now behind them. The deer looked directly into the eyes of her assailant. They were soft, gentle eyes and as Lachman looked into them he saw the fear and the dread and finally the sad acceptance of her inevitable death. His heart went out to the dying animal and he wished he could call back his arrow.

The deer's breath came in quick short gasps and Lachman knew that she was in extreme pain. He drew his dagger from its sheath on his belt and in one quick movement put an end to her agony. The boys sat side by side in silence for a while, the excitement of the chase now stilled. Then they got to their feet and went efficiently to work. There was no point in carrying the complete carcass back to the village so they decided to carve it up and salvage the skin and all edible parts of the body. Lachman ripped open the belly and one after the other, in quick succession, two full-grown foetuses fell to the ground. He was overcome with the enormity of what he had done and turned away in disgust. The feeling of revulsion was so strong that he had to bend over and vomit before he could find any relief. He turned his back towards Mulk Raj, the pain and sorrow searing through his body like flashes of burning flame. Mulk Raj sensed his cousin's pain but he did not try to reach out and offer any comfort. It was a private hell and Lachman would have to work his own way out of it.

Moments later, Lachman picked up his arrows and snapped them across his knee, one by one. He tried to snap his bow but it was too heavy and too strong. He ran up the hill, Mulk Raj running at his heels, suddenly afraid of what Lachman might do. But he need not have been for Lachman reached the top of the hill, waited for a few moments to catch his breath, then looked down into the deep, cliff-faced gorge below him, flung his arm as far back as it would go and hurled the bow down with all the strength that he could muster. They heard the bow break against a cliff.

Over the next few days Lachman rarely spoke to anyone and when he did it was in monosyllables. The parents tried to get him to talk, to tell them what was on his mind, but the answer to all their queries was a shake of the head and silence. He did not eat much, seeing which his family grew alarmed. His mother began to despair and on a friend's advice decided to take him to see a famous vaid, village physician, who lived ten miles (one mile is approximately 1.6 kilometres) away. They reached late in the evening; the vaid had finished seeing his patients. But seeing the mother's obvious distress, he abandoned his evening meal and came to attend to the boy. He took Lachman into a private room, measured his pulse and examined the colour of his eyes and his tongue. He asked a few questions and returned to the mother: 'There is nothing wrong with your son's body. It is obviously a sickness of the mind. He is not ready to tell me what is troubling him and till he speaks there is nothing that anyone can do to help him. Perhaps, you should take him to Swami Janki Prasad. He is a famous bairagi, ascetic, and is reputed to have the ability to look right into people's minds. He is at the moment camping in the forest about four miles from here. Who knows, he may be able to help your son.'

Early the next morning, escorted by a guide provided by the vaid, mother and son set out for the swami's camp. It was a makeshift camp set up in a clearing in the forest with no trappings of any kind and the swami himself was a simple, middle-aged man, with a lean body and an ascetic face. He wore his hair long. His white-flecked beard came down to his chest. He greeted them with courtesy and waited for the mother to tell him her problem. When she was done he turned to the boy, put his hand gently on the boy's head and looked into his eyes. Lachman looked back and saw softness, gentleness and compassion in those eyes.

'Your brow is troubled and your eyes swollen and I can see that you have had little sleep these last few days. Perhaps it were best for you to rest awhile before we try to deal with your problem.' He unrolled a reed palette and Lachman lay down upon it. The swami sat beside him and with his right hand caressed the boy's forehead gently, from the eyebrows up toward the hairline.

'Sleep, you must sleep,' the swami repeated two or three times, his words sounding soft and gentle with the cadence of a lullaby and then softly fading away. The mother saw that her son had at last gone to sleep with the lines of tension and pain ease from his face. Then the swami stopped, letting his hand rest on Lachman's head: 'You are asleep now and you are dreaming. What do you see in your dream?'

'I see the eyes of a deer, large, timid and afraid.'

'Why is she afraid?'

'Because I have shot her with an arrow and she knows that

she is going to die.' For some time the swami sat in silence and his hand resumed the caressing of the sleeping boy's hair. Then he stopped all movement again and asked, his voice still gentle and kind: 'What else do you see?'

'I see that the deer's stomach has been cut open. I see two full-grown foetuses lying on the ground beside her.' His voice had become agitated now.

'Hush. It's only a dream and the dream has passed. You will wake now.'

Lachman opened his eyes and looked straight into the swami's smiling face, got up and went and sat beside his mother. One of the swami's disciples put plates of food in front of them. Lachman had no desire to eat, yet he did not want to appear rude. He broke off a morsel of bread and put it in his mouth and soon found himself reaching for another morsel. His mother looked at him and smiled. Later, the swami took the boy aside and came back to the subject of his dreams. Something in the swami's eyes as he spoke of the dead deer tugged at Lachman's heart and the words flowed out: 'I have been haunted ever since by what I have done. For days I have seen, again and again in my mind, those eyes, large and limpid, looking at me with all the pain and all the sorrow of the world. I see again and again the two foetuses throbbing. The image haunts my every waking moment and I do not dare to sleep because I know it will haunt my dreams with greater horror. Those eyes unman me, leave me incapable of all other thought or emotion, and make me incapable of any action. The world has become a dreary place and my life a futile, barren existence. I feel a stranger to all that was once familiar to me – my home, my parents, my friends. I wish more than anything to be on my own, to break the old ties and bonds and drift away to seek my redemption.' He fell silent, frightened by the strong flow of words, frightened at having revealed the very depths of his soul.

'Perhaps you should go away. We leave for Kashmir in three days to undertake the holy pilgrimage to the shrine of Amar Nath. You could follow your heart's desire and leave your world and come away with us. You can go home and return in time for the departure.'

'I will stay with you now and leave with you when you leave.'

'You do not wish to take leave of your father and your loved ones?'

'I have taken leave of them in my heart already. A formal leave-taking holds no point. I am as ready to renounce the world now as I will ever be.'

1708

Swami Madho Das had come a long way from the young boy who had recoiled at the sight of the doe he had killed. It had taken him twenty-three years to reach this far and he had pushed himself to the limit on every step of the way.

After the brief but moving initiation ceremony in the clearing of the forest, he had accompanied Swami Janki Prasad on his pilgrimage to the holy places in Kashmir. For days they had travelled long distances and covered difficult terrain, and on each of these days he had pondered over the extreme step he had taken and each day had convinced him, if convincing were needed, that he had taken the right step. After the initiation ceremony he had been given a new name, Madho Das, and with this new name he had assumed a new identity. Lachman

Dev was gone forever. His mind rarely, if ever, went back to his village or to his parents, and if ever it did, it was to think of them with the calm detachment of a stranger who had passed by them on his way. He studied all the sacred texts so thoroughly that he knew them by heart. He could quote extensively and cite passages to illustrate any point he made or to serve as an example or parallel to any incident in life. This deep knowledge of the holy books earned him the reputation of being a learned man and other holy men, much older than he, turned to him for help when they needed the authority of the scriptures to support them. Yet one memory did come back, sometimes, to haunt him. It was the memory of that young man in the forest near Haripur and he would wonder where that stranger was now.

He had taken, like all bairagis, the vows of celibacy and of poverty, his life was simple and uncluttered and he was free to pursue his studies with complete dedication and to learn all that was to be learnt from his guru, Janki Prasad. He learnt the art of hypnosis and the skill of mental telepathy and worked them to such perfection that he had only to look into a face to be able to read the mind. People regarded this ability as miraculous and credited him with magical powers. He learnt the power of silence. In arguments with other sages he would hold his peace. This strong, calm silence would provoke the other party to betray the weakness of anger and Madho Das would emerge the stronger from all such debates.

From Kashmir they travelled south and camped in the thick forest near Nasik. Madho Das continued to spend long hours in meditation and exercised such abstinence and self-control that he developed almost supernatural inner powers. The great Swami Amarnath initiated him into the most esoteric yogic practices. The young fifteen-year-old boy, who had been so full of self-loathing and self-revulsion that he had renounced the world, had through his long years of meditation and study, become a sage whom people looked upon with reverence. When the swami said that he had nothing more to teach him, Madho Das had broken away and set up his own ashram in Panchvati, near Nanded. Over the years his ashram had become a place of pilgrimage. Thousands of people came to seek his blessings. They were sure that with his miraculous powers he could grant them their heart's desires: a child for the childless, a son for those who had only daughters, a suitable husband for a daughter or merely worldly success and riches. It was natural that some of those who visited the ashram would be granted their wishes. These fortunate few gave the credit for their boons to Madho Das. They spread the word of the swami's powers far and wide and returned to the ashram bearing rich and expensive gifts. It seemed that Madho Das who had willingly shunned all the trappings of worldly existence, was now, at the height of his spiritual power, in danger of being tangled in the material web again.

But, he remained, as ever, impatient with his fame and with the adulation and reverence that was showered upon him. All he could feel was a deep weariness. It was weariness not of the body but of the spirit. It was weariness born out of his inability to deal with the restlessness that had been growing within him. Increasingly he was convinced that after years this was still not the destination of his life.

One day, on his way back to his ashram, as the boat skimmed gently over the placid waters and touched the landing, Madho Das jumped on to the stone steps with an agility that belied his thirty-eight years and bounded up to the platform where he conducted the morning prayers. At one corner of the platform was a little stone shrine of Lord Krishna. He had built the shrine himself, stone by stone, and whenever he left or returned to his ashram he always stopped there to pay obeisance to his Lord. Nitya Nand, one of his most favoured and learned disciples, stood near the shrine and with him were two young acolytes bearing torches, waiting to light his way home through the gathering darkness. A simple earthenware oil lamp had been placed in front of the deity to facilitate Madho Das's prayers and, as he stood there looking at his God, a wind stirred and the flame flared and in this dancing light the eyes of the deity also leapt and danced. Madho Das wondered what secret trick the God of mischief intended to play upon him.

His prayers over, Madho Das turned to Nitya Nand: 'Come, let us be on our way and while we walk you can tell me what it is that troubles your mind.' He put his hand on his disciple's shoulder and with the torchbearers beside them they took the path to the ashram. As they walked the disciple spoke: 'We have a visitor at the ashram. He came this morning with a large group of followers, asking for you. When we said that you were away he said that he would wait. His followers address him as "guruji" and from the radiance of his face he does, indeed, seem to possess great spiritual powers. And yet his followers have slaughtered two goats in a corner of the courtyard and even now the meat is being cooked for the evening meal.'

Madho Das stopped dead in his tracks. He was a staunch Vaishnavite, a vegetarian with great respect for all animal life. He felt pain at the killing of those poor animals and anger that it should have been done in his ashram. But in a moment he gained control over these negative emotions and resumed his walk, saying nothing. Nitya Nand felt constrained to continue: 'He is much like you, swamiji, he is the same height and the same build. But he wears a turban on his head and his followers call themselves Sikhs.'

That name rang a bell. He had heard of them, heard that the

Sikhs were a religious sect with their own guru. But being so far away from the Punjab, the stories that had come his way of their activities had at best been sketchy and occasional. He could not recall any details. When he came into the guru's presence, he realized that there was something familiar about him, that he had seen him before but could not recall where and when. He greeted the guru by touching his feet: 'You are more than welcome to this humble dwelling.'

'It is kind of you to make me welcome,' the guru said. 'But I sense reservation in your eyes and your tone just as I sensed reservation in the manner of your disciples. What is it about my coming that does not meet with your approval? Be honest with me, for I respect honesty.'

Madho Das took a deep breath before he spoke: 'You are a guru and I am but a humble ascetic. Far be it from me to say anything that would amount to a criticism of you, especially now that you are my guest. But you have asked me to be honest and your asking is my command. For me all life, whether human or of other species of animals, is sacred. As a Vaishnavite, the killing of any animal is a sin. The killing of an animal in this ashram profanes it. Blood has been shed in this courtyard which has sullied the sanctity of this place.'

'I seek forgiveness both for my men and for myself and because it is within your power and your nature to forgive me for my sin, I know that you will forgive me.' The guru placed his hand upon Madho Das's shoulder as he spoke: 'I respect you for the concern that you have for all forms of life and I can feel the pain that you feel at the killing of these goats. But tell me, do you feel no pain at the killing of thousands and thousands of people who have been victims of Mughal tyranny through all these long years? You will perform certain rites for the killing of these animals, sprinkle the holy waters of the River Ganga and wash away the stains of blood and with this sprinkling you will atone for the sin that I have committed. You will say prayers, asking your God to dull your pain and in due course the sanctity of your ashram will be restored and your soul will be once again at peace with the world and with itself. Tell me, Madho Das, what waters have you sprinkled to wash away the blood that stains this vast land of ours, the blood of these thousands and thousands of helpless men and women who are being butchered so mercilessly? What rites have you performed to restore the sanctity of our country and what prayers have you recited to seek deliverance from the pain of these countless individuals?'

Madho Das was silent and after a long pause the guru spoke again: 'Speak to me, Madho Das. I am told that you are a man of great wisdom, a man of many words. Tell me how you have come to terms with this pain and perhaps I too can learn a lesson from you and come to live with the ache in my heart.'

The silence stretched on. At last when it seemed that there would never again be any words, the swami's voice stole into the silence, soft and quiet and confused: 'I am a bairagi, guruji, I have renounced the world. I have cut myself off from all men and I am no longer a part of their pain and suffering.'

'And yet they come to you with their problems. All this day, while we have waited for your return, there have been dozens, hundreds, waiting for your help and for your blessings. They believe that you can make a difference to their lives. In the face of this belief, can you truly say that you have cut yourself off from other human beings and that you cannot feel the pain and the sorrow of those around you?'

The swami pondered over the guru's words and as he pondered the veil lifted from his mind and he saw at last the truth of his own position. Isolated, though he was, he had heard stories of the brutality and the repression being practiced day after day. He had occasionally come face-to-face with victims of this tyranny and tried to offer them solace and the comfort of prayers. But he had deliberately shut his mind to it all, unwilling to let it disturb the equanimity of his existence. He looked up into the guru's eyes but could not find the words to say what he wanted to. The guru saw that look and smiled: 'There is no need for you to speak, for I have seen my answer in your eyes.' He smiled again and at last Madho Das knew where he had seen the guru before. He was the stranger whom he had met in the forest at Haripur. 'Why have you come to me? After all these years, why have you come to me?'

'I have come to you because I need you.' Once again the guru smiled and Madho Das felt, as he had felt at that moment long ago, the presence of someone strong and pure. At last the restlessness passed from him and he found the deep, still centre of his being. He fell at the guru's feet. 'I am your Banda, your bondsman, waiting for your command.'

The guru lifted him up, put his arm around him and said: 'Rise, Banda. Your place is at my side, not at my feet. Your rightful place bairagi, is not here in the ashram, but at the head of a band of men fighting this oppression and cruelty that has come to blight all our lives. Come with me and I will tell you what you must do.'

Madho Das left his ashram. His flock of disciples and the hordes of pilgrims who flocked to him, too followed the guru. In the days that followed Madho Das was one among the crowd of followers. He listened to the guru as he addressed the Sangat, the congregation and he listened to his followers as they spoke to each other. Every day he learnt something new about the guru's life, his personality and, gradually, the inner peace that he had found on that first day, strengthened itself and replaced completely the earlier restlessness. He knew that the guru had given him a purpose in life and would now show him the path that he must take to achieve the purpose. He also learnt about the lives and teachings of the earlier nine gurus.

It was during this period that he first heard of Bulleh Shah, the poet mystic, who through his poetry, sought not only to show people the right path in life, but also attempted to effect social reform. He listened to the singing of one of his kafis (a verse form used in Punjabi and other poetry) and found in it a mirror image of his own current state of mind and emotion:

> My fasts, my pilgrimages, my prayers, O mother,
> My Beloved has made me forget them all!
>
> As soon as I realized the Beloved,
> My logic, my grammar were all forgotten!
> Such was the unstuck melody that He played!
> My fasts, my pilgrimages, my prayers, O mother,
> My Beloved has made me forget them all!
>
> When my Beloved came to my house,
> I forgot all expositions, all erudition!
> In every object is He now seen,
> His splendour is visible within and without:
> And the deluded people know it not!
> My fasts, my pilgrimages, my prayers, O mother,
> My Beloved has made me forget them all![1]

What Mir Bulleh Shah Qadiri Shatari, had attained through his contact with his murshid or master, Inayat Shah Qadiri, Banda attained through his contact with his guru, Guru Gobind Singh. Like Bulleh Shah, Banda had experienced a radical change. No longer did he feel the need to perform rituals and fasts or go on pilgrimages. Nor was he interested in logic, learning and scholarship any more. His master had enabled him to see the Lord pervade everywhere, to realize Him within himself.

Banda came to know most of the close circle of the guru's disciples, men who had been with the guru for many years and had given him their unstinting loyalty, love and support. Amongst them he had been close to Bhai Binod Singh, a veteran of the guru's army. Binod was much older than Madho Das, but their friendship had the easy camraderie of men of the same age. From Binod he learnt the details of all the guru's battles and it was Binod who brought him back to the practice of archery and introduced him to other martial skills.

Over the following months Madho Das sought every opportunity to listen closely to each word that the guru spoke in his discourses, his discussions and in private meetings. There was much that he learnt which would influence his thoughts and actions in the years to come – about the political situation, the socio-economic conditions, the zamindari system which had become an instrument of oppression in the hands of the Mughals and without whose destruction there could be no true freedom, and the strategies of war and tactics that were essential for individual battles. There was an air of expectancy and suppressed excitement that pervaded the camp and every time the guru spoke of military matters his words were greeted with a hushed silence as if his audience was afraid to loose a single syllable.

The guru told his leaders the measures they should adopt to counter their initial disadvantage in terms of smaller numbers and lack of training and emphasized the need at all times to have a strong intelligence network, which would be easy to establish as the common man was groaning under the yoke of Mughal tyranny. It would provide them with information of the enemy's strengths and weaknesses and help them prepare for every battle, every clash. The guru advised that as far as possible the battlefield should always be of their choosing as they would be familiar with the topography and would be able to take advantage of each little fold that existed. Their strongest weapon in battle would be the element of surprise, which they should use to harass the enemy in a series of skirmishes and ambushes: every enemy soldier killed would be one less soldier to face them in open battle, every gold coin or bullet captured from the enemy was the diminishing of the enemy resources. There was no shame, in abandoning a battle as a war was rarely made of a single battle, but was almost always a series of battles. Only when there was no hope of another battle must they continue to fight against overwhelming odds to the very end and die as martyrs to the cause and thus serve as an inspiration to the generations to come.

The guru frequently addressed Madho Das directly and sought his company when he went on his long solitary walks along the River Godavari. He would remind him that by making himself the guru's bondsman he had become the bondsman of the Panth, the community, and he must place its interests and welfare before all else. He must retain his humility and simplicity of life and abjure all trappings of power and wealth – in his dress, food and daily living. Only then would he truly be able to serve the guru's followers. The guru, had in fact, prepared Madho Das for the role that he had chosen for him in the forthcoming war against the Mughals. Soon, all knew that Madho Das had been chosen as one of the leaders of the community and began to look upon him with deference and respect.

The evenings were Madho's favourite time of the day.

The evening prayers had been said; he had eaten his simple meal, spent an hour in meditation and now sat alone, lost in thought. The die had been caste for the coming campaign. Hukumnamahs, religious orders, had been sent to all the Sikh leaders of the Punjab – they were to marshal as strong a force as each of them could muster and wait for the guru's return to join him in his war against the Mughals. The guru's camp was gripped with excitement and enthusiasm as they were returning at last to their native Punjab and what was more, they were returning to revive their war against tyranny and oppression. Madho Das too could not help but be swept along in this excitement.

Suddenly there was a noise, which startled him out of his thoughts. It was the sound of excited voices and running feet. Madho Das slipped into his sandals and joined the crowds that surged to the guru's abode. As he ran amongst the press of people he learnt that while the guru rested, the two Pathans, Gul Khan and Jamshed Khan, who had recently attached themselves to the camp, had attacked him. The intruders had been killed but not before the guru had been seriously wounded. By the time Madho Das reached the guru's room, Bhai Binod Singh had taken charge and the guru's wound had been bandaged tightly to stop the flow of blood.

'Do not look so morose,' the guru said to his followers, the smile on his face emphasizing the paleness from the loss of blood. 'My time has not come. The flow of blood has been staunched and I have been administered medicine. The pain is bearable.'

Other than his breathing there was silence all around. The seconds stretched into minutes and minutes into hours. Yet, everyone waited – motionless and silent – for further directions. Madho Das looked towards Binod Singh and the other senior leaders, hoping that one of them would take the lead and establish the next course of action. When he caught Binod Singh's eyes there was a look of expectancy in them. He went out to the crowd of followers, moved from group to group and reassured them that all was well with the guru, and asked them to go and rest. One by one, with great reluctance, the men slipped away into the darkness.

The wound was a grievous one and required the skills of an experienced surgeon. Madho Das had great faith in the physician who attended upon the guru but he was not too sure of his surgical skills. The emperor Bahadur Shah was camped a few miles away and his personal surgeon, Dr Cole, was reputed to be a surgeon of great ability. At this time, though the personal relations between Bahadur Shah and Guru Gobind Singh, had become strained because of the former's refusal to rein in his cruel and tyrannical governors, there was not the total breach that was to occur later between the two. Bahadur Shah still retained some iota of gratitude for the support the guru had given him in his war of succession. Hence, it was not far fetched to presume that he would loan the guru the services of his surgeon. Madho Das sent Bhai Daya Singh to the emperor with the news of the attack and a request for Dr Cole's services. Within a short time Daya Singh returned with the doctor who was quick to examine the patient and suture the wound, seventeen stitches in all. He assured the assembled leaders that there was no cause for concern and that he would come back soon to re-examine the wound and to change the dressing.

A fortnight later an emissary arrived with news from the Punjab. The guru called a meeting of all his leaders. 'The time is now ripe to resume our fight against the Mughals. My hukumnamahs have been received and have been responded to. Sikhs forces are marshalling all over the Punjab, ready to join us in our battle. The Phoolkian sardars have promised large contingents and it is now time for us to return to the Punjab, organize the diverse forces into a coherent army and launch our campaign. Any delay at this stage will be detrimental to our interests. An idle mind is open to evil influence and nowhere is this more true than in a body of soldiers who are kept waiting to go into battle. As such, it is imperative that we return to the Punjab as quickly as possible and take charge. Unfortunately, the good Dr Cole has said that I am not yet fit enough to travel and has advised against my making this journey. If I am to be an effective leader in the coming war, then I must respect his advice and resume my role as your leader only when I am physically fit to do so.

'But as I said, the contingents that are collecting must not be kept waiting, someone else must take the lead. I know that you are all aware of the choice I have made regarding my deputy. I speak of Madho Das. If there is any reservation at this choice voice it now, your opinion will be heard and will be respected and if it is a strong one, it will influence all of us to change our minds.'

There were murmurs of approval, and then the seniormost in the hierarchy, stepped forward one by one, and voiced their support.

'It is done then. Madho Das will be your leader till I am well enough to return to the Punjab and resume charge. You have observed him these last few months and you know that in following my instructions and my wishes he has learnt to be a true follower of the faith. He is a Sikh in everything but in name. But to be the leader of the Sikhs this shortcoming must also be rectified.

The baptism ceremony was a simple one. Sugar crystals were

added to water in an iron cauldron and the water was stirred with a sword to the reciting of prayers till the sugar dissolved. The guru gave this amrit, nectar, to Madho Das to drink. 'I give you the name of Gurbaksh Singh. It is an apt name because you are indeed, for me, a bakshish, a reward from God. But in my heart I will always think of you with the name that you gave yourself, Banda. May you always be my Banda Singh Bahadur.'

Dozens of others from the congregation too asked to be baptized. When the last baptism had been performed the guru addressed the congregation again: 'I enjoin upon all my followers to give Banda Singh Bahadur complete and implicit obedience in the time to come. As a pledge and token of my faith in him and of my faith in our final victory, I bestow upon him five arrows from my quiver.'

Suiting the action to the word, the guru pulled five arrows from his quiver and held them out to Banda Bahadur, who fell on his knee, took the arrows from the guru, touched them reverentially to his forehead, and then placed them in his own quiver. 'I also give you a Nagara, a drum and a flag as symbols of the authority that I have vested in you. The Nagara will call upon the faithful to join you in your sacred mission and the flag will serve, as all flags do, as a rallying point for all those who believe in our cause and come to help us in our endeavours against the Mughals. Now, Bhai Binod Singh, Bhai Kahan Singh, Bhai Daya Singh, Bhai Raj Singh and Bhai Ram Singh step forward and come to me.'

The Sikhs so addressed, got to their feet and came before their Guru. 'Look carefully into their faces, Banda. They are your Panj Piarey, the first five to be baptized, and they represent the Khalsa, the Panth, they represent me. They are your counsel and you must consult them in whatever you do. You must place your trust in them and allow yourself to be ruled in all things by their advice.' He turned to the five leaders and addressed them: 'You must exercise your responsibilities with honesty, intelligence and diligence. You must put all personal considerations aside and give Banda Singh Bahadur your complete loyalty and support. But you must always remember that no individual is above the Panth, the community. You five are the Panth. When you feel that what Banda Singh says or does is not in conformity with the tenets of my teachings or is against the Sikh maryada – the tenets of the Sikh religion – it is your duty to speak and speak out loud and clear without fear of offending or hurting your leader. The maryada of the Sikhs is in your hands now and you must protect it and guard it with jealous zeal.'

There was a pause and he turned again to Banda Bahadur: 'There is no time to lose. You will take with you a small group of twenty-five men that I have handpicked myself. You will proceed with caution, taking care to avoid any encounter or confrontation with the enemy or its representatives on the way, even if this means that you have to take a longer and more circuitous route. Your destination is Buria, where you will meet the first of the detachments that have rallied forth to join us in our campaign. You are the leader now. You must assess the situation and make your own decisions. If the situation demands that you march into battle immediately, without waiting for me, then you must proceed accordingly. You must make an early start tomorrow. Those going with you all have preparations to make and have little time in which to make them.'

The Sikhs who had been chosen for this mission came forward to seek the guru's blessings. He led a prayer for their success and then retired to his chambers.

In spite of the burden that had been laid upon his shoulders, and the tensions and anxieties regarding his impending journey and the outcome of his mission, Banda slept soundly. He woke up long before it was time for them to leave and slipped through the darkness to the guru's chamber. There was a single, tall taper burning in the room and he saw the guru sitting in the lotus position, deep in meditation. Having made his obeisance, he sat opposite the guru, looking into that serene face. The outside world, the impending separation from his master, all fell away from him. The peace and stillness within was as deep as the peace and stillness of the still sleeping world. He had never known such peace and quiet before, never known the strength that he now felt. At last the guru opened his eyes and saw Banda and broke into a quiet smile: 'I knew you would come.' There was silence again and they both sat looking at each other, the dancing flame of the taper reflected in the guru's eyes, giving them a strange, hypnotic gleam. 'Are you sure of what you have to do?' Banda nodded his head in the affirmative, still loath to speak. 'Are there no doubts? No questions?' Again Banda shook his head.

'Is the shaking of your head all that you will give me? Have you no words for me?'

'Is there any need for words? All doubts fell away with your act of choosing me; all questions were answered. You know that I will do the best that I can to lead our people till you come to take charge.'

There was silence again, a long silence. Then the guru smiled and this time, even in the tenderness of the smile, there was a hint of mockery. 'And what if I am not able to come?' Banda felt his heart churn within him, yet he held the guru's steady gaze because he knew that his master was testing him.

'If it is god's will that you do not come, then let it be so.'

'Will you not miss me?' The mockery in the smile was

stronger now.

'Did you not tell me that your spirit and your soul would always be with me? And if I have your spirit and your soul, how can I miss your body?' With these words the churning in his heart was stilled and Banda felt no sadness even in the knowledge that this was his last meeting with the guru.

'You are indeed now ready for the task that I have assigned to you, my Banda,' he said. 'Come, let us pray together one last time and then you must be on your way.'

The guru led Banda in the recitation of the Japji Sahib, the morning prayer, and when it was done, Banda touched the guru's feet and the guru laid his hand upon his head. Banda strode from the room, then stopped in the doorway, turned and looked long at the guru. There was no need for words. He turned and hurried out into the still, dark world.

Chapter Two

More and more highly motivated men came forth to join Banda Bahadur. Not only Sikhs, but large numbers of Hindus and Muslims, fed up with the stifling conditions that prevailed in the Punjab, saw in Banda a messiah who would lead them to freedom and a better way of life. If further motivation were needed, it was supplied by the Sikhs of Nanded, who wrote to all the prominent Sikh leaders of the Punjab, reminding them of the brutalities of the Mughal rulers who had not spared even the guru and his sons.

THE JOURNEY HAD BEEN A LONG AND DIFFICULT ONE, long not so much in terms of distance as of time. He had taken almost a year to cover 1,700 kilometres. These were deeply troubled times and there was turmoil in the area between Nanded and Delhi. Banda and his group had followed the guru's advice and done everything possible to avoid suspicion and confrontation with representatives of the Mughals. They had broken up into smaller groups and leapfrogged from one destination to another, getting together and regrouping at intervals of three or four days. They studiously avoided the highways and used circuitous, rarely used tracks deep in the arid areas of Rajasthan.

The news of the guru's death was brought to them when they had been seven days on the move. Banda with his group of four, after a long and tiring journey, had found shelter for the night in the ruins of an old fort that was now used as a serai, an inn. They had eaten a frugal meal and wrapping themselves up in their blankets, had curled up for a well-earned sleep, when they were awakened by the approach of galloping horses; the hoof beats sounding loud and clear in the stillness of the night. They all sat up with a simultaneous start. The feeble light from the still smouldering campfire lit up their tense faces. The confidence with which the hoof beats had rung out had made it abundantly clear that men in authority were riding the horses. Under the circumstances they could only be officials from the

Mughal army. Banda look closely at his followers and smiled reassuringly: 'This is our first real test. I do not think God would have set us on this mission if he had wanted our journey to end so soon. Wrap yourselves up in your blankets again and assume the pretence of sleep. Drop this pretence only when you perceive a definite threat.'

The Sikhs did as Banda advised. The horses came to a halt and then they heard a loud voice hail the keeper of the serai by name. It was clear that these soldiers were frequent visitors to this place. There was an exchange of greetings, the telling of jokes, laughter and then the sound of the clatter of earthenware and of water being poured as food was served and eaten. There was a lull in the conversation for a short while broken only by the gurgle of hookahs. Then, there was a session of questions and answers, an update of the latest news and rumours. 'So, there is nothing new in the developments in the Deccan?' the keeper asked.

'No, there is nothing new. There is a stalemate as far as the emperor's campaign is concerned and no fresh gains have been made. But yes, there is one piece of news that might interest you. Gobind Singh, the guru of the Sikhs, is dead.'

Banda heard the sharp intake of breath from the 'sleeper' besides him. It was a terrible and tragic news, news that would provoke reaction from his followers. But if one of them did react, they were sure to be discovered. Banda himself did not move and prayed that the others would be still as well. The moment stretched on and the speakers resumed their conversation.

'But I had heard that his wound had healed and he had recovered.'

'Yes. So it was said. But he was given the gift of a powerful bow. He had an obsession with weapons and could not resist trying out this wonderful new bow. It required great strength and as he drew the string, the strain became too much and his wound reopened. He bled to death. They say that even in the face of his impending death he remained as always, serene and strong, giving advice to his followers and in the end, reciting prayers.'

There was a long silence and then a deep sigh. 'He was a great man,' said the serai keeper.

'Yes, he was a great man,' a soldier said without any reservation or grudge in this admiration. 'May Allah have mercy on his soul.' The soldiers rose to their feet and with an exchange of 'good nights', shuffled to their quarters to rest.

The Sikhs lay still, wrapped up in their blankets, overcome by the enormity of what they had heard. After the initial, momentary numbness, Banda realized that he was not as shocked by the news as he ought to have been. There was regret that he had not had a chance to say goodbye. Then his mind went back to his last meeting and he realized that the entire meeting had been in the nature of a farewell and the regret too passed from him. Banda prayed for the strength to bear this loss and to live up to his guru's trust and faith. As he prayed, the stillness came back within him and with it a resurgence of strength and confidence.

The group only came to terms with the loss of their guru four days later when all thirty-one Sikhs came together at the pre-designated rendezvous. Banda and his group were the last to arrive; the others had been waiting for him. They greeted each other in subdued whispers and then sat in silence. 'It is the will of God,' he said simply. 'And we would be failing our guru if we did not accept it with grace.' He looked into the eyes of the five senior leaders, one by one, and marvelled at how well they had been chosen. He saw in their eyes as fierce a determination as when they had received their mandate from the guru, and said:

'The circumstances have changed and with this change some rethinking is required. The Khalsa must decide how the loss of our guru is to affect the course of action that we must now pursue.'

Binod Singh cleared his throat and spoke. Even though there was firm resolve in his voice, it was soft and gentle and comforting. He too had sensed the drooping of spirits amongst some of his friends and this was his way of restoring their faith in themselves: 'Our great loss, the loss of our guru, has brought about a great change in our lives, but the circumstances that gave birth to our mission have not changed. Though the guru has gone from us, his mandate remains unchanged. If we love our guru we must ensure that we fulfil the responsibility that he laid on our shoulders. We must go out and fight – the fight he wanted us to fight. Only now it will not be under his leadership, it will be under a changed leadership and even this change the guru provided for by appointing Banda Singh Bahadur as our leader. You must take charge in the coming battles as the commander of the Sikh forces.'

'It is a heavy burden that the guru has laid upon my shoulders,' Banda said almost immediately. 'But it is a burden that I carry willingly and with pride. At this stage I can only endorse what Bhai Binod Singh has said. Our hearts are heavy with grief and our minds overwhelmed by this great loss. But even in this state of mind, we all know that we have no choice, there is only one course of action open to us. We must do our utmost to make the guru's dream come true – the dream of a Punjab where all men are equal and there is no shadow of oppression or exploitation to blight the lives of ordinary men. This is the only way in which we can show our love for our guru, the only way we can offer proof to the world that we are his true Sikhs.'

They sat late into the night exchanging news and sharing their experiences since they had last been together. Strategies for the next stage of their journey were worked out and it was decided that two of the followers would move ahead carrying personal letters from Banda Bahadur to the Sikhs in the Majha and the Doab, telling them that the time to carry out the guru's orders was now close at hand. They ended with the singing of one of the guru's favourite shabads, a hymn, in Raag Aasa, composed by Arjun Dev, the fifth guru:

> What fear have I when you are my Master?
> Who else shall I worship?
> If I have you I have everything,
> I look for no other.
> Lord such venom have I seen in the world,
> You are my shepherd, my protector
> Your name is my comfort
> You know the anguish in my heart
>
> To whom shall I tell my sorrow?
> Without your name the world is in turmoil.
>
> Only those who take Your Name find peace.
> What shall I say? Who will listen to me?
> The Lord alone can speak.[2]

The second crisis came when they were close to Bharatpur. Their finances had dried up and they had no resources left even for their day-to-day needs. They had never seen such penury before. None of them had eaten in forty-eight hours. They knew that from here onwards things would become more difficult for them, as they were now approaching Delhi where they would have to face great hostility. Even those who admired the guru would be reluctant to extend help to this suspicious group of

Sikhs for fear of inviting the imperial ire. They rummaged through their meager belongings and picked out whatever they felt could be bartered for food. Daya Singh was commissioned to take these few articles into town and come back with what food he could get.

Daya Singh strode through the gates of the city with an air of assumed confidence, though he was anything but confident. For one, he was alone in a strange new environment. Moreover, never before had he to go out on a task like the present one. Once in the main market, he looked around and hesitated, not sure which of the dozen shopkeepers he should approach. While he stood there, not being able to make up his mind, an elderly gentleman walked up to him. It was obvious that the stranger was as ill at ease as he glanced nervously over his shoulder a couple of times before addressing him: 'Are you one of the guru's Sikhs on your way to the Punjab?' his voice little more than a whisper.

'Yes,' Daya Singh said, not able to hide his surprise at having been so easily recognized. There was nothing in the other man's appearance or behaviour to suggest a threat and yet, instinctively, Daya Singh's hand went to his sword hilt.

The stranger smiled: 'Do not be afraid, my friend, I too am a great admirer of the guru. I am Sant Singh, a Lubana Sikh. I had been informed that you were travelling in this direction and was looking out for you. I hoped to extend my hospitality to you and your friends and by so doing to be of some service to my guru.'

One of Sant Singh's trusted servants accompanied Daya Singh back to the camp and escorted Banda Bahadur and his group to his master's home. Here they were entertained lavishly and with affection and after a good night's sleep when they were ready to set out again, their host took Banda into the privacy of an adjacent room and handed him some money. 'This is my dasvand, the one-tenth of my income that the guru has enjoined upon all his followers to give away as contribution to a just cause or in charity,' he said by way of explanation. 'I beseech you to accept it.'

Banda accepted the gift with grace and smiled inwardly remembering the guru's words that whenever he was in need he should pray to god for help and help would come. He had prayed in the present exigency too but had never imagined that his prayers would be answered so swiftly. There was enough money now to see them through the rest of their journey.

Once clear of Delhi, Banda embarked on a deliberate confidence-building campaign amongst all the poor and oppressed people of the Punjab, irrespective of their caste or religion. This was essential as years of living under the yoke of tyranny had broken and crushed the spirit of the people, sapped their self-confidence, and left them totally demoralized. He first came face-to-face with it near Bangar in Hissar. It was mid-morning, the day after he had set up camp, when he saw a train of refugees hurrying away from the village. They came in dozens, on foot, on horses and in bullock carts, carrying with them whatever possessions they had been able to snatch as they fled. Banda stopped two sturdy young men who were hurrying past. 'What is it?' he asked. 'What is it that makes all these good people flee in such unholy haste?'

'You must be a stranger,' one of them replied. 'Or else you too would have been on the move by now. Randhir Singh, the notorious dacoit, has sent word that he is going to raid one of the villages of Bangar. He has not specified which village and so, rather than take a chance by staying on, we are all fleeing to safety.'

Banda had heard of Randhir Singh, the dacoit whose name was bruited far and wide. He was sadistic and bloodthirsty to the extreme and when he attacked a village not only did he carry away everything of value, but also cold-bloodedly killed all the villagers who had been stupid enough to stay on. Yet, as he saw the never-ending flow of humanity streaming past him, many of them strong and well-built like the ones he was talking to, Banda could not help thinking that if these youngsters were to take a stand, Randhir Singh and his gang would find themselves far outnumbered.

'There are so many amongst you who are young and strong and, no doubt, brave. Why don't you stay and face this rascal? I'm sure you could defeat him and destroy his gang.' The youngsters exchanged a sardonic glance as one of them said: 'It is now more obvious than ever before that you are a complete stranger to these parts. If you had just once seen the carnage that he leaves in his wake, you would not ask such a question. We have tarried long enough and we must move on or else it will be too late. Pay heed to our words, abandon your camp and get away while you can.'

'Stay, and my men will fight against the dacoits with you. Together we will be able to inflict a crushing blow upon them.'

But the people had been subjected not only to the brutalities and harassments of the rulers but also to those of antisocial elements like the dacoits for too long. All fight had left them and they were convinced of the uselessness of offering any resistance. This would only bring down the wrath of the notorious dacoit on their heads with greater vehemence. Wisdom lay in abandoning their homes and belongings to the mercy of the dacoits and escaping to a place of safety. No amount of persuasion or cajoling could make them change their minds.

Once the stream of refugees had flowed past their camp,

Banda held council with his leaders. Their brief was to free the people of the region from tyranny and oppression. When this brief was drawn up it was aimed specifically against the Mughals. But they would now have to reinterpret it to include others, like the dacoits, who were guilty of exploiting the poor. Militarily too it was necessary to eliminate the dacoits because when the Sikhs finally came into confrontation with the Mughals, it would not do to have dacoits hovering over their heads, waiting to pick at the spoils of war.

Banda and his followers took positions in one of the abandoned villages. The dacoits sauntered in, supremely confident and arrogant in the belief that there could be no opposition to them. They walked straight into an ambush and were attacked from all sides. Before they had time to react or retaliate, the fight was over. A large number of them were killed immediately, and the few, who survived, fled, leaving behind the large booty they had captured from the other villages. This defeat of the dacoits served as a turning point in the lives of the villagers. They saw how just a handful of Sikhs had been able to take a stand against the ruthless, much-feared dacoits and had defeated them.

The Bangar area was riddled with gangs of dacoits and after the defeat of Randhir Singh, Banda launched a systematic campaign to eliminate them. Gradually the people too began to join in this campaign. In a few months the menace of dacoits that had been the bane of this area became a thing of the past. Banda's efforts won him many admirers. More and more people flocked to his camp to seek his help and advice, to join his forces or merely for his blessings. With the increasing numbers of visitors and followers came larger gifts of money. He also confiscated the government treasuries in Bhiwani and Sonepat and a revenue train near Kaithal. With this vast accumulation of wealth he was not only able to pay and equip his army but also continue his work of ameliorating the suffering of the poor and the needy. For himself, Banda still remained a Bairagi at heart with no attachment to wealth or to material possessions. He kept only what was needed for his extremely simple life and gave everything else away. The wisdom of the advice he gave, his generosity and his spartan lifestyle were now talked about all over the Punjab. He felt great joy in the resurgence of self-confidence and pride that he had been able to bring about in the minds and hearts of the common people who were now willing to join him in the belief that this fight would succeed.

The Punjab was going through a period of political instability. Emperor Bahadur Shah had been away in the Deccan, snuffing out the flames of revolt, for a long time. His deputies in Delhi were not able to exercise a strict control over the province of Punjab. Each of the feudal chiefs and the Mughal officials saw this as a golden opportunity to expand their territories and spheres of control at the expense of their neighbours. Though the governor of Punjab with his headquarters at Lahore was supposed to be the representative of Mughal authority, the other jagirdars, the large landowners, officials and military commanders of the smaller principalities and subas, provinces paid only lip-service to the governor and behaved more or less as independent rulers. Sirhind, Sadhaura, Malerkotla, Samana, Kaithal, Kapoori, Sunam, Ghuram, Saharanpur, Jalalabad, Karnal, Panipat and Jalandhar, were all charting their independent courses with little or no effort by Asaf-ud Daulah,

Hukamnamah by Banda Singh Bahadur to Bhayee Rupa ji.

Places visited by Banda Singh Bahadur.

Remnants at Sadhaura
The Sadhaura mud fort constructed by Banda Singh Bahadur.

Banda Singh's abode from 1713–1715. He stayed in the Jammu hills at a place now called Dera Baba Banda Singh Bahadur.

Wazirabad, city of Banda's in-laws
Photograph of an old structure in the city of Wazirabad. His wife Sahib Kaur is said to have belonged to this place.

the emperor's subedar, governor in Delhi, to impose any check upon them.

Banda realized that the time and conditions could not have been more opportune for his purpose. He would face no interference from Delhi, and with the suspicions and jealousies strong between them, the lesser rulers of the Punjab would be reluctant to come to each other's aid against a common enemy. He also knew that this situation would last only as long as Bahadur Shah remained in the Deccan. Once he returned to Delhi, he would move swiftly to reconsolidate his power in the Punjab and would concentrate on destroying Banda and the Sikhs marshalling all the Mughal forces for this purpose.

The need for quick, deliberate action was imperative, but Banda did not rush immediately into battle. He was not sure that he had sufficient strength to commit himself to open warfare. It was true that once he had entered the Punjab, men in large numbers had come to join his army. The strength of his supporters snowballed and he now had a force of 4,000 mounted soldiers and an infantry that was roughly twice this number. But he also knew that the large numbers were no indication of the true strength of his army. Almost half, if not more, of the soldiers at his command, were riff-raff, who had joined him in the hope of sharing in the plunder and loot that would ensue after each of his victories. They had no loyalty to the cause, no admiration for Banda or for what he sought to do, no concern for the welfare of the oppressed and exploited. When they saw that victory was in sight they would stay close to Banda and strip the defeated people of everything they possessed. But, if they saw any uncertainty in the outcome of battle they would abandon him and retreat to positions that would guarantee their own safety. The second large group in his army comprised the mercenaries under the leadership of generals like Ram Singh and Trilok Singh, who had been sent to him by the rulers of the Phoolkian dynasty in answer to the guru's hukumnamahs. Banda knew that these soldiers, though possessed of great skill and experience, were concerned more with their own safety and welfare than with ensuring the victory of Banda's cause. Like the first group, they could be relied upon for support only if victory was certain. But in the face of adversity, they too, would abandon the battlefield and retreat to safety. The real strength of his army was limited to a mere 1,500 men of whom a little over a thousand were infantry and the remaining were horsemen. He decided to wait till the Majhaili Sikhs were able to make the crossing at Kiratpur to join him before embarking on any major military enterprise.

While he waited, Banda worked hard to establish his intelligence network. He made contact in enemy strongholds all over the Punjab with people who were sympathetic to his cause. He was able to get fairly accurate and regular information of strategic importance: information regarding military strength and build-ups, the latest political affiliations and, most important of all, information regarding the calibre of the men he would eventually face in battle. He also held lengthy consultations with his leaders and developed broad based, general military strategies. He had no first-hand experience of war but he had listened attentively to everything the guru had said on the subject and he had elicited every detail about the guru's battles from the veterans who had fought these battles. As such, the strategies that had finally been drawn up were based largely on the guru's advice and experience.

They would, as far as possible, avoid pitched open battles and depend on the elements of surprise and speed. They would identify and single out the weakest wing of the enemy, sweep upon it, inflict swift, crushing damage and disappear before reinforcements could arrive. If the enemy strength proved too much for them, they would give the signal for a swift retreat. The enemy, sensing a kill, would give chase and when the spearheading party was well and truly removed from the main body of the enemy's army, they would turn and fall upon it and decimate it.

More and more highly motivated men came forth to join Banda Bahadur. Not only Sikhs, but large numbers of Hindus and Muslims, fed up with the stifling conditions that prevailed in the Punjab, saw in Banda a messiah who would lead them to freedom and a better way of life. If further motivation were needed, it was supplied by the Sikhs of Nanded, who wrote to all the prominent Sikh leaders of the Punjab, reminding them of the brutalities of the Mughal rulers who had not spared even the guru and his sons.

The first to arrive at Banda's camp were the Sikhs from the south followed by the Banjaras, the gypsies, dozens and dozens of trains of bullock carts, piled high with much-needed rations. Next came Fateh Singh, a descendant of Bhai Bhagu, with a large number of followers. He was to prove to be one of Banda Bahadur's most capable military leaders. A host of other Sikh leaders followed, bringing with them their own private armies. Prominent among these were Karam Singh, Dharam Singh and Chuhar Singh. Many prominent Jat and Brar Sikhs, with small bands of followers, also came to support Banda. Finally, Ali Singh and Mali Singh came with a few other Sikhs who had been in the service of Wazir Khan of Sirhind. Banda Bahadur had established contact with these two prominent leaders almost as soon as he had come into the Punjab. They had chosen not to come out in open support because they felt they could make a more valuable contribution to the cause by working as fifth columnists from within Sirhind and had provided him with vital information. This worked well till Wazir Khan, infuriated by Banda's growing power, sought to intimidate him by taking action against all Sikhs in Sirhind, including those in his service. He ordered the arrest and incarceration of all the Sikhs including Ali Singh and Mali Singh. Fortunately, Ali Singh, with his long years of service and residence in Sirhind had built up some very powerful contacts, which he used to escape along with some of his closest associates.

This was the much needed signal. All the Sikhs who could join him for the present had come in. There was no point in waiting any longer as the urgent need was to register a decisive victory against the Mughals. His own forces too were becoming restless while the fence sitters were waiting to see what show Banda and his men would put up in battle before they could cast their lot with the Sikhs.

All through their long journey, their dream had been to attack and destroy Sirhind, which was the strongest Mughal suba of the Punjab and its destruction would mean the destruction of the Mughal control in the province. It had also, in the Sikh psyche, become a strong emotional symbol of Mughal oppression and tyranny for it was the ruler of Sirhind, Wazir Khan, who had put the guru's two youngest sons, little more than boys, to death. And it was Wazir Khan, afraid that the guru might be able to influence Bahadur Shah against him, who had sent out the two Pathan contract killers to Nanded to assassinate the guru. Obviously, in the minds of his followers, there was a strong desire to target Sirhind first.

Banda understood this desire and in many ways shared it himself, but he was mature and detached enough to know that it was a desire based on emotions rather than on an understanding of the ground reality. The defeat of Sirhind would indeed, with one stroke, establish the supremacy of the Sikhs in the Punjab. But, equally, if the Sikhs were defeated at Sirhind they would not get a second chance and Banda was loath to wager his fortunes on the outcome of a single battle. He decided to move one step at a time, testing the waters as he went, with engagements involving the lesser subedars and faujdars, army commanders. Each small victory would mean a strengthening of his own position and each defeat of a petty Mughal official would mean one less force that would march to the aid of Wazir Khan when finally and inevitably they attacked Sirhind. With each of these minor victories, he would create in the minds of the common people a feeling of growing contempt for Mughal power. In the minds of the rulers he would create an impression of growing disorder and confusion, which would finally border on panic. This, in turn, would provoke them to make moves which, in a stable and balanced frame of mind, they would not have made. His own army, which had not been tried or tested in any battle, would gain experience and self-confidence with each of these engagements and would be an experience that would make them more adept in the art of warfare. This strategy would also give time for Sikhs from the central Punjab, the Sikh heartland, to come to him in answer to Guru Gobind Singh's hukumnamahs. Through patient and judicious arguement Banda won the other Sikhs to his thinking till finally they all agreed that Samana and not Sirhind would be their first target.

Samana, founded in the twelfth century by the Samanand family, was situated about eight kilometres south-west of Patiala. It was famous for its very fine cotton, next only in quality to the legendary muslin from Dacca. Many contemporary European writers have commented upon the quality of this cloth. Hence, Samana was a wealthy and powerful city. Long years of peace and prosperity had produced degeneration amongst the faujdar and the nobility who regarded the tenant farmers and the workers at their handlooms as little more than animals and exploited them to the hilt. The commoners hated the rulers but were helpless as they had no court of appeal and anyone who dared to raise his voice in complaint was summarily dealt with. There could be no hope of redressal from the governor in Lahore or the emperor in Delhi, as they were concerned with regular payments of levies, and not with just and fair governance. And Samana was very regular in clearing its levies.

Though the faujdar, who was the governor and the overlord, officially ruled Samana, there were as many as twenty-two amirs, who regarded themselves as equal in every way to the faujdar, if not better than him. The amirs were either Sayyads or Mughals. Each of them lived in a grand palace citadel and each had been granted the privilege of moving around in a palanquin by the emperor as a token of his special regard. There was no love lost amongst these amirs and they were constantly striving to be one up on each other. As a result, there was no governance in Samana, no concern for the welfare of the people, no sense of civic pride. There was only, amongst the rich and the powerful, self-centred effort to be even more rich and powerful. The city did have a wall around it but the amirs, not having experienced any external threat for many years, were complacent in their strength and their ability to face an enemy. Besides, each of them lived in a haveli with enough fortifications to keep out any enemy and with his own security assured, why need he worry about the safety of the city and of the common man? It was little wonder then that the common man would give anything to see that the power of the amirs was destroyed.

Camped at a distance of ten kos (one kos is approximately two kilometres) from Samana, Banda held a meeting with his leaders to plan the attack on the city. Their intelligence had informed them that the faujdar of Samana regarded the presence of the Sikhs with total disdain. He was convinced that they posed no threat to Samana and had made no effort to strengthen his fortification. The Sikhs knew that they would have no trouble in breaching the walls and forcing their way into the city. Once this happened the amirs would hole up in their havelis each of which was virtually impregnable.

Fateh Singh, who had been appointed commander, proposed that leaders should be appointed to lead groups of the irregulars to surround each of the havelis and convert them into virtual prisons by denying exit to the occupants. The soldiers would concentrate on the haveli of Sayyad Jalaluddin which had the highest ramparts. Once caputred its roofs and walls would give them access into the neighbouring havelis.

In the faujdar's palace the amirs too were holding a council of war. 'It is rumoured that the Sikh rabble is getting ready to attack Samana,' the faujdar led the discussion.

'Are we meeting here only to discuss rumours?' Sayyad Shamuddhin cut in. 'This rumour has been afloat for some time but no attack has materialized.' His hostility to the faujdar was apparent in his words, his tone of voice and in the arch of his eyebrows. 'If there is nothing else to discuss, I know of better ways to employ my time.' But he did not get to his feet and carry out his threat of leaving. The faujdar was, after all, the emperor's appointee and even in the emperor's absence, Shamsuddin could not throw so open a challenge to his authority. The faujdar, on his part, ignored Shamsuddin and continued his address to the others:

'We all know that the Sikhs by themselves do not pose any threat to us. Their force is made up largely of undisciplined mercenaries and dacoits whose sole aim is to loot and plunder. This rabble does not stand a chance against our well-trained and well-equipped army. But, my concern is the tenenat farmers and workers who, according to my information, have joined the Sikhs in large numbers, vowing to avenge, what they term, atrocities on them.'

This bit of information produced a ripple of laughter in the assembly. 'When did you hear of a worker or a tenant farmer taking a stand?' jeered Shamsuddin. 'The odd one may sometimes, get belligerent but at the first crack of the whip he comes again to heel like a faithful hound. You will see, even now, if there are any tenant farmers or workers in this crowd, they will support the Sikhs only till the first volley is fired from our side. Then they will cross over and beg for mercy.'

Most of the other amirs assembled nodded their heads in agreement. It was obvious that, consumed in their confidence, their sense of superiority over the Sikh forces, they did not feel threatened in any way. 'I feel we should listen carefully to what the faujdar says and to dwell seriously upon the threat posed by the Sikhs. It is never wise to underestimate an enemy no matter how weak he may appear,' said Jalaluddin, the only amir who showed a reflection of anxiety.

'Perhaps the death of their Guru Tegh Bahadur weighs heavily on your conscience, amir,' Shamsuddin's voice dripped with disdain, 'and this makes you see a ghost where not even a shadow lurks.' Some of the amirs exchanged knowing smiles. It was common knowledge that since Banda Bahadur's advent in the Punjab, Jalaluddin had lost his usual equanimity. This knowledge had given some measure of satisfaction to most of the other amirs who had resented Jalaluddin's sudden ascension to a position of wealth and eminence merely because he had supervised the execution of the recalcitrant Sikh guru.

'But you have no cause for worry. Your haveli, your palatial house is the strongest building in the city. It is virtually impregnable and your personal army is strong enough to defend it against any attack. Though, you do not need any further help, yet to reassure you, I will loan you the services of my crack detachment of Abyssinian warriors. My willingness to do without this detachment will prove to you how little I think of this so-called threat. Enough of this concern for what does not exist. Now, let us not dishonour our host by ignoring the excellent refreshments that he, with his usual generosity, has laid out for us.'

The faujdar was annoyed by the way in which Shamsuddin had taken charge of the meeting and given the signal for its end. He decided to let it ride for the moment for there would be enough opportunities to deal with the youngster's growing arrogance.

In the days before the attack, each of the Sikh leaders took it upon himself to move amongst his soldiers and motivate them further. Each emphasized the fact that Samana was home to Sayyad Jalaluddin who had supervised the brutal execution of the ninth guru, their beloved Tegh Bahadur, and also to Shashal Beg and Bashal Beg, the two executioners of Guru Gobind Singh's young sons. The defeat and destrucion of Samana would not only be the first effective blow against the Mughal power but would also provide an opportunity to every true Sikh to avenge these heinous crimes. Coupled with this was the prosperity and wealth of the amirs. The implication was clear: the defeat and destruction of these amirs would ensure that rich booty would fall to the share of each of the soldiers.

During the night of 25 and 26 November 1709, Banda, at the head of a strong force, moved swiftly to cover the ten kos distance that lay between his camp and Samana and reached the city gates, ruthlessly killing the constables manning the gates. The faujdar and the amirs, caught in a state of total unpreparedness for this attack, could think only of their personal safety. Each of them called in the detachments of his guards and sections of the army that owed him allegiance and concentrated on the security of his own haveli against the enemy. The rulers of Samana had played straight into Banda's hands as the army got divided into twenty-two groups, each holed up in what appeared to be an impregnable fortress, effectively sealed off and isolated from the other groups. They had lost all flexibility and the ability to change their positions according to the needs of the battle. The hordes of civilian besiegers knocking at the walls of the havelis insured that none of the defenders would be able to leave. With this one move, any possibility of a united, effort to protect the town was defeated. Fateh Singh performed his role admirably. He moved from haveli to haveli to ensure that the leaders who had been appointed for the purpose had indeed succeeded in mounting blockades. Having satisfied himself he brought his entire military force to aid Banda Bahadur in the siege of Jalaluddin's haveli.

For a while it seemed that the siege would be a long drawn out affair. They were just not able to breach the walls of Jalaluddin's haveli and the heavy fusillade of bullets and arrows fired upon them from the roof and rampants exacted a heayy toll.

Then one of those fortuitous accidents occurred that have so often turned the tide of battle. One of Banda's men noticed a bricked-in archway in the wall of the haveli, which lay to one side, away from the lines of fire. The battering ram was moved to face the archway, whose brickwork filling had little strength and caved in sooner than expected. The Sikhs had won entry into the haveli.

Things moved swiftly after that. The haveli was captured and the Sikh irregulars, combined with the peasants and the workers, moved in. The inhabitants of the haveli, regardless of age and sex, were all put to the sword. For too long they had oppressed the poor and now that they were in a position to extract revenge, the poor would not rest till the last representative of this hateful family, this hateful order had been exterminated. Banda Bahadur abandoned the haveli to the mercy of the mob, quickly called his soldiers to order and turned to attack the neighbouring havelis. Like a house of cards, one after the other in quick succession, all the others fell to the Sikhs.

By sunset the battle of Samana was over. The once proud and prosperous city had been reduced to piles of smouldering rubble and the streets ran with blood. It is said that more than 10,000 people were killed in this single day. Jalaluddin was caught trying to sneak out of his haveli and Fateh Singh, with one stroke of his sword, separated his head from his body. The head of the man who had masterminded the heartless execution of Guru Tegh Bahadur was fixed on a spike and prominently displayed on one of the city gates. The same fate befell Shashal Beg and Bashal Beg, the executioners of Guru Gobind Singh's two young son's, the sahibzadas, rank of princes, Zorawar Singh and Fateh Singh.

The cold winter evening was warmed by the flames of hundreds of fires that burnt and crackled as they consumed what remained of the once splendid buildings of the city and the air was filled with the acrid smoke from the burning edifices. Banda Bahadur set up camp in the courtyard of what had once been Jalaluddin's haveli. He sat in a quiet, pensive mood, staring vacantly into the flames of his campfire. Hours later he felt a hand on his shoulder and looking up, saw the face of Bhai Binod looking down at him. The flame of the fire illuminated Binod's face and Banda saw a soft, sad smile play at those lips and the gleam of compassion light up those eyes. 'Come, my brother. It has been a long and a tiring day and you have many such long and tiring days ahead of you. You must rest now.'

Banda looked back into the fire but made no move to get up. 'I wish there had been some way to avoid this carnage, this terrible bloodshed. It was the guru's command that we should be magnanimous and forgiving in victory and we have disobeyed that command.'

There was such a tone of failure in that voice that the victory of Samana ceased to exist. Binod replied: 'We all wish that there had been no killings but there was no other way. For centuries these poor people had been exploited and oppressed and once they tasted success there was nothing that could hold them back from taking the law into their own hands and for dealing in so cruel and bloodthirsty a manner with their erstwhile rulers, their erstwhile tormentors. Centuries of hatred and bitterness burnt in their hearts, centuries of frustrating impotence. There was no other way in which this could have found expression. The amirs and their families only reaped what they sowed. We cannot blame the poor people for what they did.'

'I understand that, Bhai Binod Singh. I understand their need for such total and complete revenge. But can we honestly say that there was nothing that we could have done to pre-empt this, to stop it once it started? Could we not have explained to the people the guru's desire that we forgive the vanquished? Could we not have singled out a few of the most cruel and ruthless conquerors and made an example of them so that the others would have been held back from fear of receiving a similar punishment, if from nothing else?'

'It would have made no difference. The years of suppressed anger and rage would never have been denied satisfaction. No amount of explanation, no amount of preaching of the guru's message on the eve of battle would have produced any result other than the one we have. As for making an example of a few, it would not have held back the flames of passion, and would have only turned the anger and the fire against us. They are too large in number and they would not have hesitated to include us in their anger, to embrace us with their hatred. Come, brother, you waste your time and your emotional strength in useless regrets. You know that even this is the will of God. The amirs got no more than they deserved. Their sins were so great against their people that there could not have been a lesser punishment. Do not think that you were responsible for this. If anyone was responsible, it was the amirs themselves, for they betrayed a trust that God and destiny had laid upon them. They exploited the people whom it was their sacred duty to protect.'

All through the night and for the major part of the next morning, the gold and silver, money and jewellery that Banda Bahadur's soldiers had requisitioned, was carried to some of the now ruined rooms of the haveli. A group of evaluators listed and evaluated the booty, a part of which was kept for equipping the next expedition while the rest divided equally amongst the soldiers. Banda had no source of income; no reserves from which he could pay his soldiers a regular salary. The only way he could compensate them for risking their lives for him and ensure that they had enough money to live on was to make them equal partners in the spoils of war. Booty shared, each soldier got enough to be able to live comfortably for the next six months.

Next evening, Banda addressed a gathering of his most important leaders and generals: 'This has been an important victory for us and is a cause for great rejoicing. But important as it is, this victory marks only a beginning. There will have to be many such victories if we are to ensure that tyranny and oppression are banished from the Punjab once and for all. We will have to move swiftly from one attack to the next, ensuring that each place which has been conquered at such great cost, is not left unattended to fall again into the hands of the Mughals.'

Banda's voice, loud and strong, rang and echoed against the high walls that surrounded the courtyard. The chilly evening breeze had begun to stir and in spite of the small fires that had been lit in various parts of the courtyard, many of those present shivered in the cold and drew their woollen wrappings tighter around them. He paused, looked around, and then went on to his next announcement. His five Sikhs were aware of what he was going to say as he had discussed the matter with them and there were already, smiles of happiness and satisfaction on their faces. 'This victory belongs to Bhai Fateh Singh. We would not have won without his invincible spirit, his meticulous planning and his valour. In recognition of this distinguished service, I appoint him faujdar of Samana and of its nine dependent parganas [districts].'

The announcement was greeted by a loud and sustained cheer from the assembled throng, proof not only of the general approval of this step, but also of the high regard that Fateh Singh had won for himself. Fateh Singh stepped forward and touched Banda Bahadur's feet in respect, as Banda drew him into a tight embrace. 'You have an extremely difficult task ahead of you,' Banda Bahadur said, his voice carrying even to those in the rear ranks. 'Our conquest has inflicted deep wounds and you will have to work very hard to bring peace to this troubled area and convince people that as their rulers, we will be working for their benefit. You must ensure that the zamindari system is abolished and the ownership of the land is returned to those who till it. Everything you do must be with the specific aim of restoring to the common man his pride, dignity and self-esteem. In doing so you will be carrying out the guru's command and fulfilling his deepest wish.

'Each and every one in my army fought bravely and with perseverance to ensure our victory in the battle of Samana. But there are five who fought with greater courage, vigour and persistence than the others. It is my pleasure to honour them and give them a token of our appreciation for the exemplary courage displayed by them. Bhai Bidhi Chand, Bhai Nam Dev, Bhai Ram Das, Bhai Ram Singh and Bhai Karan Singh, I know, in fact we all know, that you fought with no expectation of any reward. I bestow upon you the ownership of two hundred kilas of land each. The title deeds will be made out shortly and Bhai Fateh Singh will personally hand over possession of your new land holdings to you.' (One kila is approximately one acre.)

As Banda Bahadur had expected, this announcement was received with lukewarm applause. The tentativeness of the cheering that greeted this generous reward showed the confusion that prevailed in the minds of his listeners. Three amongst the five brave warriors belonged to the scheduled castes – people who for centuries had toiled and laboured for their masters without any recognition, without any reward. Men from these castes had never before been honoured and rewarded at a public ceremony like this one. As a result, those who attended the ceremony were confused and did not know how to react. They would learn acceptance soon because this was the practice that Banda would follow after each of his victories. He wanted his followers to understand that for his guru, and consequently for him, the accident of birth held no importance. In Banda's army it did not matter if one was a Brahmin or a chamar, the lowest caste. What mattered were actions, which if of merit, would be recognized and rewarded. He was merely reinforcing a concept that had long been introduced by the gurus.

The tradition of the langar, community kitchen, where all men sat side by side, irrespective of caste or creed, and partook of food together, had been the first step towards establishing a casteless community. These traditions sought to establish the fact that in the eyes of God all men were equal and were as brothers. By rewarding these three men of a so-called lower caste, Banda Bahadur gave further strength to this concept. What he did on that fateful evening in Samana would have far-reaching and lasting effects in the community life of the Sikhs.

> A low scavenger or a leather dresser, the lowest of the low in India in estimation, had only to leave home and join the Guru, when in a short time he would return to his birthplace as its ruler with his order of appointment in his hand. As soon as he set foot within the boundaries, the well borne and wealthy went out to greet him and escort him home. Arrived there, they stood before him with joined palms, awaiting his order.[3]

The caste system was not altogether destroyed in the Punjab, but Banda's efforts in this direction did weaken its hold considerably. The lower castes were never oppressed and exploited again in the Punjab as they continued to be in other states like Uttar Pradesh and Bihar.

Chapter Three

The desire for revenge had blinded the peasants against everything else. They had seen their quarry escape into the fort and they ranged for revenge. The rain of arrows, the gunfire and the balls of flame did nothing to lower their passion. If anything, the Mughals' efforts incited them further and their fury knew no bounds. Banda's forces had also reached the fortress walls. His leaders gave direction to the milling mobs. Battering rams and machines of war were brought into action and one by one, three of the important gates caved in before this determined attack.

A SERIES OF QUICK VICTORIES FOLLOWED. Ghuram, Thaskar, Thanesar, Shahbad and Mustafabad were captured and annexed in quick succession. While the rulers of Thaskar and Thanesar had been kind and benevolent their cities were spared plunder and bloodshed, the cities of Ghuram, Shahbad, Mustafabad suffered the same fact as Samana, as their rulers, were known for their cruelty.

The next target was to be the town of Kapoori. But before he attacked it, Banda spent the night in the village of Dalaur. He knew that his next major battle would be a battle for the control of the town of Sadhaura. Dalaur was only four kos from Sadhaura on the Barara road and he went there to collect information about the possible nexus between Kapoori and Sadhaura. In this village where lived a family of Lubana merchants, close relatives of Sant Singh, the Lubana Sikh who had come to Banda's aid with much-needed money. He had been in communication with this family and they had sent him regular reports of all troop movements and recruitments in Sadhaura. They moved in and out of Sadhaura and had a fairly easy access to strategic information. He reached the Lubana household in the evening with a small band of followers. The rest of his army was already camped within striking distance of Kapoori. Speed was of the essence because Kapoori was only four miles from Sadhaura and if the Sikh force tarried long, the rulers of Sadhaura would know of their presence and would take pre-emptive action.

His hosts made the Sikh party welcome. Though there was generosity in every word they spoke and every deed that the hosts performed, Banda sensed a wariness, a holding back. There was a note of sadness in the caring that they lavished on their guests. It was as if a tremendous burden weighed on their minds and kept them from being effusive in their hospitality. Before his host could begin to talk about the latest military position in Sadhaura, Banda referred to what he had noticed in his behaviour: 'Tell me, brother, what is it that weighs so heavily on your mind and on the minds of your entire family?'

'It is minor personal matter, not worthy of your interest.'

'Though we meet for the first time today, we have long been friends. Anything that troubles you, commands my interest. I will not go further with this conversation, will not ask the questions that I ask, unless you first tell me of your trouble.'

The merchant looked Banda squarely in the eye. 'Then come,' he said, getting to his feet and leading Banda into an inner chamber of the house. He drew the bar from across the door as the shutters swung inwards with a loud creaking sound. There was a single oil lamp burning in an alcove in the wall and by its light Banda saw a girl, a mere child. For a moment there was stark terror in her eyes as she faced her visitor. Then she gave a loud maniacal laugh. With swift, sure movements, she drew off her veil and then her shirt and her salwar, women's trousers. Banda moved forward but his host held him back. Banda looked at the merchant but the old man had eyes only for the child and in those eyes there was the misery of the entire world. Banda looked again at the girl. She reached between her legs and made an obscene gesture: 'Come, come,' she said.

'Come and do what you have come to do.' Banda stood frozen, struck dumb at the enormity of the scene that was unfolding before his eyes.

'You want me to come to you?' the girl said and laughed again, a hysterical high-pitched laugh. 'I will do what you want, anything you want but please, please do not hurt me.'

She came to the two men and kneeling before the old man, she attempted to open the drawstring of his pyjamas. He stood motionless for a moment, frozen, tears flowing soundlessly down his cheeks. Then he too knelt down upon the floor and looking into the girl's eyes, said gently: 'Look at me, my child, look at me.'

'Child?' the girl flung back as Banda recoiled at the venom in her voice, 'I am no child. I am a Mughal whore.'

The old man's fragile frame was wracked with soundless sobs as Banda bent down and put his arm around his shoulder: 'I am your grandfather, your father's father, do you not know me?'

The girl cocked her head to one side and her eyes stared fixed at the old man's face. For a moment Banda thought that he saw a flash of recognition in those wild eyes. But the moment passed and the recognition, if it had been recognition, was replaced by a questioning look: 'Father? Father's father? I have no father, no father's father.' Then there was an open leer upon that face and she laughed again, laughter that was full of mockery. 'I know you,' she said lifting her index finger and wagging it at the old man. 'You like to feel that you are doing it to your granddaughter, you dirty old man. But I will do whatever you ask. Only please do not hurt me. Yes, you are my grandfather. I love you, grandfather.' She put her arms around the old man's neck and kissed him lecherously on his lips. 'Look at this grandfather,' she said cupping a small unformed breast in one hand and holding it up towads the old man. She held that pose for a long moment and then as she turned away, Banda saw in the faint light of the oil lamp, deep bruises, welts and burn marks on her back. She lay down on the floor and spread her legs. 'Come grandfather, come.' And before Banda could take his eyes away from her nakedness he saw the marks of torture that ran all over her legs and her abdomen.

They heard a sound behind them. It was the girl's mother. She moved swiftly to the girl and slapped her firmly, once, twice, three times, across the cheeks: 'Put your clothes on at once.'

'Yes. Yes,' the girl struggled quickly into her clothes.

'Now go and lie down.' The girl moved quickly to do what she was told. The mother took a glass of water from the alcove and shook some powder from a little paper packet into it. Then she stirred it with her finger: 'Now drink this.'

'No. I don't want it. It is bitter.'

The mother slapped her once again and the girl snatched the tumbler from her hand and drank the opiate in one quick gulp. 'Now go to sleep.' The girl lay down on the cot, her knees drawn up to her chin. The draught took effect and in a few moments she was asleep. Only then did the mother permit herself the luxury of grief. She slumped to the floor and her body shook with silent weeping.

'Come,' the old man said and Banda followed him out of the room. There was no need for questions; the girl had answered all of them, even before they were asked. And yet Banda felt constrained to say something and he asked a question even though he knew the answer already.

'Who?'

'Kadam-ud Din, the ruler of Kapoori.'

Banda knew the story well.

Aman Ullah, the last nawab of Kapoori, had been a wealthy and enlightened man. He had used his wealth to turn the village into a veritable heaven. All civic amenities were provided for and the villagers enjoyed the benefits of free healthcare, free education and pensions for the old. It was in every sense a model welfare community, a glittering sun-sparkled jewel of compassion and caring in the all-pervading darkness of Mughal tyranny and oppression. But this idyllic state of affairs was short-lived. Aman Ullah, who had done so much to broaden the minds and outlook of his subjects, failed to do any thing with the mind of his son, Kadam-ud Din who grew up to be self-centred, vicious and debauched. On succeeding to the throne he quickly undid all his father's good work. The welfare state collapsed. Kapoori and its people existed only for the pleasures of their ruler. He squeezed every penny that he could from them and spent it all on himself and his pleasures. Sexual exploitation of the oppressed classes was a well-established practice among the ruling elite of the day but Kadam-ud Din developed it into a fine art. Every young girl from the village who was due to be married had to spend the night before her wedding in the Nawab's bed, every bride who came to the village had first to come to him before she could go to her husband. Not satiated with this he had bands of scouts who scoured the country for pretty and desirable girls to be brought back to his palace.

After they had sat together in silence for a long, long time Banda Bahadur drew the old man gently to the matter that was now at hand.

'No,' the old man said in answer to Banda's question. 'Osman Khan of Sadhaura will not come to Kadam-ud Din's aid. He hates him with a hatred that is as fierce as the hatred Kadam-ud Din's subjects have for their ruler. He will rejoice in his destruction.' He informed Banda about the strength and deployment of Osman Khan's army.

Long before the first light broke Banda took leave of his host. He felt oppressively poor as the only comfort he could offer his long suffering host was a quick embrace and the words: 'I will pray for you.'

Early the next morning, the Sikh forces, augmented by the common people of the surrounding areas, fell upon Kapoori and easily overcame the resistance that was offered. The palace and Kadam-ud Din's pleasure pavilions were looted and destroyed and all his minions perished on the sword. It would have been in the fitness of things, given us a sense of poetic justice, if we could know that Kadam-ud Din was captured, tried and punished with a slow and painful death. In the sound of his cries of agony there would, perhaps, at last be a silencing of the poor child's manic laughter, of her pleas that she be not hurt any more. But history gives us no such relief for the chronicles are silent as to what fate befell him. Perhaps he escaped far, far away where no man knew him, lived out his life in secure anonymity and died at a ripe old age. And we are left haunted by the image of the child and the echoes of her voice and of hundreds like her whom he had destroyed.

It was time now for Banda Bahadur to turn his attention to the town of Sadhaura, which in recent times had earned for itself a reputation for religious intolerance.

Sadhaura was originally sadhu-wara, the abode of the sadhus. During the period when Buddhism had been the predominant religion of north India, Sidhaura had been an important religious centre. Much later the town had been captured and held by the Tusi Pathans. In 1414, Sayyad Nizamuddin drove the Pathans out and was given this town as part of a jagir by the emperor in Delhi. Sayyad Nizamuddin's son, Shah Abdul Hamid, and his grandson, Shah Abdul Wahab, were saints in the true sense of the word. They were venerated during their lifetimes and worshipped after their deaths. Their mausoleums became dargahs. The tomb of Shah Abdul Hamid was known popularly as the dargah of Ganj-i Illam and that of Shah Abdul Wahab as the dargah Qutab-ul Aqtab, the title by which he was worshipped by his followers. The dargah of Qutab-ul Aqtab was located in the Shahwani quarter of the town, which though a predominantly Muslim locality, was so strong in its secular teaching that the few Hindus who lived there, had always been treated with great respect and affection.

Jaswant Rai's family had lived in this quarter for close to two centuries. They had a beautiful haveli and a large walled garden with ornamental canals, fountains, flowers and flowering shrubs, and trees that spread their perfume over the garden both night and day. But Jaswant Rai and his haveli, as indeed all of Sadhaura, had fallen on evil days ever since Osman Khan had become the ruler and the official caretaker of the two shrines. He had not learnt anything from the lives of the two saints buried there and was a bigot in the worst sense of the word. He was convinced that Allah had sent him to this world with the express purpose of converting every kafir, infidel, in Sadhaura to Islam. He regarded this as his divine mission and pursued it with the relentless zeal of a fanatic and set about forcibly converting all his subjects to Islam in direct contradiction to the teachings of the two saints whose tombs he so dutifully protected. He raised the rate of jeziya, the tax on non-Muslims, and passed edicts by which no non-Muslim could hold any government office, nor could he gain admission to seats of higher learning. Any non-Muslim who travelled to and from Sadhaura was burdened with a crippling pilgrim tax. Non-Muslims had to register all births, deaths and marriages, a process which was made extremely cumbersome and expensive. He imposed such heavy taxes on the movement of goods both in and out of Sadhaura by non-Muslims that within a few years non-Muslim traders were financially crippled. While those with the weakest spirits fell in with Osman Khan's designs and converted to Islam, others abandoned their homes and businesses and fled from Sadhaura. A few, very strong minded amongst the non-Muslims stuck on, determined to outlast the oppression of their ruler. Amongst this small band was Jaswant Rai, now well into his sixties and content to leave whatever business remained, in the hands of his sons Hakumat Rai and Ram Rai.

The two brothers, by tacit and secret agreement, had quietly moved the major part of their business out of Sadhaura, though for the sake of appearances they still kept a semblance of business interest in the town of their birth. The families still lived in the town and because of this Jaswant Rai could claim to anyone who cared to listen that like a venerable old tree the roots of his family were too deeply rooted in the soil of Sadhaura to allow transplantation.

The times were difficult, very difficult, yet when deterioration set in, it first appeared in almost unnoticeable stages and then suddenly snowballed into total ruin. Every year, before Diwali, the haveli would get a new coat of paint as a sign of welcome to the Goddess Laxmi. Then one year the family could not spare the money for this annual coat of paint and the goddess of wealth was not made to feel welcome. The next year the family seemed to have even less money. Soon no one could remember when the haveli had last been painted. First, a few rooms and then entire wings fell into disuse and disarray. Windows and door shutters hung awry on hinges that had given way. There seemed to be no money even for essential repairs. Termites ate into the wooden door and window frames. Stone balconies, which had been fixed on to the brick walls with metal plates, fell off after storms and heavy rains and no one thought of putting them back. Soon the plaster on large sections of the walls had crumbled and then the brickwork itself began to give way.

With the next rain, a section of the wall of the old garden wall came down and was not rebuilt. By the third year the gardeners had all been dispensed with as the gardens, which had become one vast stretch of tangled weeds, undergrowth and unkept shrubbery, were now regarded as an unnecessary luxury. The fountains and the canals had fallen into disuse. More of the wall had given in, providing access to wanderers from the street. They came in, at first curious to get a glimpse of something that had been denied to their sight for years. Then later, when the curiosity had worn off, they came in because they regarded the once beautiful gardens as a convenient place for defecation. A part of the garden became a garbage dump and soon the entire quarter was dumping their garbage there. There was, during the day, a cloying, sickening smell of putrification and rot. But in the night there was the perfume of the now wild growing jasmine and the queen of the night that filled the cool air and stirred haunting memories of the beauty that once had been.

At one end of the gardens was a small, very quaint and private temple to Goddess Laxmi, who had been adopted by the family when she had made them the special beneficiaries of her blessings. Jaswant Rai's grandfather had built the shrine and since then the family had taken special pride in it. Jaswant Rai, like his father and grandfather before him, went every morning and evening to the shrine to lead the prayers. One morning, on his way to the shrine, he saw the entire family and its retainers standing in small groups, talking to each other in excited whispers as if joined together in a conspiracy. The moment they saw Jaswant Rai they all fell silent. He was intrigued by this strange behaviour. He walked across the stone platform and once at the doorway peered in. Then he ran to the edge of the platform and leaning over, vomited with loud retching sounds. There in the sanctum sanctorum, at the very feet of the goddess, was the severed head of a cow. Jaswant Rai walked away never to return. The abode of his goddess had been defiled, his goddess had fled and he did not have the means to make her come back. The temple, like the major part of the haveli and the gardens, fell into disuse.

The sons knew that their sojourn in Sadhaura had come to an end. They knew that the haveli was doomed. They had learnt to accept this and were already in discussion as to where their new home should be. This discussion, like the moving of their business, was kept secret from their father. He would not be able to understand or endorse their desire to move and would be pained by it. And in the twilight of his life they did not want to cause him pain. So they kept their plans and their discussion from him.

Osman Khan had fired one final shot at the non-Muslims some time ago by issuing an ordinance that no dead body, which was carried past the holy mausoleum, could be consigned to flames. Doing this would be an act of sacrilege because the dead saint had been a devout Muslim and the act of consigning a body to flames was anathema to a devout Muslim. Such an act would call upon the heads of all the inhabitants of Sadhaura, the wrath of God, both in the earthly domain and in the domain of the spirit. Since the only way out of the quarter went past the mausoleum, the dead would have to be buried according to Muslim rites and the non-Muslims, in effect, would be accepting a conversion to Islam. The few remaining non-Muslims in the Shahwani quarter fled. Jaswant Rai stuck on. This was where he was born, he said, and this is where he would die. In these troubled times this was the only way he could assure eternal rest for his soul. As long as he remained in good health his sons showed no urgency in their pleas that he should move. There was an amused exasperation at his constant and firm refusal to leave Sadhaura. Then, forces beyond the family's control intervened. Jaswant Rai fell ill with a strange illness beyond the ken of all the brilliant vaids and hakims who were called in to attend him. It was a wasting away of the body, a weariness of the soul. Yet the surer he was that his end was near the more resolved he became to die in his haveli. His sons, if they were dutiful sons, would find some way to get around the hateful ordinance. But when the days stretched into weeks and the weeks into months and he became progressively weaker, he realized that his persistence in staying on would, after his death, endanger the lives of all the loved ones who stayed by his side. He could not leave, of that he was certain, but he was also certain that he had no right to put the lives of his family in jeopardy. He called small groups of his family to him, prevailed upon them to move to a safer place, bade them goodbye and sent them on their way. The large and cohesive family was broken up into small, irregular units and sent off to different and unstated destinations.

    At last, only Ram Rai stayed on at Sadhaura with this father. Jaswant Rai tried to make him leave. If he stayed he would cremate his father's body and would then have to face the wrath of Osman Khan. Disobeyed imperial orders meant instant and terrible death and though Ram Rai retained his equanimity in the face of this certitude, his father could not at first accept it. His repeated pleas went unheard. He pleaded again and again but all the response it elicited was a secret smile, a holding of the father's hand or a caressing of his forehead. Then in sheer exasperation the father said: 'Why don't you say something? Why do you always answer my pleas with that infuriating smile?'

'You know that I will never let your body be buried, father. You will be cremated like a true Hindu. It is only those unfortunates who do not have sons who have their funeral pyres lit by servants and friends. You have not one son but two and your pyre will be lit by a son.' He held his father's withered hand in both of his and then raised it to his lips in a rare display of affection. 'You have been the most wonderful father, both to me and to my brother. It would be a sin and God would never forgive us if one of us failed to perform this final duty for you. So let me be father, you cannot persuade me to abandon you and abandon the duty that I must perform for you.'

Members of the well-to-do Muslim families who had been Jaswant Rai's friends and neighbours came in to see how their old friend was doing. Looking into their faces the son saw no concern for his father's illness. He saw only a deep curiosity, an impatient wait for his death to see what the son would do in the face of Osman Khan's ordinance.

The flame finally flickered and was extinguished. Jaswant Rai after a long and eventful life, breathed his last. The grief-stricken and shame-faced son went through the preparations for a Muslim burial. At last the coffin was lowered into the grave and he threw a few clods of earth upon it. As he scanned the faces and looked into the eyes of those who had turned out, one last time, to pay their respects to his father, those who had worked for his father, who had been the beneficiaries of his father's generosity and charity, he saw a look of shame, almost of sadness that they had been powerless to prevent this humiliation of the dead. But in the faces and eyes of the rich and powerful who had once been his father's friends, he saw only triumph, triumph that yet another once proud Hindu had been humbled. He showed no reaction to this but seethed inwardly. His eyes scanned each face again and again and stored each face in his memory. He promised himself that he would make them pay for this, each one of them.

The funeral was over and the mourners all went their separate ways. What they were not to know was that at some stage in the ceremony Ram Rai had snatched a few private moments with his father. He had removed the body from the coffin and weighed the coffin down with stones. For two days and nights after the so-called burial he sat in a secluded room in the sprawling haveli beside his father's body. The neighbours left him alone, convinced that overwhelmed by his grief and by the shame of what he had been forced to do, he did not care to face anyone. In those two days the body putrefied and decayed and the closed room was filled with the smell of rotting flesh. On the third day he filled the room with wood – piles of shavings of dried wood, small pieces a little bigger than twigs, and then pieces as large as small logs. He arranged all this dried wood very carefully around and over his father's body and even after a generous pyre had been built he continued to put on more and more logs of wood till the pile of wood almost reached the ceiling. Then he set fire to the wood, closed the door carefully and stole from the haveli into the remains of the garden and made his way out of the compound.

The town was still asleep. By the time it awoke the fire would have consumed his father's body and the haveli itself would be close to total destruction. If perchance the fire was doused and some remnants of the dead body were found, it would be concluded that the son, maddened by guilt and grief, had set fire to his house and perished in the flames. He hoped that the two days between the funeral and the fire would be enough to remove any suspicion of what had actually happened. He reached the end of the street and turned back to look at what had once been his home.

There was no sign of the fire, not yet. He looked and felt a rush of sadness sweep over him. It had been a happy home, a good secure home, a home full of memories: of his father and of his childhood, which had been overlaid with images of his infant children. It had been a house that had been made a home by the passage of many generations and of the oral history of what so many of them had said and done. And now he had been forced to destroy it. The sadness gave way to anger as he remembered those smug triumphant faces at the funeral. He remembered each of them. He did not know Osman Khan and so there was an element of objectivity in the tyranny and oppression that the ruler had unleashed on his non-Muslim subjects. But he did know the people at the funeral. They were all friends and neighbours of Jaswant Rai's family and now they had turned against that family. He for one would not forget or forgive.

When Banda Bahadur at last made the attack on Sadhaura he was joined by Hakumat Rai and Ram Rai and thousands of other highly motivated men who had neither forgotten nor forgiven the insults and injuries that had been done to them over the years. His bigotry apart and despite the cruel persecution of his Hindu and Sikh subjects, Osman Khan was a strong ruler. He was a powerful man, much dreaded not only for his atrocities against the non-Muslims, but for the total ruthlessness with which he crushed all opposition. He had watched Banda Bahadur's progress into the Punjab and had realized quite early that he would, sooner or later, be a target of Banda's attack. Sadhaura was a rich and prosperous town, its fortifications and defences strong and well-maintained. There was no surprise attack that Banda could hope to mount here, no sneaking in secretly into the fortifications. For the first time he was facing an enemy who had measured his strength, who knew exactly what to expect from Banda and who had dug his heels in for the inevitable confrontation.

From his assessment of Osman Khan's character and military ability, Banda knew that he would not fall into a trap by responding to any diversionary tactics. The siege of Sadhaura would be an open, face-to-face battle. Banda by this time had a force of 400 mounted soldiers and 8,000 foot soldiers. His intelligence had told him that though Osman Khan had about 1,500 mounted soldiers, his infantry was roughy of the same strength as that of the Sikhs. The cavalry could be neutralized if the fort were attacked while Osman and his force were inside. Banda looked at the vast sea of peasantry that swarmed over the plain, eager to storm the fort and to wreck revenge on those who had oppressed and exploited them with such extreme cruelty. He could no longer feel any remorse at the blood thirstiness that his attack would perpetuate. With cynical detachment he welcomed this desire for revenge as a motivating force that he could harness to serve his own ends.

His battle plan evolved quickly and clearly. He would meet the leaders of the peasantry and each leader would be allocated one of the eight gates of the fort. Each segment of peasantry would then swarm these gates with the persistence and vigour of a swarm of locusts. Their numbers were so great that the fort would not be able to hold out against them. His own soldiers, both infantry and cavalry, were divided into contingents and also attached to specific gates they would march through once the peasantry had breached them.

Battle orders were drawn and the Sikhs and their supporters encircled the fort and fell quickly upon it. They were still a few thousand yards from the walls when they saw the Mughal cavalry ride out from the gates followed closely by the infantry. Obviously Osman Khan had assessed the situation in his own way. If they waited in the fort, the vast multitude of peasants would form a living wall and trap them inside. Then, like a pack of hungry wolves, they would overcome the defences and devour every obstacle that came in the way. He decided that it would be far better to ride out and attack the besiegers and take advantage of his superior cavalry.

When the Mughal forces rode out in full strength, the peasantry momentarily halted in their tracks. They had not anticipated this move. Banda Bahadur too held back, not sure how he should react to this unexpected move by the enemy. While he pondered on what he must do, the matter was taken out of his hands. He heard loud blood-curdling battle cries from the groups of peasants. These cries echoed and re-echoed from the walls of the fort. So strong was the desire for revenge that the peasants were now prepared to take on the imperial forces in a head-on collision in an open field. The destruction caused by the superior skills of the Mughal forces was tremendous. Thousands of peasants were killed, which only served to strengthen their resolve. Though each horseman killed as many as ten peasants, sheer numbers finally overwhelmed him. The horse had to pull up against a wall of humanity and the horseman was dragged down and quartered without any mercy. There was nothing that the Mughal cavalry or infantry could do against this overwhelming onslaught. The ranks wavered for a while and then, as if on a prearranged signal, abandoned the battle, turned and fled to the safety of the fort, the peasants in hot pursuit. Though the imperial forces gained the gates well in time to close them against the peasants, their position remained precarious. The desire for revenge had blinded the peasants against everything else. They had seen their quarry escape into the fort and they ranged for revenge. The rain of arrows, the gunfire and the balls of flame did nothing to lower their passion. If anything, the Mughals efforts incited them further and their fury knew no bounds. Banda's forces had also reached the fortress walls. His leaders gave direction to the milling mobs. Battering rams and machines of war were brought into action and one by one, three of the important gates caved in before this determined attack. The peasants streamed into the fort. The imperial forces had taken up strategic positions and once again the untrained and unskilled peasantry was subjected to large-scale killing. But the Sikh infantry and cavalry had by now taken control and fell upon the Mughal forces in full fury. The fate of the battle hung in the balance for a while. Then a cry went up from the Sikh detachment: 'Osman Khan has been killed.' This was all that was needed to signal the Sikh victory. The imperial army fell back, totally demoralized and disarrayed and the Sikhs, both the peasants and the soldiers, fell upon the Mughals and butchered them. The entire city was raised to the ground. Some attempts were made to burn the two shrines but Banda Bahadur intervened and thwarted them. The shrines survive to this day, drawing pilgrims and devotees from all faiths.

When it was obvious that the battle had been lost, many of the terrified Sayyads and Sheikhs took shelter in the haveli of Shah Badar-ud Din. The presumption was very clear. The Shah was popularly known as Sayyad Budhu Shah. He had fought side-by-side with Guru Gobind Singh in the battle of Bhangani and as a punishment for this support to the guru, Osman Khan had killed him. It was natural that Pir Budhu Shah had come to be venerated by all sections of the Sikh community. The Sayyads and the Sheikhs, who had taken shelter in his haveli, presumed that their lives would be spared because the Sikhs would not attack the abode of one they respected so greatly. If the Sikh peasantry were aware that the haveli, which sheltered their enemies, had once been the home of the Sayyad saint, they did not show it. They fell upon the haveli and butchered every Muslim who had taken shelter there. The haveli, or at least what remained of it, came to be known as the Qatalgarhi.

When the evening sun sat low on the horizon, the battle was in its final throes. The Sikhs had won though minor skirmishes and encounters continued with what little pockets of resistance still remained. It had not been an easy victory. Thousands on both sides had lost their lives. The frenzied mob, their eyes red and bloodshot with their desire for revenge, fell upon the civilian population of the city and slaughtered all.

Hakumat Rai and Ram Rai, with a strong band of supporters, combed the Shahwani quarter for any of their former friends and neighbours. They killed them in cold blood, ignoring their frantic pleas for mercy. Finally it was clear that not one of their quarry remained. They paused at the ruins of what had once been their home, exhausted in body, mind and spirit. Then the two brothers made their way through the rubble, the garbage and the overgrown vegetation in what had once been a splendid garden. They came at last to the little shrine where their father, their grandfather and great-grandfather had prayed so often. Miraculously the small marble statue of the Goddess Laxmi still stood where they had abandoned it.

Chapter Four

The battle of Ropar was seen as a successful blow against the faujdar of Sirhind. This once invincible official was now vulnerable and many who had been sitting on the fence, decided to cast in their lot with Banda, who spent the remaining winter months in organizing and training his army.

Banda divided his soldiers into jathas, a loosely organized group of soldiers corresponding to a battalion in a modern army. The soldiers in any one jatha came from the same part of the Punjab or belonged to the same tribe or caste. By doing so Banda was able to give each group a strong sense of cohesion, of loyalty and of fellow feeling.

ALL EYES WERE NOW ON SIRHIND, WHICH POLITICALLY was a valuable prize to be won.

Historically, the city of Sirhind was next only to Lahore in importance in the Punjab. It was one of the oldest cities in the region and its origins were lost in the mists of antiquity. It was strategically located on the important trade route which served the entire Indo-Gangetic plain. Hiuen Tsang, the famous Chinese pilgrim and traveller, had written of Sirhind in glowing terms. 'Sirhind was an opulent town, with wealthy merchants, bankers, tradesmen, men of money and gentlemen of every class; and there were especially learned and religious men in great numbers residing there.' [4] During the Sultanate period in Delhi, Sirhind assumed importance as a frontier defence post, the last major out-post between Delhi and Lahore. An important military cantonment was established here and Firoz Tughlaq built a major fort. One of the many canals that he built ran past Sirhind, bringing prosperity to the region and also enabling the rich aristocrats to design and plant elaborate gardens. Soon Sirhind gained the reputation of being a garden city.

When Bahlol Lodi usurped the throne of Delhi in 1451, he built a tomb to commemorate the memory of his son-in-law Mir-i Miran. The Mir, an extremely pious man, had earned the reputation of a saint. It was no surprise that in a very short time his tomb became a major attraction for pilgrims and Sirhind became a centre of pilgrimage. An institute for the teaching of Islamic theology and literature was also set up here. Sirhind was given greater religious importance by the fact that it was the home of Sheikh Ahmed Sirhindi, the great Naqshbandi saint and teacher of Muslim theology and mysticism. His mosque too became an important place of pilgrimage.

During Akbar's time, Hafiz Sultan Rakhana of Hirat was the governor of Sirhind. He built many beautiful buildings and laid out exotic gardens and it was claimed that in these Sirhind had no parallel in India. There must have been some substance to this claim because property values in Sirhind outstripped those even of Delhi and Sirhind became the second largest revenue earner for the Mughals. Under the Mughal emperors Jehangir, Shah Jehan and Aurangzeb the city of Sirhind gained considerably in prosperity and fame and became a major centre of trade and the inhabitants, by and large, were well-to-do individuals.

By the time of Banda Bahadur's arrival in the Punjab, the town was spread over an area of three kos on the banks of the Hansla river. The population had increased considerably and the walls to the north-west had been dismantled to allow for the expansion of the town. This new quarter of the town was a model of excellent town planning. Sirhind at this time boasted of 360 mosques and, since traditionally a mosque always had a maktab or Islamic school attached to it, Sirhind became an important centre for education.

For centuries the Hindus and Muslims had lived in perfect amity. The majority of the Hindu population belonged to the Sood community who earned their living by leasing agricultural land from the government and wealthy landowners. They were simple, down to earth people, who lived frugal, spartan lives and taught their sons to earn their own living and not expect an inheritance from their fathers. 'Over the years, the Soods became an extremely wealthy community, who were also completely loyal to their Mughal rulers. When Raja Man Singh, as governor of Kabul, set out to quash a Pathan rebellion, five thousand well-equipped volunteers from this community joined his forces. As a result of this loyalty the community flourished further. A chaudhry from each Sood family was appointed as an important official in the court and as many as twenty-two of their leaders had been granted the privilege and honour of being palki-nashin, the right to travel in palanquins.'[5]

In recent years this long-standing cordiality between the two communities had been severely strained. Wazir Khan, taking his cue from the bigotry of Aurangzeb, launched a policy of discrimination against the non-Muslims and subjected them to acts of great cruelty and barbarism, a policy which reached its peak in the martyrdom of Guru Gobind Singh's two young sons in 1704.

In theory Lahore was the seat of Mughal power in the Punjab where all authority emanated from its governor. All the faujdars and amirs of Punjab were subject to his orders and had to seek his approval for all important decisions and actions. But, the then governor of Lahore, Samad Khan, was a weak man. The emperor had been long absent from Delhi and without his support Samad Khan found his authority in Punjab eroded by Wazir Khan, governor of Sirhind. Aurangzeb had vested in Wazir Khan the authority of the dewan, the amir and the faujdar and after Aurangzeb's death, he took advantage of the political instability to establish his independence. He paid mere lip-service to Samad Khan and exercised his own authority in all matters of importance. Since Samad Khan dared not reprimand him for this lapse, other faujdars too began to ignore the authority of Lahore.

They increasingly turned for help and advice to Wazir Khan and soon it was Sirhind under Wazir Khan that became the real seat of Mughal power in the Punjab. Hence, the capture of Sirhind would leave no doubt that it was no longer the Mughals who ruled Punjab but the Sikhs. Banda waited patiently for the Majhaili reinforcements to cross the Sutlej and reach him. But, when he saw Sher Muhammad Khan's success in holding off these Sikhs, Banda decided to ride out and facilitate their crossing.

Sher Muhammad Khan was alarmed by Banda's advance. He realized that if he remained where he was there was every likelihood of his being squeezed between Banda's forces and the Majhaili Sikhs. So he sent a large contingent under his cousin to meet the threat of Banda's advancing army. The Majhailis sensing their opportunity attempted a crossing of the river, which Sher Muhammad Khan with his depleted strength was not able to hold back. But, Sher Khan was not one to give up easily. While the Sikhs were still rejoicing over their successful crossing at Ropar, he made one final effort to destroy them.

On the surface it was an unequal battle. The Pathans of Malerkotla had in their ranks the highly skilled detachment of soldiers, which Wazir Khan had sent to their aid and the Rangars of Ropar equipped with sophisticated artillery, had now joined them. The Sikh forces were smaller in number and had no firearms or guns worth the name. They had come to battle in the name of their guru equipped with this name and swords and spears.

All day long the battle raged with great acts of courage and valour being performed by soldiers on both sides. Towards late afternoon the tide appeared to turn in favour of Sher Muhammad Khan. A westerly wind began to stir, first gently, then increasingly stronger and with it came a darkening of the skies. Providence seemed to be taking a hand in the affairs of men. An unseasonal dust storm started. The skies became darker and the fury of the winds stronger by the minute. As if on a prearranged signal, both forces withdrew to their camps for the night. During the night, braving the fury of the wind and the sand, the Sikhs who were still on the other side of the river, crossed over and joined their brethren at Ropar.

The day dawned fresh and clear. The Sikhs firmly believed that the sand storm was an omen, a sign that God was clearly on their side. This belief and the arrival of the reinforcements, gave them strength of heart and they were determined to defeat the force from Malerkotla. The Pathans, too, after a good night's rest, were confident of victory, led as they were by the indomitable Khizir Khan. They swooped down upon the Sikhs, determined to destroy them once and for all. The battle was reduced to a frenzied close hand-to-hand combat, where it seemed that brute strength would prevail. As was to be expected, there were numerous casualties on both sides. Suddenly, a stray bullet struck Khizir Khan. The Pathan forces were shocked at the fall of their leader. Uncertainty prevailed for a while. The Sikhs pounced upon them with renewed vigour. Soon, the Rangars and Pathans were driven back by the Sikhs.

Sher Muhammad, accompanied by his cousins Nashtar Khan and Wali Muhammad Khan, came forward to lead his forces in person. But his soldiers by now were highly demoralized. Both Nashtar Khan and his brother were killed in the scuffle while Sher Muhammad Khan was seriously wounded. The Pathans were left without a leader and were no longer in a position to prevent the Majhailis from joining Banda's army. Banda advanced upon the town of Banur and captured it without having to strike a blow. He secured the citadel and moved towards Ropar to meet the Sikhs who came to join him from the north. This memorable meeting took place between Kharar and Banur.

In the public imagination this success assumed far greater significance than the minor military victory warranted, for the battle of Ropar was seen as a successful blow against the faujdar of Sirhind. This once invincible official was now vulnerable and many who had been sitting on the fence, decided to cast in their lot with Banda, who spent the remaining winter months in organizing and training his army.

Banda divided his soldiers into jathas, a loosely organized group of soldiers corresponding to a battalion in a modern army. The soldiers in any one jatha came from the same part of the Punjab or belonged to the same tribe or caste. By doing so Banda was able to give each group a strong sense of cohesion, of loyalty and of fellow feeling. The irregulars, the highly motivated Sikhs, Muslims and Hindus, peasants and small-time businessmen, who had come seeking revenge on their oppressors, were also organized into groups, each of which was attached to one of the jathas and in the short time available were taught the skills of sword fencing, archery and some battle tactics. By April, the seemingly undisciplined horde of followers got the semblance of a regular army.

Banda had realized that he was highly disadvantaged as far as his strength in artillery and cavalry was concerned. So, while he was busy training his soldiers, he sent out bands of agents to scour the countryside and to requisition or purchase arms, ammunition, horses and elephants.

Wazir Khan had looked upon Banda's march into the Punjab with something akin to amusement for he could never imagine that this ascetic, who had lived a life of renunciation for so long, could achieve success as a general and lead his soldiers to victory. This amusement, which turned to incredulous amazement, soon gave way to alarm after the sack of Kapoori and Sadhaura. Stories of the acts of cruelty perpetuated upon the inhabitants of these two towns were in wide circulation. They could not but create panic amongst the inhabitants of Sirhind who knew that a confrontation with the Sikhs was inevitable. Wazir Khan turned to his trusted adviser Suchanand, who had advised him to kill Guru Gobind Singh's captive sons, for advice.

Suchanand's advice followed predictable directions. His first suggestion was that a thousand soldiers, under the command of his nephew, take on the guise of disaffected rebels and appear to desert the Sirhind army. They were to approach Banda Bahadur and offer him their services as Banda always welcomed deserters and discontented soldiers with open arms because they provided a highly motivated force against a common enemy. Once these thousand soldiers had been assimilated into the Sikh army, they would provide an extremely effective counter force to be used as and how Wazir Khan desired. It was a plan worthy of Suchanand's deviousness and Wazir Khan's treacherous nature. It might perhaps have succeeded if Ali Singh and Mali Singh, former residents of Sirhind, had not recognized Suchanand's nephew and suspected his treacherous designs. They warned Banda Bahadur who was able to take adequate precautions to foil Wazir Khan's designs. The thousand soldiers with their commander were designated as an independent jatha and segregated from the rest of the army and other leaders warned against their possible treachery. As a result, Suchanand's nephew found himself in a state of total isolation. What he did not know was that Bhai Binod Singh was using him as a conduit to send disinformation to Wazir Khan.

The second measure suggested by Suchanand and adopted by Wazir Khan was the calling of a conclave of zamindars and rich land owners, both Muslim and non-Muslim. Wazir Khan emphasized the need for all zamindars to unite in the battle against Banda Bahadur who was committed to the abolition of the zamindari system. Wazir Khan was able to garner the support of many non-Muslim zamindars.

The final measure suggested by Suchanand showed the level of cynicism to which he had allowed himself to sink. He, a twice-born Brahmin, advised the faujdar to call upon all the mullahs to declare a holy war, a jihad, against the infidel, Banda Bahadur. Fatwas were issued making a passionate and fervent appeal to all fundamentalists. Soon, a large numbers of gazis, or soldiers of God, sallied forth from every nook and corner of the Punjab. They came with contingents of soldiers, some small and some large in number, but all highly motivated, to join Wazir Khan's forces in the holy war. The coming battle, at least on Wazir Khan's side, had been reduced to simple but ominous terms – a holy war between the Muslims and kafirs. It was a jihad and God's hand would be with the true believer in this quest of conquest and defeat of the infidel.

While Banda Bahadur made his preparations for the coming battle, the daily routine in his camp continued to cater for the morning and evening prayer meetings, at one of which, he became aware of an elderly woman who sat patiently on one side, waiting to catch his attention. There was something that was faintly familiar about her. But absorbed as he was in his prayers, he could not spare the mental effort that would establish who she was and where he had seen her before. Once the meeting was over and the devotees got up to leave, one by one, his eyes turned again to the woman. There was anxiety in those eyes and uncertainty. Perhaps she doubted his ability to be able to help her. At last it was her turn.

'What is it, mother?' he asked gently, hoping God would give him the power to help her. She smiled. It was a small sad smile.

She knew that the term 'mother' had not been used as a term of specific endearment but as a general term of respect.

'Do you not know me, my son?' He recognized the love in that endearment, recognized that she was his mother. He felt no joy, no flood of warmth, and no sadness that they should have come in contact like strangers did. He felt only a deep stillness. They had been mother and son, but that had been in another world, in another life and had no bearing on the present. He had been able to put it all away. But, he was not sure that she had been able to do so. She spoke, as if in answer to his thoughts.

'I would not have come to you. I gave you birth but I have known for long that you have severed the bond that once bound you to me. I expected this. Found pride and joy in what you do for others, found comfort in the thought that from being my son alone, you have become the son of thousands of mothers. I come now, not as your mother but as a supplicant, one among the dozens whom you have comforted today. My husband is dying and his breath will not leave his body till he catches one last glimpse of he who was his son. He is too sick to come to you. I beg you to come to him to bring him moksha [freedom from the cycle of birth and death].'

She reached forward and held his feet so firmly, it seemed that she would never let go. He put his hand on her head. 'Come,' he said. 'From what you have told me, mother, there is little time to lose.' And still he used the term as a term of general respect and not as an endearment. She was, as she had said, only one among the hundred supplicants.

They travelled through the night and reached Buttana in the early hours of the morning. The sky was lighter though the sun had still not broken over the horizon. There was the twittering and chirping of birds before they took flight in their daily search for food. On the outskirts of the village, they met a few farmers, carrying their ploughs over their shoulders, guiding their oxen to their fields. Each of them slowed their pace as Banda and his group passed and turned to stare at them. No words were exchanged and each went his way. Banda broke from the group and strode ahead, walking through the once familiar brick-paved street. There was the smoke of morning fires in the air, the pungent smell of burning cow-dung cakes. There was the sound of voices raised in prayer and in devotional song. There were the voices of girls calling out to their friends to join them as they made their way to the village well. He saw the first stirring of life in his village, once so familiar and well loved, now still remembered but lacking the ability to move him.

He came at last to what had once been his home; the door was wide open and he strode through it and across the paved courtyard. There was a small, hushed group of people sitting outside his father's room. They made way for him as he strode to the door. He stood at the doorway and looked down at his father, an oil lamp burned on the ground beside his father's head, casting its light on the disease-ravaged face. The body was wracked with agonizing gasps, each breath a painful labour and there was pain too in the eyes as they looked up at him. He realized that he was silhouetted against the morning light and his father could not see his face. He stepped into the room and at last his father saw him. The unseeing eyes became curious and then at last recognition dawned on them. The face broke into a radiant smile and all the pain and disease disappeared and he saw his father again as the once handsome man he had known. The radiant smile remained in place for a long moment. The old man raised his head and stretched out his hand. Then the head fell back on the pillow, the painful wracking stopped. The face still wore the warm radiance of that last flash of happiness and joy; the eyes still retained that excitement of recognition as they glazed over. Banda Bahadur reached down and closed the eyelids.

Later that morning, he bathed the dead body and in the afternoon lent his shoulder to the bier that carried it to the cremation grounds. Here, he supplied the flame that set the pyre burning and two days later, he bore the fragments of bones in a cloth bag to Haridwar and cast them in the holy waters of the Ganga. He returned to Buttana for the mandatory funeral feast that they must host for the village. All through, there was a sense of detachment. When at last all was done and he turned to take leave of his mother, the stillness left him and in its place was a soft, throbbing pain. He knew it was not pain at the loss of his father, because his father had long ceased to be anything but a stranger, someone whom he had once known and who had now ceased to be a part of his life. Try as he would, he could not find an explanation for this pain and this failure caused such confusion in his mind that he was not able to put it away from him.

On his way back from Buttana he and his small group stopped at a hamlet to seek refreshment. While they ate, Banda looked up and saw on the peak before them the fort of Mukhlispur. He remembered it clearly from the many hours he had spent there with Salim Khan all those long years ago. Feeling an overpowering urge to revisit it, Banda took leave of his companions for a couple of hours. Once inside the fort, through the massive front gate, he saw that nothing had changed since he had last been here. It had been built so strong that the intervening years had been but a pause and had done nothing to hasten the process of decay. He stopped to drink at the spring, the waters as cool and sweet as they had always been and then he climbed to the turret at the highest point of the fort. He could look down across the low foot hills to the plains that stretched as far as the eye could see. On two sides the hill was enclosed by rivers and he could sense from the sound that the waters were too deep to allow easy fording. On the fourth side he looked up at the hills ranging higher and ever higher. He knew these hills as he knew all the ravines and forests, like the back of his hand. Even now, after all these years, he was sure that he could find every tree, every fork in the rivers, every spring, every waterfall, every haunt of the birds, the bees, the rabbits and the deer that he had known in his childhood. But even while he surveyed the calm and peaceful countryside, the pain remained.

Why? Was it remorse at having abandoned his parents? Or guilt at never having thought to get in touch with them? Then he remembered his mother's words: 'For myself I would never have come to you. I come to you for another.' His pain was because his father had never let go of him. The pain that he felt was his father's pain. Tears came and at last the pain ceased. He walked down to the spring, washed his face, drank from the sweet waters and walked back to rejoin his group.

That night the memory of Mukhlispur came to haunt his dreams. He saw a fort in good condition of repair, the buildings still intact, and the defences needing a minimum effort at reinforcement. He saw a fort impregnable from three sides; its only access over a steep treacherous climb, which the Mughals would not dare to use. He saw a fort with its independent source of water and the ability to hold out against a long siege. It was an ideal place to establish his stronghold, an ideal place from which to administer the areas that he had conquered, an ideal place from which, if the need ever arose, to melt into the safety of the surrounding hills. Banda took an immediate decision, which could provide him with an important stronghold in his struggle with the Mughals. The moment he returned to the camp he took steps to secure the fort of Mukhlispur. Gyasuddin, the master builder with vast experience in construction work of this nature, was given charge.

With the advent of May, Banda knew that he was as prepared as he would ever be to take on the forces of Wazir Khan, and to capture Sirhind. The forces were more or less equally matched. Banda had under his command 35,000 men. Of these 11,000 were mercenaries and professional robbers and thieves. As opposed to Banda's actual strength of 24,000, Wazir Khan had 15,000 well-trained and disciplined soldiers. He also had the support of 5,000 gazis who had come to him in answer to the mullahs' call of jihad. The gazis were experienced, highly motivated soldiers. Though Wazir Khan had a smaller number of soldiers, his army was much better equipped than the Sikh army. He had at least two dozen cannons, a sufficient number of arms and ammunition and at least half his force consisted of mounted soldiers. He also had a large group of elephants. The Sikhs, on the other hand, had no artillery, no elephants and very few horses. Few of the soldiers were armed with matchlocks. With such great disadvantages the superiority of number became negligible and Wazir Khan felt that he had the advantage, provided he took the lead.

Wazir Khan was an experienced soldier and strategist. He often stood on the ramparts of his fort and watched his army perform military manoeuvres on the plains below. The sight had filled his heart with pride. They had all, every single person,

'Tazkiratus-Salatin Chaghata'

Details of the battle of Chapar-Chiri as written by Muhammad Hadi Kamwar Khan in his 'Tazkiratus-Salatin Chaghata':

"A large number of persons belonging to the class of sweepers and tanners, and the community of banjaras and others of base and lowly castes, assembled around him (Banda Singh) and became his disciples. The person (Banda Singh) gave himself the title of *Fath Shah* (Patshah). First, he ravaged the township of Sadhaura and after that he destroyed and burnt a large number of villages and towns and having killed the Muslim inhabitants and their families, he headed towards Sarhind. Wazir Khan had since long been holding the faujdari of that place; he was descended from Wazir Khan Akbar Shahi.

He (Wazir Khan) came out for a distance of 8 Kurohs from Sarhind and a fierce battle and heavy slaughter took place, and his (Wazir Khan's) principal officers were killed. He too was driven by his sense of pride to engage these faithless heretics (Sikhs) and so tasted the drink of martyrdom. His son, relatives and friends and the pirzadas (men of mystic families) of Sarhind, along with their families, fled towards the capital (Delhi). These rebels who were as numerous as ants and locusts, reached Sarhind in a twinkling of the eye, and collected about rupees two crores in cash and goods from the effects of Suchanand, Wazir Khan's *peshkar* (clerk) and other Muslims of this place. They (Sikhs) left no stone unturned in inflicting insult and humiliation and burnt that beautiful town and its good buildings. They strengthened its fort and turned their attention to other towns and villages".

Source: *Nishaan*, Issue II/2010, p. 8

performed their movements with exemplary precision and meticulousness. He had moved from cannon to cannon as his gunners carried out practice firing and had been amazed at their accuracy. Surely the Sikh army would not be able to withstand such an accurate barrage of gunfire. His archers too, when they let fly their arrows in unison, seemed to be like some divine retribution sent by God, whose first flight of arrows could strike terror in the hearts of the enemy. Learning from the experience of Samana and Sadhaura, Wazir Khan decided not to wait for the enemy but ride out and meet it at Chappar Chiri, ten miles from Sirhind.

He deployed his cannons in a carefully designed semicircle so that the fire from his batteries would contain the Sikh forces. Behind the cannon were his archers and musketeers who would fire upon any formation that came successfully through the cannon fire, with his cavalry, ready to charge at any of the enemy who still broke through, forming the third line of defence.

Banda got news of this careful deployment of troops and raced towards Chappar Chiri and reached the battlefield in the evening. There was still enough light for him to ride out to a strategic height and view the enemy deployments. Wazir Khan had indeed seized the advantage and laid the ground for an open battle where he could make optimum use of his superior artillery and cavalry. Banda returned to his camp and, in the fading light, called a council of war. Their effort would be to press on in full strength and trust their numbers and their spirit to carry them past the cannons. Going by the assumption that in the deployment of artillery that he had seen, the weakest are usually placed in the middle of the arc, Banda decided to aim his major thrust at the four batteries in the centre. For this thrust he chose the Malwa Sikhs, who had been the longest with him and entrusted the command to Bhai Fateh Singh, Karam

Singh, Dharam Singh and Ali Singh. Raj Singh, with the Majha Sikhs was placed on the left flank and Sham Singh, with the Doaba Sikhs was placed on the right flank. Banda himself would be positioned on the left of the battlefield, on a mound high enough to give him a vantage view of the battle, from where he would direct the movements of his army.

The twenty-second day of May 1710, dawned bright and clear and promised to be a hot, scorching day. Banda had taken up position long before the break of dawn. As the sun rose over the horizon, the opposing forces got full sight of each other. Silence descended upon both the armies. Banda sized both forces – the enemy with its semicircle of cannons, the gunmen besides them, waiting for orders to fire, the archers and the musketeers and then the infantry – all formed up in military precision, all turned out smartly in uniform. Then on his own side, he saw the restless rabble, a swarming sea of humanity dressed in all kinds and colours of clothing, armed with the most varied motley of weapons that any army had ever possessed. But he felt no doubt, no uncertainty. There was just one thought in his mind, one feeling in his heart: 'Let God's will be done.'

As the sun rose higher and the heat shimmered in waves above the plain, Banda saw his army advance with little semblance of order in their movements. Some segment of the army moved faster than the others and were well ahead before the leaders called a halt and waited for the rest to catch up. It was a staggered movement, lacking all precision, all practice. Then, as if on an unheard command, the first cannon thundered, followed by others in quick succession. The cannonballs fell with deadly accuracy among the front ranks of the Sikhs. Smoke, reeking of the smell of gunpowder filled the air. Severed heads and limbs flew into the air and the survivors of this first onslaught, their faces and bodies smoke-stained and splattered with blood, looked with horror at the remains of those who had once been their friends and fellow soldiers. Before they could recover from their shock, the next round of cannon shots fell upon them. Banda saw from his vantage point bodies of men detach themselves from the rear of each of the jathas by the simple expedience of stopping in their tracks. These were the thieves and robbers who had joined only for plunder. Now that their lives were endangered they had lost all stomach for battle. He had known that this would happen. After a while he saw, on the left flank an entire body of soldiers break away from the battlefield. These must be the men from Sirhind. Banda Bahadur seemed to sense a holding back, an uncertainty among his soldiers. They stood on the battlefield, unmindful of the cannon balls raining upon them with unfailing regularity. Just then Raj Singh rode up to the mound: 'The dakus do not join the fight and the thousand from Sirhind have deserted.'

'Yes. I can see that. The others stand undecided. There is not a moment to be lost. Come, we will ride together and give the lead.'

The Sikhs in the vanguard saw their leader ride down from the mound and through the cannon fire into the very thick of battle. They took fresh heart. A cheer went up from the soldiers and passionate war cries echoed through the smoke-filled air. In spite of the heavy casualties inflicted by the Mughal artillery, the musketeers and the archers, the Sikhs swarmed past the cannons and engaged the Mughal infantry in a hand-to-hand combat. On all sides there was the sound of steel striking steel, of loud war cries and of cries of agony of the wounded and the dying. Mixed with the smell of the gun powder, was the equally strong smell of blood, both human and animal.

Wazir Khan had been fighting where the battle was thickest.

He came face to face with Fateh Singh and through the smoke recognized the brave commander: 'Say your prayers, if you have prayers. For this is where you meet your end.' He drew his sword and rushed upon Fateh Singh, who did not waste his breath on words. He drew his sword and with one quick movement severed Wazir Khan's head. The Sirhind soldiers saw their commander's head fall to the ground and roll under his horse's hooves. The fight went out of what remained of Wazir Khan's army and they fled to the safety of the fort. 'Not a man of the army of Islam escaped with more than his life and the clothes he stood in. Horsemen and footmen fell under the swords of the infidels who pursued them as far as Sirhind.'[6]

The Sikhs had routed the Mughal forces. Yet they had suffered such heavy losses both in terms of the dead and the wounded that it took them two full days to regroup in sufficient strength to attempt the final assault on the fort, ten miles away, where the survivors of Wazir Khan's army were holed up to make one last brave effort to stave off Banda's attack. Every time the Sikhs rushed at the gate, one of the strategically placed guns fired steadily upon them, forcing them to fall back. During the course of a few hours, 500 Sikhs had fallen under its deadly fire. They could no longer afford such heavy losses, nor could they afford to be held back much longer as the battle-weary soldiers would lose heart. It was imperative that the gun be silenced. Ali Singh, who had long lived in Sirhind, told them of an abandoned brick kiln. From its height a sniper could take the gunmen and provide a safe passage into the fort for Banda's soldiers. Sham Singh, who had deadly accuracy with a musket, was entrusted the task.

In a diversionary tactic, Banda Bahadur mounted a fresh attack at the gate. While the cannon thundered down at the others, Sham Singh and Ali Singh moved quickly and took up position on the mound of the abandoned brick kiln. Banda and his men fell back and the gunners relaxed, unaware of the danger that lurked. They broke cover and in two quick shots Sham Singh killed both of them. The cannon was silenced, the gates broken through. The mob descended first on Wazir Khan's palace but the inhabitants had all fled to Delhi the moment they had heard of his death. In savage fury at being deprived of their revenge, the mob fell upon the palace and plundered and looted everything they could lay their hands on. It tore the palace apart brick by brick.

Another section of the mob made its way to Suchanand's house. Not finding him there, it's fury knew no bounds. One of the servants, on the promise of his life, led them to another house, where he was found hiding in a jar in the granary. He was pulled out and marched into the market square where a huge crowd had collected to see his execution. The once proud and arrogant dewan was reduced to a pitiable state. In the scuffle, his clothes had been torn and he stood there with a few tatters hanging from his body, his face smeared with soot and mud. He expected no mercy, none was shown. His body was hacked to pieces, care being taken to keep him alive as long as possible. There were people who knew Suchanand and who said that he had only got what he deserved. '... have heard from reliable people of the neighbourhood that during the time of the late Khan there was no zullum that he had not inflicted upon the poor subjects, that there was no seed of which he now reaped the fruit, that he had not sown himself.' [7]

The rabble had tasted blood and would not be denied. Muslims had become the main target. The mob went from house to house seeking out the inhabitants, pulled down the trousers of all males to establish from the fact of their circumcision if they were Muslims or not. Many Muslims managed to escape to the Sood quarter of the town and found asylum in the homes of their Hindu friends. All through the day the nightmare of death and destruction continued.

Banda walked through the streets. He saw a doorway littered with the shards of broken pots while from inside he heard the wailing of a woman and the voice of a man begging for mercy. He went in. Kneeling on the bare mud floor was a poor Muslim, his hands raised in supplication. Above him stood a Sikh soldier, his naked sword raised high, ready to swoop it down to strike the poor man. In the shadows he could see the dark figure of a woman, two small children clutched tightly to her sides, wailing in the face of inevitable death.

'What is it, Bhai Singha? Who is this man? Why do you seek to kill him?'

'He is a Muslim, my lord.'

'But he is a poor potter. He could not have been cruel to anyone, could not have harmed or oppressed anyone. Why do you seek his death?'

'He is a Muslim. Wazir Khan's soldiers were told that they must kill all Sikhs, that their war was against the Sikhs. So our war must be against the Muslims and we must kill all Muslims.'

Banda reached forward and raised the potter to his feet. Then putting his arm around the Sikh's shoulder he said: 'Do you forget that Guru Nanak's closest friend and confederate was a Muslim? Do you forget that Muslims composed some of the most beautiful verses of our Gurbani? Do you forget that a Muslim laid the foundation stone of the Harmandir Sahib? No, my son, no matter what Wazir Khan and his mullahs said and did, our war is not against the Muslims, it is against all oppression and tyranny, whether it is the tyranny of Wazir Khan or the tyranny of Suchanand.'

Banda and his leaders, with bands of followers, combed the streets of Sirhind, calling a halt to this gruesome dance of death. He sat in silence, overcome by the death and destruction that he had unleashed upon this once proud city. As the evening shadows lengthened, Binod Singh stole upon him: 'Bhai Sahib, it is time for Rehras [the evening prayers].' Banda put his thoughts aside and got to his feet to lead the congregation through the evening prayer. As always, prayer brought him comfort and peace and by the time he had finished some measure of equanimity had returned to him.

Amongst the crowd of supplicants waiting for his help was Dev Dutt Sood, one of the leaders of the Sood community. He had brought a large offering of money and pledged support of the entire Sood community. Then, after a pause, he added: 'There is one petition,' he said. 'And I make it with the confidence that yours is a benign and forgiving soul.'

'There is no need for flattery,' Banda cut in. 'Come to the point. What is it you want of me?'

'There are many Muslims who sought safety in our quarter. I beg you to forgive them for whatever crimes they may have committed and to spare their lives.'

Banda smiled at him: 'And you have brought me their ransom. There was no need for this. We are all weary of the killing and they would have lived even without your intercession.'

Contrary to the commonly held and widely accepted belief, Banda did not cause the city of Sirhind to be raised to the ground. He made every effort to stop the rack and ruin that he had seen perpetuated upon the cities of Samana, Sadhaura and Kapoori. Though in the initial stages of his occupation a few buildings were set afire, most of them, including the dargahs, remained intact. It was fifty-four years later, on 4 January 1764, that the Sikhs under Jassa Singh Ahluwalia captured Sirhind and raised it to the ground.

From Sirhind, Banda Bahadur moved to subjugate Ghudani, Malerkotla and Raikot in quick succession. No resistance was offered; defeat accepted and heavy ransom and tribute paid. All three towns were spared the carnage and destruction that had been the signature of Banda's earlier conquests. At Malerkotla, late in the evening when the terms of surrender and subjugation had been worked out, Banda attended a special prayer meeting, which was a thanksgiving to God for the easy success of the guru's mission. All through the prayers Banda was conscious of a woman, dressed all in white, who stood a little apart from the rest of the congregation. As always, after the prayers, those who sought Banda's help and advice came up to him one by one. She was the last to stand before him, old and frail, unable to lift her eyes to him, unable to speak.

'What is it, mother?' he asked gently, getting to his feet. 'You need not be afraid. You can tell me what is in your heart.'

She looked up at last and smiled at him: 'I'm not afraid,' she said. 'Not any more. Fear, like grief, left me a long time ago. I was overwhelmed to be at last in the presence of my guru and I was at a loss.'

'Don't do this to me, mother. You know I am no guru. I am merely Banda, the guru's bondsman.'

'In my eyes and in my heart you are my guru and nothing that anyone might say or do can change that.'

Banda recognized the futility of argument. 'What can I do for you, mother?'

Chappar Chiri
Present-day Gurdwara on the edge of the historic battlefield
(the battle took place on 12 May 1710).

Jama Masjid at Banur
Maulana with his kids standing on the roof of the tunnel that
was connected underground to the Gurdwara of Chhat (7 km from Banur).

Wall paintings inside Dera Baba Banda Singh Bahadur at Riasi (Jammu).

Manimajra Fort, Chandigarh

Burail Fort
Hidden in the dense 'concrete jungle' of Chandigarh, this fort still has some traces left.

'My name is Sada Kaur and I come to you for help. Not for myself but for my granddaughter. Her name was Anoop Kaur, beautiful and strong, the apple of my eye, the reason for my existence. She was a maidservant in the household of my guru. Then in the confusion after the battle of Chamkaur, she caught the eye of Sher Muhammed Khan of Malerkotla. He lusted for her and had her made captive and brought here to Malerkotla. He thought that like all his conquests this one too would be an easy one. He had not made consideration for the fierce spirit of my child. When he sent for her that night, they found her dead, a knife driven into her heart. Like a true Sikh, she had preferred death to dishonour.' She paused and Banda thought it was to collect her emotions, but there had been no break in her voice, no clouding in her eyes.

She took a deep breath and swept on: 'When the news of her death was brought to him, he raged like one who has gone insane. He had never in his life before been cheated of what he had desired. He had been cheated now and he could not forgive her, not even in her death. I begged him for her body but he only laughed in my face. He buried her in a grave as if she were a Muslim. When he saw me weeping over her grave, he mocked me,' her voice came in sibilant whispers through her toothless mouth, giving a ghostly quality to her words, "See how I make her suffer even in her death, because she did not give me what I wanted from her while she lived," he taunted me.'

In the dancing lights of the torches, Banda looked closely at the old woman's face. There was no sadness there, no weakness, only the strength of a fixed determination. 'I would go each day to the grave and each day I knew my Anoop would find redemption. I heard of your coming and prayed for your success. And now you are here, I beg of you to exhume her body and give her the last rites that are due to her so that her spirit will at last find rest and peace.'

'We will go to the grave tomorrow and do as you ask.'

'No.' The monosyllable was a quick sharp cry of pain. 'Not tomorrow. Today. Now. I have been patient all these years for I had no option but to be patient. Now with you here, I cannot be patient. I do not think that I would be able to live through the night.'

In the eerie atmosphere of a torch-lit night, in a private courtyard, Anoop Kaur's body was at last exhumed from her grave. For a moment Banda was afraid that the old woman would ask for the coffin to be opened so that she could get one last glimpse of her beloved granddaughter. He heaved a sigh of relief when she made no such demand.

The funeral pyre was built carefully log by log and the coffin placed upon it. Appropriate prayers were recited and Banda himself lit the pyre. They waited long enough to ensure that the fire would complete its task. As Banda stared into the flames, he pondered over the short tragic life of the unknown girl. It was God's will and he had seen this will work itself out in stranger ways than this. He turned to look for the grandmother. She sat patiently on the stone step, staring at the burning pyre.

'Come, mother. Your work is done.'

'I would like to sit a little longer here.' Banda hesitated. 'Do not worry about me,' she said. 'I have made this journey from my hut to her grave so often before, I could make it now even if I were blindfolded. Don't worry about me. I will not die on you. Now that the burden of all these years has been lifted from my shoulders, there is much that I wish to live for.'

Chapter Five

There is no greater excitement than that which accompanies the birth of a state and if the capital of the state is also born at the same time, all the excitement focuses on the new town. So it was with Lohgarh. The entire region was gripped by a raging fever. After centuries of rule by foreign invaders, the natives had at last come into their own. After centuries of dominance by Muslim rulers, control had passed into the hands of non-Muslims.

IN THE MONTHS THAT FOLLOWED, THERE WAS A LULL IN HIS military activity and whatever attacks he mounted were in the nature of mopping up operations, which met with little or no resistance. Bahadur Shah, after his campaign in the Deccan, chose not to return to Delhi but to move to Rajasthan to crush insurgency there. Banda decided to take advantage of this opportunity to consolidate his hold on southern and central Punjab. In quick succession he annexed Saharanpur, Behut, Ambeta and Naunta. In a short time Banda and the Sikhs had become the undisputed masters of the entire area from Sadhaura to Raikot and from Machhiwara to Karnal. He had conquered the area between the Jhelum and the Jamuna and was soon governing it through his deputies. He called a council of leaders to seek their opinion and advice.

'While the Mughal emperor is busy with the Rajputs we should move to establish administrative control over the areas we have conquered.' He paused for breath and scanned the faces of his leaders. The younger ones among them nodded their heads in agreement but the veterans, the ones who had come with him from Nanded, sat silently, looking at him with watchful eyes. As the wars had taken a heavy toll, the few who remained seemed now to be wary of him. He waited for them to speak, but the silence stretched on. He had hoped for vocal support for what he was suggesting. Even, the youngsters who had nodded their heads with vigorous assent a short while ago, now sensed a conflict in the offing and chose to hold their peace.

'Do you not agree?' he addressed his question to Bhai Binod Singh and the handful of veterans who still remained. Binod exchanged glances with the others and Banda sensed that the matter had been discussed behind his back. 'Come, Bhai Binod. You know that I am dependent upon your opinion and advice and bound by the decisions of the Khalsa even when they go against my own beliefs and judgement.'

Even as he said this he admitted to himself that this was not strictly true: never in the recent past had the Khalsa taken a decision, which went against his own wishes. He realized with sudden and complete clarity that true democracy had ceased to exist amongst the ranks of his followers. Most of his leaders were youngsters, who had assumed leadership only in recent months to fill the vacuum created by the loss of many of the veterans. These youngsters were awed by his stature and his achievements. Legends about their leader were the staple diet of their formative years and they would have considered it sacrilege to question anything that Banda Bahadur proposed. They would sense his mood and give voice to their support and before the veterans could express a difference, the pendulum would swing in favour of Banda's proposal.

The veterans held their peace, not wishing to appear to be in conflict with their leader, not wishing to create a rift in the ranks of the Khalsa. But obviously the decision regarding their next course of action was so important that they could not quietly accept their leader's viewpoint without an open discussion on the subject. They knew what was in their leader's mind and were in disagreement with him. Their sullen silence had reflected it and the younger leaders too held their peace. Banda had no option but to bring their disagreement out into the open. 'What is it, Bhai Binod Singh? Your silence tells me that you have reservations.'

'Yes, my lord,' Binod replied, looking him straight in the eye. 'We have our reservations. If advantage has to be taken of the Mughal emperor's continued absence, it must be to subjugate Lahore and Delhi. Our power is at its zenith; the emperor's deputies in both places are weak and indecisive. One determined push would topple the Mughal empire.'

Banda smiled: 'You have given voice to the wish of my heart. How often have I wished to give the order to rush our forces to Delhi and to raise our standard on the ramparts of the Red Fort but have fought the temptation to do so with all my strength. Look around you, Binod, see how many of those brave and trusted warriors who helped us win our battles are with us today. Our strength, after the Battle of Sirhind, is sadly depleted. We cannot be sure of the support from the areas we have conquered, not sure that they will not rise when we march to Delhi and be an enemy at our backs.'

He paused and looked around, waiting for his words to sink in. 'True, Lahore and Delhi are not the forces they once were. True that we would in all probability be able to overthrow them. But we have come too far to risk a probability. When we attack these two important bastions, these symbols of Mughal power, it must be with certainty of success on our side, as we did in the case of Sirhind. And this certainty can only come if we consolidate our position and are certain of the support in men and arms and in food from the areas that we have conquered.'

'We have destroyed the rulers and all their ilk – the common man, irrespective of caste or creed hails you as his saviour and will do anything to show his gratitude. He will not rise against you. Rather if you marched to Delhi, he would march by your side to ensure the fall of the Mughal capital,' replied Bhai Binod.

Banda smiled. 'Are you sure, Bhai Binod?' Those who knew him sensed a touch of sadness in his voice. 'Are you sure?' He paused for a moment and before Binod could reply, he swept on: 'I am not. After the fall of Sirhind I saw some of our Sikh brethren indulging in the mindless killing of Muslims, even the poor and the impoverished, who themselves had been the victims of tyranny and exploitation at the hands of their Mughal rulers. Look around you at the congregation now. So few of our Muslim friends remain with us.'

Banda paused and Binod looked around. Many of the familiar and well-loved faces of the Muslims who had become leaders in their movement were missing. 'After Sirhind our movement has taken on a communal colouring. From a war between the oppressor and the oppressed it is in danger of deteriorating into a war between Muslim and non-Muslim.'

'It is Wazir Khan who must bear the full responsibility for this,' Binod's voice seethed with vehement, passionate anger. 'He did this by getting his mullahs to declare a jihad, a war between the true believers and the infidels. It was this that created the divide.'

Banda smiled again, this time at the passion in Binod's voice. 'True. It was Wazir Khan who started this. And we compounded matters by senseless and indiscriminate killing. It does not matter who was responsible. What matters is that many who believed in us, have now turned against us. We used them in our war by making them feel that it was a war of freedom and having achieved victory, we put them to the sword.' His voice was louder now and rang even in the ears of the furthest ranks of the congregation. They all sat in silence as the enormity of his words sank in. 'We were a popular movement when we came. We are now in danger of becoming another much-hated invader. So, before we turn our eyes to Delhi or Lahore, it is this perception that we must correct, it is this damage that we must repair.'

Banda saw at last the doubts slip away from Binod's eyes to be replaced by the light of understanding and he nodded his head in grudging acquiescence. 'We must move quickly to establish a competent administration over the areas we have conquered. And through this administration we must convince the average Muslim that though some excesses have been committed, these were aberrations rather than the norm. That we are here to give him a rule which is firm but both benevolent and kind, a rule under which his self-respect will be restored to him and he will at last find his place in the sun. We have the land of the Mughals; we must now fight to win over the hearts and minds of the people who inhabit this land. It is only then that we will have their whole-hearted help and support in our march on Delhi, and with this support the fall of Delhi will not remain a probability but will become a certainty.'

Banda had proven to be an able military leader. The guru had spoken to him extensively about the military strategies to be employed against the Mughals and he had learnt his lesson well. With each of his battles he had gained experience and each victory had given him greater self-confidence, not only in the strength of his forces but also in his own ability to lead them to victory. In the field of administration he found himself on less certain ground.

The area he had conquered corresponded roughly to the area covered by the three Mughal subahs, provinces of Hansi, Samana and Sirhind. So, with minor realignment of boundaries, he retained these three administrative units, naming them as the subahs of Thanesar, Samana and Sirhind. Of these, Thanesar was the most strategic by virtue of its proximity to Delhi. When Bahadur Shah mounted his counter-campaign against the Sikhs, as he was bound to, Thanesar would have to bear the brunt of his attack. Binod was the most tried and tested soldier amongst those of the original twenty-five who still remained. He, more than anyone else, was capable of holding back the emperor's advance till reinforcements were rushed in from the other two subahs. So he was appointed the governor of Thanesar.

The equally redoubtable Bhai Ram Singh was appointed joint governor to help Binod in his difficult task. Sirhind was not only the most important of the three subahs as far as eminence and prosperity were concerned, it was also at that moment of history, the most sensitive. Banda required a kind and compassionate ruler who could apply balm to the wounds caused by the indiscriminate killing of Muslims. Bhai Baj Singh, Banda's closest companion from Nanded, was best suited for this delicate task and was appointed governor of Sirhind. Samana had been destroyed and the immediate requirement was to rebuild the fort and restore to the city the strength that it had once possessed. Bhai Fateh Singh was confirmed in his position as Subedar of Samana and assigned the task of reconstruction. All the faujdars of the recently conquered twenty-eight parganas were replaced and the entire area extending form the Sutlej to the Jamuna and from the Shiwalik hills to Kunjpura, Karnal and Kaithal was now governed by men who were loyal to Banda Bahadur and faithful to the cause.

The two major thrusts by the new governors were their efforts to destroy the zamindari system and the abolition of jeziya. There were at the time two kinds of zamindars. The first of these were the landowners who owned huge tracts of land either through heredity or thorough grants of jagirs by the rulers as a token of gratitude for services rendered. These zamindars held the power of life and death over their tenant farmers, a power they did not hesitate to use, sometimes without any provocation. The farmer lived an existence of abject penury and often was not able to keep body and soul together.

The other class of zamindar was the official who had been given the right to collect revenue for the ruler. This class of official was equally cruel and savage. In his greed he bled the farmer to death. Banda Bahadur saw that if any social justice was to be achieved this class of people must go and zamindari, in either form must be abolished. The huge landholdings of the zamindars were confiscated and distributed among the landless peasants. Zamindars of the second type were called upon to surrender or face dire consequences. They were all removed from their posts and men whom Banda knew to be fair and honest appointed in their place. With this step, empowerment was given to a class of people who for centuries had lived the lives of slaves and been exploited by the zamindars. These peasants became at last their own masters, owners of the land, which they had tilled so diligently over the years with little or no share in the harvest that they reaped. The batai system of revenue collection was introduced whereby the peasants retained two parts of the produce and the amils or revenue collectors took one part for the state. By introducing this revenue reform Banda Bahadur achieved far-reaching effects on the economic life of the Punjab. The peasants, who had at last come into their own, were to provide the backbone of all future struggles against foreign dominance.

Islamic law made a distinction between two categories of non-Muslim subjects – the pagans and the dhimmis, the latter being those who based their religious beliefs on a sacred book. The Muslim rulers tolerated the dhimmis and allowed them to practise their religion, but in return charged them a special tax called jeziya. The rates of jeziya and the method of its collection varied from state to state and from province to province. In

India the Hindus and the Sikhs were treated as dhimmis by the Mughals and had to pay jeziya. But over the years, specially in the Punjab, the jeziya had become so exorbitant that along with the lagaan, land tax, that had to be paid to the zamindars, it crippled the common man and kept him close to starvation levels. Hence, the abolition of jeziya not only gave the common man the much-needed financial relief but also provided him with a strong symbol of freedom and liberty.

Banda also took steps to win over the Muslim masses. The mullahs' call for jehad had given his war a communal colouring, which had been reinforced by the excesses committed against the Muslims at Sadhaura and Sirhind. It was important for the Muslims to understand that Banda's struggle was not a war of revenge but a war for social and religious liberty and for economic equality. Among the new officials appointed, care was taken to appoint such Muslims as well, the most noticeable being Jan Muhammad who was appointed as zamindar of Buria. According to Bhagwati Das Harkara's report submitted to the emperor on 28 April 1711:

> Banda Singh Bahadur had given a word and expressed his resolve not to harass the Muslims. Therefore, all those Muslims who joined him were given daily allowance and wages and were properly looked after. He had permitted them to read khutba and offer prayers. Thus 5000 Muslims joined the service of the rebel Sikh leader, with freedom of azan and namaz. These Muslims felt comfortable in the army of the rebels. Banda Bahadur's movement became genuinely a movement of the depressed classes and men from all walks of life, all castes, creeds and religions flocked to his banner. [8]

Banda then decided to visit Mukhlispur to see how work was progressing and rode into the fort through a new gate. It was of an orthodox design – thick wooden planks reinforced with iron plates and studded with sturdy iron spikes, the standard defence against the battering from attacking elephants. Banda stopped a few yards down the main street and alighting from his horse, washed his hands and face at the spring from which he had drunk a few months ago. It was no longer the quaint, modest spring that it had been. There was a beautiful stone lion head fixed on the stone wall and through its mouth a generous spout of water flowed into the huge stone-lined bowl below. The light of the late morning sun glistened on the surface of the waters and ripples from the falling spout spread to the edge of the bowl. Banda could look down to the very bottom of the bowl and the waters sparkled clean and fresh.

The air was full of the sounds of construction and repair, the sound of the hammer and chisels of the stone masons as they dressed stones for the walls and arches and columns, the sound of the carpenters' saws. There were the cries of gangs of labourers as they hauled heavy beams of wood and stones and raised them to their appointed places, cries that took the form of a refrain raised in unison to enable them to unify their labours and thus produce more dramatic results. There was the sound of the grinding stones as they whirled to grind the lime for the mortar. There was the sound of joyous laughter of the labourers' children who ran around busy in their games, oblivious of the monumental work that was going on around them. There was a wealth of smells too – the smell of freshly sawn wood, of coal fires on which the welding and soldering of metal was being done, of melting tar and of the midday meal being cooked.

From where he stood, Banda could see little of the work being done, but from the sounds and the smells he could visualize the hundreds of workers who were busy in the work of restoring the fort. He wanted to go around it to see for himself how much work had been done in the last few months. As if on cue, the moment he turned away from the spring, Gyasuddin, the master builder came down the stone-paved central street to greet him.

'You come upon a wish, my lord. I was to send to you tomorrow morning to say that though much still remains to be done, the fort is now habitable.'

'Come, show me what you have done.' For the next two hours Banda and the master builder went around the fort. Banda was indeed impressed, both at the amount of work that had been done and by the quality of the work. The ramparts had been repaired and strengthened and there was nowhere along their entire length any sign of the decay, which had been so obvious when Banda had last been there. To Banda's practised eye, they seemed well-nigh impregnable. All along the ramparts, at strategic points, platforms had been constructed for the mounting of guns and storage space for ammunition had been created. The residential quarters stood in neat half moons in the centre of the fort. The masonry had been well-restored, new doors and windows had been fitted to a few, while a team of carpenters could be seen working on the rest. Close to the residential complex were the once vast stables. Because their own cavalry was of much smaller strength than that of the Mughals, the master builder had wisely calculated that their need for stables would also be limited. As such, he had converted part of the stables to provide granaries and godowns for other supplies. He had also created an armoury and an arsenal and provided strong rooms for the treasury. While walking around the fort Banda saw three more enlarged springs like the one he had stopped at. The old dungeons had been redesigned and converted into underground water tanks. To feed these, pipes had been laid from the rivulets upstream. While the springs would ensure an adequate supply of drinking water, the tanks would supply water for bathing and washing. An addition to the fort was a large assembly hall, a gathering place for the congregation in times of inclement weather. Another was the two new lookout towers, which had been built at the two ends of the southern wall.

At the end of their tour Banda and the master builder climbed up one of these and surveyed the surroundings. What he saw took Banda's breath away. He had been right. It was indeed a very strategically placed fort, situated on a hill that rose steeply at the end of a low ridge. To the north the hills rose, criss-crossed by craggy rock faces and ravines. It was a forbidding and hostile terrain to any Mughal force attempting to attack from that direction. To Banda and his followers it was a familiar and friendly terrain, ideally suited, if the need arose, for a quick and complete retreat. To the south the hill fell almost vertically down to the plains, in a drop of over a thousand feet, precluding any possibility of attack from that direction. Along the east and west walls of the fort ran the two rivulets – the Pamuwali and the Oaskawali khools – which formed a more perfect line of defence than anything that man could have devised. From the height at which they stood, the two streams appeared as thin, harmless ribbons of water. But Banda knew that even in this dry season both of them were virtually unfordable for as far as the eye could see. In the monsoons they would become raging torrents, impossible to cross. He turned again towards the south. Beyond the drop of the hill, the plains stretched till the far horizon. It was a bright, clear day and the eye could see forever. Should an enemy force advance towards them from the plains, it would be sighted in ample time for the inhabitants of the fort to prepare for the attack.

A soft cool breeze, most uncharacteristic for this time of the year, had begun to stir and Banda lingered at the top of the watchtower. He had seen all that he had come to see and yet he remained, the seed of an idea forming in his mind and germinating quickly into a major decision. He had sought the refurbishing of the Mukhlispur fort with the intention of using it as a holdout in case he ever found himself with his back against the wall. For his capital he had always thought of Sirhind, which had been the fountainhead of Mughal power in the Punjab and also the symbol of all the tyranny and oppression practised by them. For the Sikhs it was also the hated place where the guru's two younger sons had met a cruel death. Making Sirhind the centre of Sikh power would obliterate forever these hated memories from the Sikh mind. Sirhind had drawn its strength from its strategic location. With its strong fortifications and a broad sweeping view of the plains around, it had been the ideal place from which the imperial forces could enforce their rule. But Banda realized that this very location, which had been a source of strength to the large imperial forces, would now be a source of weakness for the Sikhs. They were smaller in number, not so well equipped. When the Mughal emperor ordered the attack on the Sikh capital Sirhind would, by its very location, be exposed and vulnerable. It offered no route of escape should escape become necessary. The Sikh capital should be remote and forbidding. It should be located in a position which denied its attackers easy access, provided them with no launching pad for their attacks. Mukhlispur answered this description better than any other place that he knew. Yes, he would make Mukhlispur his capital.

He returned to his camp and after the evening prayer, addressed the congregation and presented his proposal: with the departure of the four stalwarts to take up their governorships, there could be no reservations. Young Prem Singh asked a few questions, but they were all of academic interest: How many people would the fort accommodate? What number of cannons would be mounted on the ramparts? Was there an adequate supply of water? There was no hint of conflict or disagreement either in the tone or content of these questions. Yet, because they had been raised, they provided a certain legitimacy to the decision Banda took at the end of the meeting. In appearance, at least the proposal had been questioned and democratic norms observed while taking this important decision. Mukhlispur would be the capital of the new Sikh state and Banda Bahadur, with his immediate entourage, would repair there in four days time. Their taking up residence would motivate Gyasuddin's men to complete the remaining work in the shortest possible time.

'Henceforth the fort of Mukhlispur will be called Lohgarh – the iron fort, to reaffirm in our minds that it is invincible and well-nigh impregnable. The change of name will also destroy whatever connotations the fort holds with its origins and history. With its new name it will be thought of as a new fort, as our fort.' He paused, looked around at the congregation and was pleased at the impression this announcement had made.

'Perhaps some of you will remember that the guru's fort in Anandpur was also called Lohgarh. By using this name we will emphasize the continuity of our endeavour. And when we take up residence at our new capital we will remember the courage and the sacrifices of all our Sikh brethren who gave their lives in the defence of the guru's Lohgarh. This memory will motivate us to follow their example in valour and steadfastness of purpose.'

There was wild cheering form the congregation. When some semblance of order had been restored Banda Bahadur asked Bhai Daya Singh to lead them in prayer and the congregation broke up to the triumphant cries of: '*Bole So Nihal. Sat Sri Akal.*'

There is no greater excitement than that which accompanies the birth of a state and if the capital of the state is also born at the same time, all the excitement focuses on the new town. So it was with Lohgarh. The entire region was gripped by a raging fever. After centuries of rule by foreign invaders, the natives had at last come into their own. After centuries of dominance by Muslim rulers, control had passed into the hands of non-Muslims. A new order had been established and there was a surge of hope in the breasts of those who had never known hope before. People flocked in large numbers to admire the new fortress capital. Many came as volunteers to fight under Banda's standard. These he quickly organized into regiments that were divided amongst his three subahs. Many came in the hope of finding a home and employment, traders and merchants flocked to Lohgarh, sensing the opportunity of making quick money. Craftsmen of all kinds, artists, musicians and wise men alike came to Lohgarh seeking patronage. Banda did all he could for these people, but he was still struggling to establish himself. His state was an infant one and it was too early in his rule to be able to provide the kind of security that the arts needed in order to flourish.

In spite of his growing power, his spreading fame, Banda remained in essence, what he had always been, a bairagi. He lived in a modest one-room apartment, making over the rest of his haveli to various administrative offices. In spite of the variety of foodstuffs that were now available, he still ate his frugal meals. His dress too was the simple choga, a flowing gown that all the Sikhs wore. Sometimes, the visitors who thronged the fort were hard-pressed to recognize the legendary leader and had to ask for him to be pointed out to them.

Gradually order was restored to the human chaos that had descended on the fort. Visitors were carefully screened before they were allowed inside. Shops were allotted to selected tradesmen so that all essential needs of the inmates could be met. These tradesmen were given living quarters within the fort so that they became permanent inhabitants of Lohgarh. Care was taken that the total population of the fort did not become so large that it was unsustainable. Captured cannons from Sirhind were mounted on the platforms of the ramparts and the gunners went through regular practice, training and firing their guns on selected targets. All the booty from the various conquests was brought to Lohgarh and stored in the treasury and the revenue and the tribute from the conquered territories were sent here for safekeeping and for necessary distribution. Banda spent a major part of the day in overseeing the training of his soldiers and in designing war games, which would prepare them for the expected confrontation with the Mughal army. He also made time to meet people who came from far and near to seek his advice and blessing. There were also regular audiences with messengers from his three subahs who brought him an update of the state of affairs there.

A few days later, while attending to the supplicants who thronged to him for help and advice, Banda was surprised to see Bibi Sada Kaur standing in their midst. He got to his feet and strode through the throng to greet her. 'You bring me joy with your presence,' he said as he bent to touch her feet. 'Come, mother, come and sit beside me.' He led her back to where he had been sitting.

'I hope all is well with you, mother. What brings you here? Is it something that you want of me?'

She turned and smiled up at him and then reached out and touched his cheek: 'I come to bask in the radiance of my guru's light, to see for myself the glory of your new capital. And having seen it all I can do is to call the blessings of the almighty upon you. Blessed am I to have lived to see the birth of a Sikh state with a Sikh capital, governed by a Sikh overlord.'

'I am no overlord, mother, I am merely the guru's bondsman – an instrument of his will. If gratitude has to he given for this blessed state of affairs, it must be offered only to Wahe Guru who has made it possible.'

The old woman looked into his face again and there was a mischievous twinkle in her eyes. Knowing all that she had been through, Banda marvelled that she could still summon up such mischief. 'But you are the Wahe Guru's agent and since I cannot see my maker and thank him in person, I must do the next best thing and thank you.'

From the cloth bag that hung form her shoulder she brought out a beautiful, maroon, velvet robe, embroidered richly in gold. 'I have brought you this as a measure of my gratitude,' she said while opening the folds of the robe for all to see. There was a collective gasp that went up from those nearest to her – surprise and awe at its beauty and richness.

'You mock me, mother. You know that I could never wear a robe of such richness. This is a robe that is fit for a king.'

'You are my king, both of the temporal kingdom in which I live and of the spiritual kingdom in which I pray. I started working on it when I heard that the guru would soon be returning from the Deccan. Then, when the news of his assassination reached me, I folded it and put it away. Now when you came and gave my granddaughter Anoop, her liberation, I took it out again and completed it for you.'

Banda looked closely into her twinkling eyes, then smiled and firmly shook his head: 'I cannot wear the robe that was meant for my guru.'

'But you already wear his mantle and stride in his shoes. We all look to you to complete the tasks the guru began. We all know that he chose you and delegated to you his own responsibilities.'

Banda could see the smiles on the faces of those nearest to him, could sense that they were in agreement with the old woman. 'You are too kind, mother. As I have said before, I am my guru's bondsman – not worthy to touch the hem of his robe, leave alone to wear it.'

The old woman sighed and went silent. It seemed that she had accepted Banda's decision. She looked down at her feet for a moment and then looked up at him again. Her eyes sparkled but this time with the shine of unshed tears. She did not take her eyes off him as she refolded the robe. 'They say you are a kind and compassionate man. But in your refusal I see only a cold, inflexible hardness. An old woman has sat through the dark lonely nights and by the dim flickering light of a single lamp, embroidered this gown for you, bringing to each stitch all the love that her tired old heart is capable of feeling. Her eyes have ached and she has turned half blind with her labour. Her only hope has been to see her guru, if only for a moment, dressed in the robe that she has made with all her love – just a moment to know that her love has been accepted.'

Banda did not know what to say. He did not want to hurt the woman, yet he could not bring himself to wear that rich robe even for a moment. In a sudden movement she threw herself at his feet: 'Will you let my labour be in vain? Will you deny your mother the one last happiness that she seeks in this life?' Her voice broke and her body was racked with sobs. He reached down and raised her to her feet and held her close.

'If it means so much to you, mother, I will wear the robe for a moment,' he said taking the robe from her hands and slipping it over his head. He pulled the hem down to adjust the folds. There was pin-drop silence as all eyes were turned upon him. He stood erect and proud, the richness of the robe lending a glow to his handsome face. He was the same height as the guru and the same build. Now as he stood there in that richly embroidered robe, many believed that the guru had come back to them. Many fell to their knees and hailed him as a collective cheer went up from the crowd. Quickly, Banda pulled the robe off and stuffed it into the old woman's bag. Then he put his arm around her shoulder and led her to his apartment.

Later, when he was alone with Bhai Prem Singh, the topic of the robe came back again. 'For the moment when you wore that robe and all eyes were turned on you, even a rank stranger would know at once that you were Banda, the leader of the Sikhs. And that is the way it should be. Strangers should be able to recognize you with a single glance and should not ask for you to be pointed out to them.'

'I would be too embarrassed to wear clothes so rich and gaudy.'

'That I know my lord, your aversion to all kinds of ostentation is well known and respected. But your robes could be distinctive without being extravagant.' And so it was that Banda began to wear robes in colour and style that were distinctive and easily recognized.

The size of his congregation kept increasing. Many of them

stood in serried ranks at the back, craning their necks to catch a glimpse of their leader, straining their ears to hear his words. His followers soon started the practice of seating him on a raised platform from where he could be easily seen and heard. At first his leaders sat with him on the platform, but later when the size of the congregation increased still further and the height of the platform too had to be raised, he alone sat on it. Both in his dress and his seating he set himself apart from his fellow Sikhs. He allowed the expediency of the moment to make him forget one of the basic tenets that the guru had enjoined upon him.

In the months that followed, Banda took three important steps to herald and celebrate the birth of the new Sikh state:

> Banda Singh aimed at national awakening and liberation of the country from the oppressive government of the Mughals. Guru Hargobind and Guru Gobind Singh had transformed the Sikhs from a peaceful people into a class of warriors. They never took any offensive and fought only defensive battles against the government. They did not acquire territory, did not take prisoners, and did not seize the enemy's property and wealth. But the seeds of sovereignty were sown and they germinated during the time of Banda Singh Bahadur.[9]

The first step that could be regarded as a declaration of this sovereignty was the setting up of a mint in Lohgarh where a new coinage was struck and brought into circulation. The coins

Obverse

Reverse

The Banda Bahadur Coin (from Saran Singh collection)

were of four different denominations but the basic design was the same. Unlike the kings and rulers who had gone before him, Banda did not strike the coins in his name. His coins were struck in the names of his gurus, Nanak and Gobind. According to the well-known numismatist and a renowned specialist on coins of the Sikh period, Jyoti M. Rai:

> The first Sikh coin was struck by Banda Bahadur in 1710; these silver coins were unique as neither the ruler's names nor title or portrait appeared on them. Instead, they were inscribed with couplets which paid tribute to the glory of the gurus. The verse on the obverse later came to be known as the Nanakshahi couplet and Sikh coinage itself came to be known as Nanakshahis or money of (Guru)Nanak.
>
> These coins were minted after Banda Bahadur's victory at Sirhind and a new calendar was established by the Sikhs starting with year 1. These silver rupees carried the regnal years 2 and 3 which pertain to this new era and in all probability, from the honorific names given to cities at the time; these coins were minted at Banda's stronghold Lohgarh. The new coinage carried a message to all Sikhs; they had the blessings and support of the Gurus. They could take on their Mughal oppressors without fear or defeat or be forced to renounce their faith. Thousands of Sikhs were tortured and executed as they refused to convert; this was Baba Banda Bahadur's fate a few years later in 1716. The Mughals seeing what significance these coins had for the Sikhs, banned them and anyone caught possessing one was executed. A few samples survive today, showing us the spirit of the eighteenth century Sikhs, who believed that with the help of the Gurus they could never be vanquished.
>
> Another interesting silver coin which gives one

an insight into the very essence of the Sikh persona is surprisingly a Mughal coin belonging to Emperor Shah Alam Bahadur (1707-1712). In 1710, Baba Banda Bahadur, alongwith his forces sought blessings at Harmandir Sahib in Amritsar before marching towards Lahore. Here, on the outskirts of the city, a fierce battle with the Mughals raged on for many days. During this time the Sikhs managed to put a Khanda on some of the Shah Alam coins of the Lahore Mint. The sheer audacity of this action was felt all the way to the Mughal capital; the outraged emperor with his ample resources made preparations to proceed for the Punjab. On hearing this, Banda abandoned his siege on Lahore and got back to defend his territories, leaving behind some Sikh coins with a Sikh emblem for posterity.

Each coin bore the following inscription in Persian:

Sikka Zad Bar Har Do Alam Fazl Sachcha
Sahib Ast Fath-i-Gur Gobind Singh
Shah-i-Shahan Tegh-i-Nanak Wahib Ast

(Coin struck for the two worlds [spiritual and secular] with the grace of the true lord, Nanak, the provider
And the victory of the sword [power] of Guru Gobind Singh, King of Kings and the true Emperor.)

On the reverse was the inscription:

Zarb Khalsa Mubarak Bakht
Ba-Aman Ud-Dahr
Zinat At-Takht
Mashwarat Shahr

(Struck in the haven of refuge of the world,
The beautiful city,
The ornament of the blessed throne.)[10]

He used these titles of honour for Lohgarh just as each of the emperors, when they coined new coins, used honorific titles for their imperial cities.

The second measure adopted by Banda was the introduction of an official seal for all official correspondence – his hukumnamahs and firmans, his orders and letters. It was a square seal and bore the inscription:

Degh, O Tegh O Fateh O Nusrat Bedrang.
Yaft az Nanak Guru Gobind Singh

(By the blessings of Guru Nanak and Guru Gobind Singh achieved the victory over the enemy and started ever giving, charity for the poor.)

This had reference to the two strongest symbols of the Sikh gurdwara, symbols that had proved to be the most powerful source of the Sikhs popularity and power. The 'degh' was the cauldron in which the food for the gurus' langar was cooked. It became at once the symbol for the attempt by the Sikh religion to abolish the caste system: all followers of the gurus, irrespective of caste or creed ate collectively from the food cooked in the cauldron. The 'degh' was also the symbol of charity, the means used to feed the poor. The 'tegh' was the sword, the symbol of the power and might of the 'Khalsa'. It was the symbol of their war against the oppressors and their tyranny, a symbol of the protection offered to the weak and the helpless. The third

Detail, with khanda and kirpans.

The Shah Alam Bahadur Coin, Lahore Mint.
Year AH 1122–AD 1710
(from Jyoti M. Rai collection)

measure that Banda adopted was the introduction of his own calendar, his era, beginning from this victory of Sirhind.

In the adoption of these three measures – the striking of new coinage, the use of his own seal and the adoption of a new calendar – Banda was doing no more than what each new ruler did on gaining power. Through these three measures the ruler emphasized not only his own individual strength as distinct from the strength of his predecessors, but also sought to show that he was a totally independent ruler, not subservient to any other ruler of the time. By striking the coins and the seal in the name of his gurus, Nanak and Gobind, Banda sought to silence any criticism of imperial design. He claimed through these measures that the gurus were his guardian angels and all his power and prosperity was a boon from the gurus and had nothing to do with his individual achievements. But in the months to come, the new coinage and the use of the seal came to be associated with imperial might and it was clear as daylight that this might have emanated from the personality at the centre. No matter how earnestly Banda eschewed the use of the word 'king', he had in every sense, except in name, become a king.

Lohgarh also drew numerous performing artistes, all hoping to win favour and patronage from the new chief. There were singers, both solo and group, folk dancers, acrobats and even travelling animal shows. Among these performers was a group of marasis. Like minstrels everywhere, the staple themes of their songs were stories of valour and courage, of miracles and the supernatural and of love and romance. The story of Banda's

छप्पर चिरी युद्ध 1710 के 300 वर्ष
300 YEARS OF THE BATTLE OF CHAPPAR CHIRI 1710
बंदा बहादुर द्वारा ढाला गया पहिला सिख सिक्का
FIRST SIKH COIN STRUCK BY BANDA BAHADUR

"दो दुनियाओं में घड़ा पहिला सिक्का
गुरू नानक की तेग से आश्वस्त
गुरू गोबिंद सिंघ शाह-ए-शाहान की विजय
सच्चा साहिब की कृपा से"

**"COIN STRUCK IN BOTH THE WORLDS
UNDER THE GUARANTEE OF GURU NANAK'S TEGH
VICTORY OF GURU GOBIND SINGH SHAH-I-SHAHAN
WITH THE GRACE OF SACHA SAHIB"**

The special cover shows the first Sikh coin which was the model for later Sikh coins. The Persian writing reads (see next page):

"Coins struck in both the worlds
Under the guarantee of Guru Nanak's tag
Victory of Guru Gobind Singh Shah-i-Shan
With the grace of Sacha Sahib."

The cancellation shows Banda Bahadur in armour.

life had given them enough material to compose songs telling of the conversion of the young hunter to a bairagi, of the supposed miracles he had wrought as a bairagi – miracles of healings both of the body and of the mind. They sang of his meeting with the guru and the guru's choice of him as his deputy, of his military victories. Their latest song had been composed specially for the visit to Lohgarh. They performed on a stage which had been hastily set up for them. The singers formed a semi-circle as their leader stepped forward and bowed to Banda who sat facing them. All around were row upon row of listeners. Those who could not find a place to sit stood in serried ranks and a few enterprising ones had even climbed on to the branches of the overhanging trees to get a better view. The marasis were good, they sang well, their melodies were hummable and could easily be picked up and their lyrics were simple and direct. They had already won the attention of the listeners who now waited with bated breath for what they knew would be the climax of the performance. The leader spoke in the pin-drop silence: 'We bring you now a song which has been composed only for this occasion. It is a song celebrating the birth of the first Sikh state and the glory of the first Sikh ruler.' He knew he was treading a thin line as Banda had repeatedly restrained the use of the titles of guru and king for himself, but got around by using milder synonyms. Very often during the announcement and the actual singing of the song, Banda was tempted to put an end to the performance. But he knew he was fighting a losing battle. How many words could he forbid the use of?

It was a beautiful song, beginning on a slow and gentle note. It spoke of the guru, his beauty, his strength, his courage and his achievements, of his dreams and ambitions for his people and of his unfulfilled plans. Each of the four lead singers would, by turn, step into the centre of the semicircle and sing a verse each and then step back into his position. At the end of each verse the entire group would take up the chorus. Slowly but steadily the song gained momentum, the beat became more vigorous and the drummers sounded their instruments faster and louder.

Finally, they sang of Banda. The song moved quickly through brief descriptions of his beauty and strength, of his military successes, of the splendour of Lohgarh – a splendour that had still to be fully realized. They sang of the conquest of Delhi and in the final stanza spoke of Banda standing at the foot of the Mughal throne. Abruptly, almost as if someone had slit the singer's throat, the song ended, something that even the audience did not realize. The silence was complete. And in this silence each of the listeners saw in his mind's eye, Banda ascending the Mughal throne. Banda, angry and embarrassed as he was, could not but admire the sophistication of the composer. By ending the song where he had, he had sought to escape all censure from Banda Bahadur. And yet, he had painted a vivid picture of Banda becoming emperor of Hindustan. At last the audience realized that the song had ended and broke into tumultuous applause.

Then Banda got to his feet and turned to address the audience: 'These singers are extremely talented and they have sung exceedingly well. They are not only talented singers but are also extremely clever. They know that I have expressly forbidden anyone to refer to me as "guru" or "king". They did not use these terms but used other ones to describe me, leaving no doubt that they look upon me as a guru and a king. I cannot condone what they have done and to ensure that no one else will be tempted to emulate them I must punish them.'

He paused for breath. The joy and pride that had flowed through the audience a few moments before was replaced with dread. What punishment would their leader impose upon the hapless singers? 'For what they have done, I banish them forever from my presence. They will never again sing for me.' He stopped for a moment and then in a clearer, firmer voice, added: 'I forbid them and anyone else from singing that song ever again.' He turned and strode away without a backward glance and the audience too broke up in hushed silence.

Banda had no way of knowing that the song echoed the aspirations of a large number of his followers. With that one performance, a torch had been lit that would never again be completely extinguished. No matter what he said, what he did, there were many who would look upon him both as a guru and as a king. Even his ban on the song was not strictly observed for both in melody and structure, it was too beautiful to be abandoned. It gave Banda an image that was larger than life, an image that reinforced his role as the guru's successor and as the first Sikh ruler of the Punjab.

A few months later, a delegation of Muslim leaders came to meet Banda. When ushered into his presence, he was mystified by their appearance for they did not look like Muslims at all. They all had long untrimmed beards and wore their turbans in the Sikh fashion. Banda made them welcome and waited for them to state the purpose of their visit. One of the delegates stepped forward, establishing with that one movement that he was the leader of the delegation. He was tall and well built and his face, handsome as it was, shone with the radiance of a spiritual light.

'My lord, you do not perhaps recognize me, I am Dindar Khan and I ranged myself against you in the battle of Kapoori.' He signalled to the wiry athletically built individual who stood beside him. This man was considerably older than Dindar and yet had an aura of great physical and spiritual strength about him. 'And this is Mir Nasir-ud Din, the newswriter of Sirhind.'

'I know you well Nasir-ud Din, you are one of those whom the Soods ransomed, are you not?'

'Mir Nasir-ud Din and every man in this delegation. We wish to be baptized into the Sikh faith.'

Banda smiled at his visitors. 'Sikhism is a way of life and baptism is a solemn pledge that you will abide by all that this way of life enjoins upon you. There is no merit in seeking baptism if you do not practise this way of life.'

'We have made a humble beginning in understanding this way of life. Our community will not now let us live amongst them because of what we have set out to learn. Through baptism we will be able to live amongst the community of Sikhs and learn to practice all that they practise.'

Banda surveyed the assembly of Muslims who stood before him. Each had a look of great earnestness about him. He knew what posterity would say of him if he acceded to their wish. Historians would say that he had forced them to convert on pain of death. Other chroniclers would say, with an air of authority, that he had allured the Muslims into conversion by promising them material advancement. And yet, as his eyes scanned each face, he knew that he did not care how the future would judge him for this deed. For the first time Muslims had come forward, not as individuals or in ones and twos, but in a large group, seeking to embrace a new faith.

'It will not be easy,' he warned. 'The embracing of a new faith brings exultation but the abandoning of an old faith brings pain and tears. There can be no easy conversion.'

'It is not easy,' Dindar Khan replied. 'Daily we are condemned by the mullahs for our interest in Sikhism. They denounce us before their congregations and they pray for the wrath of hell to be poured upon our heads and condemn us to eternal damnation. They tell all Muslims to shun us and we live a life of ostracism. Yes there has been pain and there have been tears, both in the struggle within ourselves and with the world around us.'

Banda got to his feet and put his hand on Dindar's head: 'May God give you strength and may this baptism bring you peace and serenity.'

Preparations were made and the Muslims were baptized to become Sikhs. According to convention they were to be given new names, but there were so many names that were common to both Muslims and Sikhs, that Banda adopted the simple expedient of adding the suffix 'Singh' to the first names. Thus Dindar Khan became Dindar Singh and Mir Nasir-ud-Din became Mir Nasir Singh.

After the evening prayers, while they waited for their turn to eat at the langar, Banda called Dindar and some of his close associates to his side. 'Tell me what is it that inspired you to take this important step to abandon all that you have always believed in and adopt new beliefs?'

'We have not abandoned all that we believed in. There is so much that is common to both our religions that much of the old still remains with us.' This was true because Nanak had sought to bridge the gulf between Islam and Hinduism with his teachings. 'But yes, if you are asking for specifics, there are two things which exercised an immediate and urgent influence upon us. First, the spirit of the Sikhs as they went into battle. We saw poor, undernourished, emaciated peasants, with little more than their sickles and their scythes in their hands, transformed into fierce warriors when they heard the call to battle. We saw this transformation happen again and again, marvelled it and sought to understand the force that had wrought it.'

'And the second?'

'This,' he said with a sweep of his hand that took in the entire range of activities connected with the langar. As each new group took their places to be fed, volunteers placed trays and bowls of brass and copper before them. Other volunteers ladled vegetables and lentils from bucket-like containers into these bowls. Still others served hot chapattis from baskets. On the other side a group of young men kneaded flour into dough. A group of women rolled balls of dough into rotis and tossed them on to the huge tavas (iron plates on fires). Volunteers sat rubbing the used trays and bowls with ash and washing them clean. 'Everywhere there is an air of complete harmony, of belonging to one family, of all being equal. The community service binds everyone together. There is no more eloquent symbol of your religion than this.' Banda was moved by Dindar's words.

Having received what they had come for, the new converts did not tarry long in Lohgarh. After the morning prayers, they took leave of Banda, who stood at the edge of the courtyard watching them go till a bend in the cobbled street took them away from him. Then he mounted the ramparts so that he could watch them long after they had left the fort. He watched their diminutive figures till they were lost in the distance. Their conviction had seemed strong enough and their desire to become Sikhs had been firm. Would they remain devout Sikhs if Bahadur Shah were to overthrow the Sikhs and re-establish his power in the Punjab? Or would they, with a strong survival instinct, re-convert to Islam? No matter what happened, he prayed that some of the understanding of the Sikh religion that Dindar had shown in his description of the langar would always remain in their hearts.

The faith of the new Sikhs was put to the test sooner than anyone could have expected. Many of them belonged to the village of Unarsi in the district of Deoband. Jalal Khan, the faujdar of Jalalabad, ordered the arrest and persecution of all new converts. An appeal for help was sent to Banda Bahadur in Lohgarh, who could not ignore the same and sent messages to Jalal Khan seeking the release of the Sikhs. But Jalal Khan humiliated the messenger, and said that he would destroy all Sikhs and called upon Banda Bahadur to try to stop him if he dared. Banda swung into immediate action. At the head of a large force he sallied forth to subdue Jalal Khan. It was the first time that the Sikh forces had crossed the Jamuna. Banda met with little resistance till he reached the walls of Jalalabad and laid siege to the fort. The siege lasted twenty days and there was great loss of life on both sides. The defenders fought with great courage in spite of the great hardships they had to endure due to lack of food and water.

The monsoon had set in. The area around the fort was reduced to one vast stretch of marshland, denying Banda any kind of foothold and the overflowing waters of the Krishna washed the very foot of the walls of fort. The Sikhs made every effort to breach the wall and gates with their battering rams, but met with no success. At the end of twenty days Banda had to admit that they had reached a dead end. Hampered as they were by the inclement weather and held at bay by the courage of the defenders, their chance of a quick victory seemed to be receding with each passing day and if victory did not come to them quickly they would soon be themselves cut off from the rest of the Punjab by the swollen waters of the Jamuna.

The deciding factor came in the form of an urgent appeal from the Sikhs of Jalandhar who were under siege in the fort of Rahon and sought immediate help in their attempt to defeat the Mughal faujdar. Banda decided to beat a retreat, cross the Jamuna before its waters reached flood proportions and send relief to the beleaguered Sikhs at Rahon. Jalalabad would have to wait.

The victory over Sirhind had served as a source of inspiration to the Sikhs, who in the north waited with growing impatience for Banda's arrival so that they could throw in their lot with him and drive the Mughal rulers out of the rest of the Punjab. When they saw that Banda would be some time in reaching them, they took matters into their own hands. At the end of a few months, with the exception of Lahore, the Sikhs controlled the whole of the Majha region, which extended till Pathankot, embraced the Rearki and Kandhi areas and all the land from Machhiwara to Karnal. The ruler of Jalandhar was a ruler only in name and the rebellious Sikhs had become a force to contend with.

Suddenly there was a fresh wave of hostility amongst the Muslim leaders, with the religious ones projecting the conversion of Dindar Khan and his followers to Sikhism as the worst kind of assault on Islam. What had been an external and physical threat to their religion had now invidiously crept into the minds of some believers and become a far more dangerous and pernicious threat as it was a threat from within. They saw a distinct possibility of more and more of their co-religionists following the example set by Dindar Khan and his group. Hence, they were now, by and large, fired by a fanatical fervour to defeat and obliterate the Sikhs. Many Muslim traders and aristocrats sold off all their belongings and used the money to procure men, horses and equipment for the Mughal armies. The

Sikhs, smaller in number and ill-equipped, used time-tested techniques to defeat the Mughal forces. This tactical superiority was displayed most of all in the battle of Rahon where the Sikhs finally gained ascendancy of the Jalandhar region.

> If defeat befalls their armies, take it not as a defeat, oh youth. Because it is a war tactic of theirs. Beware, beware of it. Their tactic is such that in wreaking defence, their defeat is changed into victory.
>
> The army that pursues them is cut off from reinforcement. Then they turn upon their heels and even if their pursuers try water they set fire to it.
>
> Did you not witness how during the battle they took to flight to deceive their pursuers?
>
> And then they drew a cordon round the Khan and caught him in such a manner as if he were taken in a circle.[11]

After the battle of Rahon the Sikhs made inroads into areas that were considered part of the Delhi region. The governor of Delhi, Asaf-ud Daulah was a weak, wavering man and did not have the courage or the determination to march against the Sikhs. It was doubtful if he would take a stand in the event of a Sikh attack. Sensing this, many of the aristocrats began an exodus to the eastern provinces to find shelter from what they saw as an impending storm. With each passing day it became increasingly clear that any further delay by Bahadur Shah in dealing with the Sikhs would result in the loss of Delhi, as Banda Bahadur had by now consolidated his hold over major parts of the Punjab. He had won over the peasants completely to his side and was looked upon as the saviour of the poor. He had convinced the Muslims that he was not an enemy of Islam.

The peasant and the worker had come into their own, free from exploitation and oppression and were willing to follow wherever Banda Bahadur led.

And yet, inexplicably, Banda failed to make that final thrust.

Chapter Six

Banda smiled at this. 'I have always advocated the wisdom of recognizing that moment in battle when the tide has turned firmly against us, to bow to the inevitable and so live to fight another day. But to run away even before battle is joined will be an act of cowardice and not an act of wisdom. You would not want to make a coward of me both in the eyes of my followers and my enemy.'

THE TWENTY-SECOND DAY OF JUNE 1710, HAD BEEN A DAY OF INTENSE heat. The sun had blazed mercilessly from a blanched sky on to an earth that had long since yielded all trace of the moisture that it had once held and could now only turn up a dry, parched face to the unyielding heat. From the early morning, when the blood-red orb had first appeared over the eastern horizon, to the late evening when it had dropped as suddenly over the western rim, there had been just one long stretch of burning time. Even with the lengthening of shadows there was no respite. There was not the slightest trace of breeze to fan away the heat that still shimmered from the earth's surface.

The emperor sat alone in his tent. Ever since his exile in Kabul, as a prince, he had grown to dislike sleeping under a solid roof. He needed time to be by himself, to go over the events of the day and to take important decisions as to the course of action that he should pursue. For this he needed to be alone to avoid being confused or influenced by those around him, even by Munim Khan, his trusted and faithful wazir.

This detour to Ajmer on his return march to Delhi from the Deccan, had been occasioned by the need to subdue the recalcitrant Rajput chiefs Jai Singh of Amber and Ajay Singh of Jodhpur. He had tried to deal with them before on his march to the Deccan when he had set out to defeat his brother Kam Baksh and bring to end the long drawn-out war of succession. He had kept the two Rajput princes in his camp under house arrest. But while they were camped at Mandeshwar, the two had escaped. They had formed an alliance with Raja Amar Singh of Udaipur and worked to undermine the Mughal influence in Rajasthan by resisting the authorities and inflicting heavy losses in encounters with the imperialists. However, Bahadur Shah had decided that Kam Baksh's insurgency posed a greater threat than the rebelliousness of the Rajput chiefs and adopted a conciliatory attitude towards them. He restored their mansabs but held back permission to return to their capitals. Now, after the destruction of Kam Baksh he moved into Rajasthan to bring the two chiefs to heel.

The Rajputs, alarmed at the emperor's personal resolve to lead an army against them, sought the intervention of their old friend Asad Khan, Wakil-i Mutlaq and governor of Delhi. Bahadur Shah knew the princes well enough to understand that they would seek Asad Khan's help. Hence, when he received a dispatch from the governor while camped at Toda, he knew what the contents would be. The dispatch spoke of the grave danger and threat posed to Delhi by the Sikh uprising in the Punjab and described in detail the conquest of territories and the control that the Sikhs now exercised. It spoke of the excesses committed by the Sikhs upon the Muslims and in very strong terms, impressed upon the emperor the urgent need to come to an immediate settlement with the Rajput chiefs so as to move quickly to the Punjab to subdue the Sikhs. The emperor smiled to himself while he listened to the reading of the dispatch. The wily old Asad Khan had sought to obtain lenient treatment for his Rajput friends by exaggerating the extent and urgency of the Sikh problem. The reports from the news writers also mentioned the Sikh uprising. Hafiz Khan Diwan, Hassan Raza Kotwal, Muhammad Tahir and Darwesh Muhammad all wrote about the Sikh uprising but, their language was so hyperbolic and ornamental that they made the Sikh problem sound a minor irritant and not a major threat. Asad Khan's dispatch stood discredited in the emperor's mind and he decided to move on against the Rajputs.

The emperor was welcomed into Ajmer with open arms. Flowers were strewn in his path and two contingents of Bundela Rajputs under Raja Udet Singh Bundela and Raja Chatarsal Bundela had ridden out to meet him and pledge their support in his war against Amber and Jodhpur.

While his camp was being set up in a garden outside the city, the emperor had gone barefoot, the soles of his feet searing in the burning sand, to perform sajda at the shrine of Khwaja Moinuddin Chishti. Bahadur Shah was a deeply religious man and this pilgrimage brought to him a calm and serenity. He returned to his camp at peace with himself and with the world, the weariness and the exhaustion of the long campaign lifted from his heart. This serenity was short-lived. Soon after his midday meal his wazir, Munim Khan, informed him that a delegation from the Punjab was waiting to see him.

'What do they seek?' he asked, a little irritated, as he had looked forward to a restful siesta during the long, hot afternoon.

'They have been the victims of extreme cruelty at the hands of the Sikhs and have been stripped of everything that they possessed. They come as supplicants to seek your help.'

The emperor was amused at what he thought was a fresh ploy by Asad Khan to soften his anger against the Rajput princes. He was sure that a few riff-raff had been recruited by Asad Khan and trained to recount tales of extreme victimization at the hands of the Sikhs. It would be interesting to listen to their tales of 'woe' and then expose them for the charlatans they were. After the rigours of his Deccan campaign he could do with some entertainment. But as he listened to them he realized that there would be no entertainment here. It was a large group that had been ushered into his presence. And none of them could be dismissed as riff-raff by any stretch of imagination. They were divided into two broad groups – one, richly dressed, with a proud mien even in their distress, was obviously from the landed gentry; the other, from their solemn dress and presence as much as from the way they wore their turbans and beards, were the custodians of Islam. After the exchange of formalities, they took up positions – one group on each side of the emperor and waited, their eyes cast to the floor. Bahadur Shah turned first to the men of religion: 'Speak, holy ones, tell me what it is that you seek from me.'

One of the group stepped forward, bowed once again and then raising his eyes, began to speak. His voice was soft and low when he began, but as he saw the interest in the emperor's eyes it became gradually louder till it filled the entire khaima: 'Jahanpanah, we are the Pirzadas of Samana and Sadhaura. We are all that are left of a once large and strong community. We were the caretakers of the holy mausolea and were greatly respected and revered by Muslims and non-Muslims alike. Then we became the victims of the scourge who calls himself Banda Bahadur, the king of the Sikhs.'

Turn by turn the Pirzadas spoke and told stories of the blood-curdling cruelty that they had been subjected to. When they were done it was the turn of the landlords. Each story told of the brutal and senseless killing of innocent Muslims, of rape and ravaging, of plunder and loot. They told of the desecration of graves, of the digging up of bodies of long-dead Muslim women and of consigning these bodies to flames in imitation of a Hindu cremation. They spoke of the forcible conversion of Muslims on pain of death. As the emperor listened he felt the hair on his forearms stiffen and a knot at the pit of his stomach. The speaker concluded:

> He is a *shaitan* (devil). With all the magical powers of the *shaitan*, when he rides into battle, flames issue from his tongue and throat and burn the Muslims who dare to confront him. He can turn bullets and arrows from their course and direct them back to the one who fires them. His spells weave an invisible shield around him and his followers, so that spear and sword have little or no effect upon them. [12]

On and on the stories went, describing Banda's powers and strength, his lust for battle and his invincibility. The emperor was deeply disturbed. Even if he made allowance for the exaggeration that despair produces, there was enough substance in these stories to cause deep alarm. The power of the Sikhs had grown considerably, hostile and strong, so close to the capital of his empire, that it posed a grave and imminent danger. At last when he could bear to listen no longer, he dismissed the supplicants. He dismissed his attendants and his trusted wazir. Now, alone in his tent, he pondered over what he must do.

The Rajput chiefs had challenged his power and if not subdued soon, they would set an example that others would follow. He would lose his hard-won control over Rajasthan. But they, at least, had no territorial ambitions. There was a chance, through careful negotiations, of working out a face-saving compromise with them. If they were confirmed in their principalities they might eschew open confrontation. The Sikhs, it seemed, had become the more pressing problem. Not only was their rebellion fired by territorial ambition but also by communal hatred. They had captured most of the Punjab and had consolidated their hold over the territories that they had conquered. They were now virtually knocking at the gates of Delhi and if he did not move immediately against them there was every danger of his losing his capital to them.

His mind went back to his association with the last guru, Gobind Singh, a man of great beauty, both physical and spiritual, a man of strength, truth and purity. Bahadur Shah had admired the guru greatly and been grateful for his help in the war against his brother Azam. They had fought side by side in the battle of Jaju. The guru had tried to prevail upon him to take disciplinary action against the tyrannous and oppressive faujdars like Wazir Khan of Sirhind. Bahadur Shah was well aware of the cruelties practised by Wazir Khan and others and secretly admitted that at some stage he would have to take action against them and curb their excessive power. But he was not sure if the time was right for such an action. He himself was new to the throne, still struggling to secure his succession. He could not afford to antagonize the powerful and important Mughal officials in the Punjab. With his absence in the Deccan, disgruntled officials like Wazir Khan would be free to create trouble against him, which he could not risk at this stage. The guru had seen through this, broke camp and went his separate way. In the years that followed Bahadur Shah had often regretted his lack of action against Wazir Khan and the others, by punishing whom he would have won a permanent friend in the guru and the Sikhs would always have been strong and dependable allies, stronger and more dependable than even the mighty Wazir Khan.

But this was no time for regret. Between the Rajputs and the Sikhs, the Sikhs were the greater and more pressing evil and he must deal with them at once.

The emperor clapped his hands and Gul Muhammad, his old

and trusted attendant came into the now darkened tent. 'Have the lamps lit, Gul Muhammad, call for some rose sherbet and then send for Munim Khan.'

As if to confirm the emperor's newfound decisiveness, a breeze stirred and blew through the open sides of the tent, bringing with it the coolness of the desert night.

'We have decided to make peace with Jai Singh and Ajay Singh. We will confirm them in their territories and grant them audience on my march. They will have leave for six months to visit their capitals, after which they must return to serve as subedars to the provinces we assign them.'

'As always you are most generous, Jahanpanah. You will win them over with this forgiveness.'

'Call Muhammad Yasin, the firman writer, and draw up separate firmans for the two chiefs. When they have been signed and sealed, send them on tonight. We wish now for a speedy conclusion to this matter.'

He invited Munim Khan to join him at dinner. Munim Khan had been an obscure official in Bahadur Shah's establishment in Kabul, when he had been governor. Munim had been appointed in charge of finances in 1703 and under his careful control the governor had become a rich and powerful man. Munim had been raised to the rank of Diwan of Kabul and Naib-subedar of Punjab. In preparation for the inevitable war of succession that would follow Aurangzeb's death, Munim Khan had gathered a war chest for Bahadur Shah and also silently collected herds of camels and oxen, which would carry and drag cannon and boats – boats which would ferry them across the rivers of the Punjab and cannons that would help them win the war. With these preparations, when news did at last come of Aurangzeb's death, Bahadur Shah was able to move quickly to Lahore and then to Delhi. He took twenty-eight lakh rupees from the Lahore treasury and thirty lakhs from the Delhi treasury, and used this money to pay his soldiers and assure himself of their loyalty, something his brothers had failed to do. It was on Munim Khan's advice that Bahadur Shah moved swiftly to Agra to gain control of Shah Jehan's fabulous and legendary collection of gold and jewels. The possession of this wealth was to be a key factor in his victory in the war of succession.

It was little wonder then that the relationship between the emperor and his wazir was one of warm friendliness, if not of familiarity. The wazir was one person who could dare to contradict the emperor and be sure that his contradictions would be listened to with great attention. They sat together, the emperor on a more elevated seat than the wazir as protocol demanded. The emperor, like his father before him, was a man of simple, austere habits and the food, as always at his table, was frugal.

'We have decided to concentrate on quashing the power of the Shaitan,' the emperor began, coming straight to the point. 'We are told that he has collected a large force of misguided Hindus and even some half-mad Muslims in his support, along with a large body of his own Sikhs. You heard what one of the zamindars said today – Banda's strength is over forty thousand men. We have, already, the forces of the two Bundela rajas in our support. We must send a message to Asad Khan to mobilize an army and get it ready for an immediate advance against the Sikhs. Also, call upon the subedar of Oudh, the faujdars of Barha and Moradabad, and the nazim of Allahabad to bring their forces and meet me on my march to the Punjab.'

Munim Khan ran over the names in his mind. He would have to draw up these orders in the morning, without any notes to assist him; it was his memory that he had to depend upon, which fortunately was exceedingly sharp.

'And who will lead this joint expedition?'

'We will.'

Munim Khan lapsed into silence and Bahadur Shah, sensing a contradiction, asked: 'What is it?'

'It is not proper that you should lead this expedition,' Munim said without a moment's hesitation. 'It is a mere uprising of peasants. By leading your army against it, you will give to it an importance that it does not deserve.'

'Till yesterday we would have been inclined to agree with you. But not today. It is not the peasants that we march against but this monster, this so called king of the Sikhs. You heard how they all spoke of him – with anger and with hostility. Yet while they spoke of him they lowered their voices in awe. They have made him a legend, a legend from which the power of the Sikhs emanates. Without him the Sikhs are nothing but a rabble of disorganized peasants. Without him the Muslims will once again be men and cease to be the half-men that we saw today.'

'Yes. His defeat is important, more important at this moment than anything else in the world. But important as it is, it does not deserve the stature that your presence at the head of the expedition will give it. By marching personally against him you will be adding to his strength and power, you will be making of him a bigger legend.'

He paused and the emperor looked closely at him.

'Let me go out against him. I vow by all that is sacred and beloved to me that I will bring him back to you imprisoned in an iron cage.' He paused and then added: 'Or at the very least his head upon an iron spike.'

The emperor smiled and rested his hand upon his wazir's shoulder. Peace was made with the Rajput rajas and orders of mobilization sent out to the officials.

As the emperor moved towards the Punjab and established camp at Paragpur on 7 August, further reports, purported to Banda, awaited him. Bahadur Shah realized that Banda had become a symbol, an icon, as much for his supporters as for his opponents. For the former, he was the symbol of freedom from tyranny, oppression, exploitation, humiliation and disrespect. He was the embodiment of all that was good, brave and noble for which they would follow him gladly even down to the gates of death. For his opponents he was the symbol of all that was cruel and hateful, an embodiment of all that was vicious and evil. As long as he lived they could hope for no peace. The death and destruction of Banda Bahadur had become an imperative and demanding need. This realization brought the fire of purpose and urgency to the emperor's resolve, producing great stress in his mind.

'He must be destroyed, he must be destroyed,' he muttered over and over again as he shuffled up and down the length of his tent. He was like a man possessed. There was a look of madness on his face, a wide and glittering brilliance to his eyes and though his stoop was more marked than ever before, there was great vigour even in his shuffling.

Munim Khan stood in the shadows, knowing that he must intrude; not knowing what form the intrusion may take. He stepped out from the shadows, put his arm around the emperor's shoulders and with a gentle but firm voice said: 'You will destroy him, Jahanpanah, you will destroy him. Come and be seated.' He guided the emperor to his favourite seat, looked around, raised his eyebrows and nodded to Gul Muhammad. The attendant left the tent only to reappear shortly with a glass of milk.

'Drink this,' Munim Khan urged softly. 'It will help to calm your nerves.'

The emperor did not know that the milk contained a special draught, which Munim Khan had obtained from the court hakim. He had, in recent weeks, noticed signs of strange and erratic behaviour in the emperor, which had caused him great anxiety and so he had shared it with the hakim.

'The emperor has led a hard and difficult life and this has taken its toll both on his body and his mind. It is not only his advancing years that have enfeebled him but also the stress of these long, difficult years. The symptoms you describe portend nothing but a tragic end. As time goes on he will be given to bouts of great frenzy and later to delusion. Shortly before the end he will lose all control of the mind.'

'Is there nothing that can be done?'

The venerable hakim shook his head. 'No. There is no cure. But I can give you a draught, which if taken regularly, will delay the onset of the worst part of the affliction. A second dose could be administrated at the onset of his bouts. It will help calm his nerves and ease him into a restful sleep.'

Later as Munim Khan sat besides the sleeping emperor, he prayed silently that Allah would permit him to stay long enough with the emperor to ensure the regular administration of the hakim's draught. He was a good man and had led a good life, he did not deserve so terrible an affliction.

The next morning the fit had passed and the emperor, addressed his advisers: 'While we wait for our reinforcements to arrive, this monster grows from strength to strength. We cannot tolerate it. It has become necessary to contain his further growth. For this we appoint Firoz Khan Mewati as the commander of an advance force. He will march ahead of the imperial army and do whatever he deems fit to contain the Sikh till we can reach the Punjab with the full imperial army to destroy him.'

Mewati stepped forward and knelt before the emperor, both to express his gratitude at the honour bestowed upon him and also to show that he accepted the challenge of the difficult task assigned to him. As the deposed faujdar of Sambhar, he was grateful for this chance to redeem his name and his fortunes. The emperor touched the kneeling warrior lightly on the head.

'On your way to the Punjab you must destroy the military posts established by the enemy and establish in their stead, imperial posts. You must restore to our impoverished people, Shahbad, Mustafabad, Samana, Sadhaura and other old seats of population, which have been plundered and occupied by the enemy. Go now and make preparations for your departure.'

After Firoz Khan had left the emperor turned again to address the assembly: 'Let it be known that there can be no visitors to Delhi without written permission from the wazir, Munim Khan and from officials designated by him for this purpose. Similarly no relatives and friends from Delhi can come to visit the imperial camp without express permission from the Wakil-i Mutlaq, Asad Khan.'

This announcement was greeted by a hushed silence and in the silence many of the leading courtiers looked at each other, surprise writ large upon their faces. The emperor smiled and offered an explanation: 'Situations like this give rise to all kinds of rumours the spread of which could weaken the resolve of the faint of heart amongst us and could even trigger a wave of desertions. It is to safeguard ourselves against this eventuality that we have had to take steps that are inconvenient for you.'

The imperial camp at last understood the full importance of this campaign. They were up against a strong and well-organized enemy and the emperor was taking no chances. He was moving to plug all the loopholes that might weaken them and lessen their chances of success. But the emperor had not finished yet.

When the murmuring had subsided he raised his hand to ask for silence: 'As we all know, our enemy's great strength stems from many sources. One of these is his extremely efficient and well-organized spy network. His agents have infiltrated all levels of our administration and provide him with information of vital, strategic importance. To be rid of this we order that all Hindus in our camp and in our employ, who support beards, will shave them off immediately. This is not to show a distrust of our Hindu brethren or to humiliate them in any way. We ask them to bear with us and to comply with our order in the right spirit. Through this measure we will ensure that no Sikh spy is hiding in our midst in the guise of a bearded Hindu.'

In the next few days Bahadur Shah was joined by the forces from Moradabad under Muhammad Amin Khan and from Barha under Sayyad Wajib-ud Din. The Barha forces were dispatched immediately to the Punjab to join the advance force under Firoz Khan Mewati. The imperial camp moved further north and arrived at Sonepat on 22 October 1710.

Both the advance parties had moved with such precision and efficiency that they reached the borders of the Sikh territory long before the Sikhs could prepare for the attack. The main body of soldiers under Banda had only recently abandoned the siege of Jalalabad and rushed to the aid of the Sikhs of the Doab in their fight against Shamas Khan, the faujdar of Jalandhar. The remaining Sikh forces were scattered over the territories occupied by the Sikhs. They were divided into small detachments and were manning garrisons in Sirhind, Samana,

Thanesar, Sadhaura and other important towns and cities of the Punjab. The advance force of the Mughals had the element of surprise completely on their side.

As Banda had predicted it was Thanesar, under Binod Singh and Ram Singh, which had to bear the brunt of the Mughal attack. Battle was joined outside the village of Amingarh, near Tirawri on 26 October. As usual it was the Sikhs who had chosen the battlefield. Binod had seen at a glance that they were vastly outnumbered. The large Mughal cavalry would not give the Sikhs a fair chance in a close quarter, hand-to-hand fight. So Binod, taking a leaf out of the book of Banda Bahadur's earlier battles, chose a thick grove of close growing chichra, thorny bushes, as the battleground. This would render the Mughal cavalry ineffective and force it to dismount, which would give the Sikh soldiers a better chance in the hand-to-hand battle that would ensue. They took up position in this grove and deployed their artillery and their strength of muskets in a ring at the edge of the grove.

Mahabat Khan, Munim Khan's son, led the first attack. The Sikhs waited patiently and when the Mughal forces were within range they let loose such a strong volley of fire that the Mughals suffered heavy casualities and were forced to fall back. Again and again the Mughal advance guard attacked and repeatedly they were forced to fall back under the intensity of the Sikh fire. The loss of life was so great that Mahabat lost heart and called off the attack.

Firoz Khan watched the failure of the first Mughal manoeuvre. The fate of the battle hung in the balance and what had appeared to be certain victory had now been reduced to a possible defeat. He held a hurried conference with Sayyad Wajib-ud Din of Baraha and decided that their cavalry would be of no use in this battle as the horses would not be able to penetrate the thick growth of bushes. They would have to do what the Sikhs wanted them to do – dismount and combine their cavalry with infantry. Both would form a solid phalanx and advance upon the groove.

Their numbers were large and though the Sikhs continued to fire with devastating effect, there were now a dozen Mughal soldiers to take the place of each who fell. The Mughals were able to advance to the edge of the thicket. The Sikh foot soldiers were ready for them and with loud blood-curdling war cries they charged upon the advancing enemy. Fierce hand-to-hand fighting broke out, which led to heavy casualities. For a while it seemed that the Mughal forces would be contained, but soon with a sudden surge the left wing of the Mughals pushed through the Sikh ranks and Firoz Khan realized that the battle had at last swung in his favour. The Sikh force fell back against the heavy numerical strength of the Mughal force. Retreat was ordered. The memory of all the stories of Sikh cruelty that the soldiers had heard was still fresh in their minds. They fell upon the dead and dying with frightening savagery and perpetuated every indignity they could think of. Heads were severed from the bodies and a cartload of 300 heads sent as a gift to the emperor. Many heads were hung by their long hair upon the trees on both sides of the Grand Trunk road. Groups of Mughal soldiers would jeer at these heads and say: 'Now at last we know why the Sikhs wear long hair. It is to enable us to hang their heads after we have killed them.'

The emperor rewarded Firoz Khan with the faujdari of Sirhind.

The surviving Sikhs fell back on Thanesar. Binod Singh knew that he could expect no reinforcements, so rather than wait for what he knew was certain defeat, he ordered a retreat to Sadhaura, where help could be expected from Lohgarh.

While Firoz Khan was busy with the conquest and

consolidation of power in Thanesar, Bayzid Khan, the governor of Jammu, and his nephew Shamas Khan, the faujdar of Jalandhar, marched upon Sirhind. Shamas Khan had augmented his forces with a large number of peasants from the Doab. They moved with such speed that Baj Singh, the Sikh governor of Sirhind, who was away on an expedition, was not able to get back in time to meet the Mughal attack. His brother, Sham Singh, joined with Subha Singh, to offer a bold front to the enemy.

The encounter took place in the beautiful garden of Yaqub Khan, a few miles outside Sirhind. The Sikhs, though vastly outnumbered, fought valiantly and for a while stood their ground. Then a stray bullet killed Subha Singh. The morale of the Sikh forces suffered a blow and they fell back before the Mughal force and Sham Singh ordered a retreat to the fort of Sirhind where he took stock of the situation. Like Binod, he realized that no reinforcements would be forthcoming and trying to hold out in the fort would only result in casualties without any hope of pushing back the Mughals. So when Shamas Khan attacked the fort he found it abandoned. The Sikh forces had retreated towards Sadhaura.

Bahadur Shah finally caught up with his advance force on the outskirts of Sadhaura on 4 December. Banda was entrenched in the fort, his forces augmented by the survivors from Thanesar and Sirhind. The quartermaster general of the imperial army, Rustamdil Khan and Firoz Khan Mewati, moved forward to select a suitable site to serve as the imperial camp during the impending battle. Munim Khan and his son, Mahabat Khan, at the head of their forces, accompanied them. They had advanced a mere two kos when the Sikhs rushed down upon them after subjecting them to a thick rain of arrows, rockets and musket fire. The Sikhs were desperate and their despair added a fierce determination to their courage. Among the casualties were the son and nephew of Firoz Khan Mewati. The Sikh chiefs personally led their soldiers in the charge. They made an impressive sight with their long open beards, their flowing robes, their flashing swords and their blood-curdling war cries and thus inspired their soldiers to perform ever-greater acts of courage and valour. The attack was ferocious and the number of the dead and wounded among the Mughals heavy. Unfortunately, for Bahadur Shah, the main body of the imperial army arrived on the scene at precisely this moment. Each Sikh soldier abandoned his entrenchment and came out to fight in the open. The Sikhs were vastly outnumbered. As the day drew to a close, the few Sikhs who had survived the battle retreated towards the eastern mountains and made their way to Lohgarh.

It was now a foregone conclusion that the Sikhs would be defeated in the impending battle of Lohgarh. The major concern of the Mughals was that Banda Bahadur should not escape the siege. Bahadur Shah called a council of war to emphasize this important point: 'So long as this Banda Bahadur is alive to lead the Sikhs, so long will they remain a thorn in our flesh,' the ageing monarch spoke to his commanders. His failing health and the exhaustion caused by his long years of campaigning had taken their toll. His face was etched with deep furrows. He seemed to shrink in his seat and appeared even older than his years. His once powerful voice, which his listeners had trembled on hearing, was now only a high-pitched hysterical shriek. His speeches had always been characterized by their clarity and brevity. But now his words tended to wander and lacked all precision. 'His guru was once my friend. He helped me in my succession.' He lapsed into silence, unable to remember the connection he had sought to make between his association with the guru and the need to destroy Banda Bahadur.

'Jahanpanah, you were telling us about the need to crush and destroy Banda Bahadur Singh,' Munim Khan whispered into his emperor's ear.

'Yes, we must crush him,' Bahadur Shah said, raising his voice, irritated that his wazir should need to remind him that his mind was wandering. 'He has become the symbol of the opposition. As long as he lives he will remain a beacon for all rebels and malcontents and we will know no peace. Once he is destroyed, all opposition will be stilled. Hindus, Sikhs and even some Muslims see in him the hope of fulfilling their aspirations, of advancing their lot. They see in him the hope of taking away from us our rights over them and over the property they hold in trust from us. There should be no doubt that the primary objective of our attack on Lohgarh is the capture and destruction of Banda Bahadur. This takes precedence over all else and must be achieved at all cost.'

He paused for breath. There was a sparkle in his eyes as some of the long years of weariness seemed to have fallen away from him. He sat a little straighter and his voice was more firm and strong than it had been at the opening of the conference. 'All the strategies we work and all the planning and scheming we do must be aimed at one and only one objective – the capture and destruction of Banda Bahadur.'

The emperor was only echoing the thought that was in the mind of each of his generals. Banda's capture and destruction had become the end all and be all of all their efforts. Well aware of the Sikh penchant of melting away in the face of overwhelming odds in order to regroup, the Mughals deliberated on steps to be taken to ensure that Banda did not slip away from Lohgarh when his forces came into contact with the Mughals.

Small groups of Sikhs and Hindus were still straggling across the Punjab, seeking safety within the walls of the fort of Lohgarh. It was this movement that the Mughals exploited to ensure that Banda Bahadur did not escape. A small group of Muslims, disguised as Hindu refugees, joined the Sikhs and Hindus who were still coming into Lohgarh. Their brief was to stay close to Banda and kill him should he try to escape before the capture of the fort. It was a desperate measure as there was no way of knowing that some amongst the motley of Hindus and Sikhs who had sought refuge in the fort would not be from the same area as the Muslim infiltrators. There was the risk of being recognized and exposed. But so great was the Mughal need to destroy Banda that such desperate measures were readily adopted.

The Sikhs had made their own plans. In the run-up to the Mughal siege, a series of in-camera meetings had been held by the Sikh leaders. 'We are far outnumbered and all the recent battles against the Mughals have shown us conclusively that we are not at the moment in a position to resist their advance. The battle for Lohgarh can at best be a holding action to help the civilian population escape to a safer place. We cannot hope to give effective battle to the Mughal forces.' Binod looked towards Banda Bahadur, who nodded.

'What Bhai Binod Singh says is true. Our intelligence sources report that Bahadur Shah has close to sixty thousand well-trained soldiers. Most of them are veterans of the Deccan campaign. Our number is less than a quarter and most of our soldiers are irregulars without great training or skill. We must not wager much on the outcome of this battle. Though we must, as always, fight with courage and with valour, we must regard this battle as just another backward step and buy ourselves time for a more opportune moment to face the enemy.'

There was silence and Bhai Binod Singh took the floor again: 'More than the capture of Lohgarh, more than our defeat, it is the destruction of our leader that the Mughals seek. To them as to us, he is the symbol of the war against them. They see in him an unblinking beacon, a strong, pure light that calls upon all to fight for justice. They know that our struggle has not been waged long enough for it to throw up a second line of leaders, one of whom could take Banda Singh Bahadur's place. They know that without him we will be left rudderless and our struggle will flounder and be lost. So, through the siege and capture of Lohgarh it is the capture and elimination of our leader that they seek. Even more than working out strategies for the impending battle, it is the safety of our leader that we must first and foremost ensure.'

There were strong murmurs of assent from the handful of leaders who had been invited to attend the meeting. 'Bhai Banda Bahadur must leave the fort before the siege is laid.'

Banda smiled at this. 'I have always advocated the wisdom of recognizing that moment in battle when the tide has turned firmly against us, to bow to the inevitable and so live to fight another day. But to run away even before battle is joined will be an act of cowardice and not an act of wisdom. You would not want to make a coward of me both in the eyes of my followers and my enemy.'

Binod and Gaj Singh exchanged glances and the other leaders avoided Banda Bahadur's eye. Banda knew that his leaders had discussed the matter privately and a decision reached without reference to him.

'It is not cowardice to keep the flame of our struggle alive,' Sham Singh, the defender of Sirhind, said. 'What Bhai Binod Singh says is true. There is yet no one who can take your place. We will make a stand here and I promise you it will be a strong stand. But our stand will be even stronger if we are secure in the knowledge that the safety of our leader is not at stake.'

Burail Fort
Inside view of the Burj today, now under the Gurdwara Qila Sahib Burail.

Inside view of the Manimajra Fort today.

Mud Fort of Sitaragarh
The top of Sitaragarh is a kilometre away from the Lohgarh Fort, but to this day, words spoken from Sitaragarh can be heard at Lohgarh and vice versa owing to some acoustic phenomenon.

Remnants of Lohgarh Fort
Remains of the fort still exist in the forest area. Lohgarh was the Khalsa Raj's headquarters whereas Mukhlispur was the 'capital city'.

Jama Masjid at Kalanaure.

Wall paintings inside the Jama Masjid at Kalanaure today.

Finally the leaders passed a resolution urging Banda Bahadur to abandon the fort of Lohgarh and to seek safety in the hills. Banda hesitated in his acceptance of this resolution.

'You remember the promise you made to the guru. In all important matters you would respect the advice of your leaders. You must abide by this promise.'

Banda had no choice but to obey.

To give Banda a fair chance of getting away and to keep the news of his escape from reaching the Mughals, the leaders decided to practise a deception. They looked around for a Banda Bahadur look-alike and found him in one Gulab Singh, a Hindu convert, who was a bakshi in the Sikh force. Gulab Singh, with the zeal of a new convert, was only too glad for this opportunity to serve his 'guru'. Once he had put on Banda Bahadur's robes, taken his place both in his apartment and at the head of the congregation, he was able to pass off as the leader to all except the most discerning who had all been taken into confidence by the Sikh leadership.

As dusk fell upon the ramparts of the fort, Banda disguised as a simple peasant, slipped out of a small side entrance and stole away over a steep mountain track, through the deep forest that lay between the fort and the high hills. In the days that followed, the Mughal spies, within the fort, continued to send reports to Bahadur Shah that Banda Bahadur was still in Lohgarh, preparing to lead the defence of the town.

Late in the evening of 9 December 1710, the emperor arrived at his camp on the Som, within sight of the citadel of Lohgarh. As the evening shadows lengthened, he stood at the entrance to his tent, looking up at the fort. He marvelled at the uncanny instinct, which had made Banda Bahadur choose this place as his stronghold. It stood high on a summit and the hillside before him rose up to the foot of the fort in one sheer unbroken stretch, as impregnable as the strongest, thickest, man-made wall. All around there were craggy rocks, offering little chance of a foothold for an attack. As he watched he saw, high on the ramparts, a figure striding ahead of a small group of followers. There was such confidence in that stride that it left no room for doubt that he was the leader. The chill evening breeze had begun to stir and the leader's distinctive robes flew and fluttered before the wind. Bahadur Shah saw the leader stop and point at the ramparts. He saw the group of followers rush forward to examine what had been pointed out to them. Banda Bahadur was examining his defences. Bahadur Shah looked away and caught Munim Khan's eye. The wazir smiled and the emperor smiled back. Their quarry was secure. With their spies, in place, there would be no escape for him. It was dark now and the fort was a looming shadow in the gathering gloom. The wind blew fiercely and the emperor shivered in the sudden cold and permitted to be led to the warmth of his tent.

So strong and invincible did the fort seem, that even with 60,000 troops, both on horse and foot, under his command and the support of a vast number of irregular Rohila Afghans, who had turned out in the hope of plunder, Bahadur Shah decided against a direct attack. They would encircle the fort and lie in wait. Banda Bahadur might interpret their inactivity as an expression of fear and be tempted to come out of the fort and take on the Mughals in an open engagement.

Early next morning the imperial forces, commanded by prince Rafik-us Sham, marched to the very foot of the Daber hills. This force was to circle the fort from the left. Raja Udet Singh Bundela, commanding Bakshi-ul Mumalik's troops supported the prince. Munim Khan, accompanied by his sons Mahabat Khan and Khan Zaman, commanded the right arm.

Raja Chatarsal Bundela complemented this force. Also in support were the troops of the two princes, Azim Shah and Jahan Shah. Munim Khan had had the foresight to recruit as his guides, men with an intimate knowledge of the local terrain and had obtained from the emperor special permission to advance to the Sikh pickets. The emperor had made it clear that this was to be a move purely of reconnaissance and under no circumstances was he to launch an attack on the Sikh positions.

His guides gave him invaluable aid and Munim Khan advanced swiftly and arrived within a shot of the lowest of the Sikh entrenchments. The Sikh strategy was to place tiers of small entrenchments at strategic points all around, starting from halfway up the hill. With these positions they would be able to inflict the maximum damage on the enemy when the Mughal force launched its attack. It was within range of the lowest ring of pickets that Munim Khan's force had reached. The Sikhs were not the ones to miss this God-sent opportunity. From their vantage position they let loose a rain of gunfire, arrows and fire balls on the enemy with devastating accuracy. Munim and his men held their position, but when the second round of fire was unleashed upon them, their lines wavered and began to fall back. He remembered only too well the emperor's clear order that under no circumstances was he to attack the Sikhs. At the same time he could not stomach the humiliation of a retreat, and this would be conceding defeat without even firing a shot. While he hesitated, the Sikhs cheered loud and long and the sound of their cheering was like insults and taunts being hurled down upon him for his lack of will to fight back. He could not bear this and ignoring the emperor's orders, led the attack against the Sikh picket, who put up a brave fight but were heavily outnumbered. As the Mughal forces pushed close they abandoned the picket and climbed up the hill to take up positions in the higher entrenchments.

The scene of the battle was so close to the royal camp that the emperor, the princes and all the other commanders saw every detail of the fighting. It was obvious that the Sikhs would now be pushed back into the fort. The other commanders, jealous that Munim Khan would bear the palm of victory alone, too ignored the emperor's command and led their soldiers into the fray. The Sikhs were pushed back from picket after picket but not before inflicting heavy losses on the Mughals.

By the time dusk fell, all but two of the highest pickets had been captured and the Sikhs had fallen back on their last position in the fort of Lohgarh. The carnage had been heavy and the hillside was covered with blood, both Mughal and Sikh. As the echoes of the battle receded, Bahadur Shah looked at the hillside, now littered with dead bodies and was overwhelmed by the large number of soldiers who had been killed in a single day of battle. Perhaps the princes and the remaining noblemen were overwhelmed too, because a deep hush descended upon the camp.

The call for the evening prayers resounded in the hills. Munim Khan ordered his soldiers to take positions where they were and rest for the night. The advance upon the fort would be resumed next morning, as the fort was now surrounded from all sides and their quarry would not be able to escape. Sure in this belief he returned to the royal camp, to make his peace with the emperor, whom he had disobeyed. Though the emperor's greetings to Munim Khan were more formal than warm it was obvious that in view of the resounding Mughal success his act of disobedience had been forgiven.

All was not well within the fort. It had been home to a large number of refugees over the last few months, most of whom had been in transit and had been encouraged to move on as quickly as possible to the safety of the hills. But their brief stay had depleted the stores of provisions. What was left was distributed amongst the sick and the wounded. It was clear that there was no hope of holding out against the Mughals and they decided to break through the cordon of their forces. All through the night, small groups of Sikh soldiers attacked what they considered to be the weaker points in the Mughal lines, where the exhausted, battle-weary soldiers were taken by surprise. Many of the Sikhs were able to make good their escape.

The next morning, 11 December, was cold and bleak. A heavy rain cloud had descended low over the hills and shortly before dawn when Munim Khan resumed his advance up the hill, a light drizzle began, adding to the misery of his soldiers. The engagement, if it could be called one, was swift and short. There was no opposition worth the name and the only one they encountered was from the two highest pickets, which were soon overpowered. The Mughals broke into the fort of Lohgarh, where an eerie silence hung.

After the blood and thunder of the previous day, this silence seemed ominous and threatening. It was as if the Sikhs had devised some new and unfamiliar strategy of war and the Mughals had walked straight into a carefully set trap. Their damp clothes clung to their bodies and chilled them to the bone. Fronds of cloud and mist clawed at their faces and the shadows of the trees loomed dark and sinister through the low cloud cover. The soldiers were reluctant to advance further into this hostile and frightening environment. Their officers, understanding and sharing their fears, were loath to goad them on. But the commander's orders could not be ignored and detachments of Mughal troops moved slowly up the cobbled streets, one cautious step at a time. There were one or two stray pockets of survivors in some of the buildings that the soldiers entered. But they were all civilians, old men and women, who sat huddled in corners, looking at their conquerors with large silent eyes, the silence of the condemned man in the moment before his execution.

Then, with startling suddenness and clarity, a sound broke the silence. It was the sound of a voice raised in the recitation of the Japji Sahib, the Sikh morning prayer. The voice was deep and resonant and the music of the words played upon the silence of the fort with the accomplishment of a virtuoso. Many of the Mughal soldiers stopped in their tracks, overwhelmed by the beauty of the sound and as they listened, almost miraculously, the drizzle stopped, the clouds lifted and the sun broke over the horizon. The sinister shadows dissolved and the Mughals understood that the silence was not part of a diabolical stratagem on the part of the Sikhs, but because there was no one left to make a sound. There were only the dead and the dying scattered all over the fort, the wounded too far gone to be aware of what was happening around them, too far gone to groan in pain or to cry. Then there was this voice that had come ringing out to them. They followed it and came to a prayer hall, a huge hall with just a handful of devotees sitting cross-legged on the floor, listening to their leader recite that beautiful prayer. The leader wore his distinctive robes and turban. The first soldiers paused under one of the arches, not sure what next to do. Gulab Singh looked up and caught their eyes and held up his hand, palm outwards, to indicate that they should wait. Even without this gesture they would have waited, compelled by the strength of his voice, the serenity of his face.

The prayers came to an end. The 'guru' turned and smiled at the soldiers and then strode towards them. There was jubilation in the Mughal camp as the news of Banda's capture spread through their ranks. Gulab Singh was heavily chained and fettered and led into Munim Khan's presence. With him were the few survivors who had been hiding in the abandoned buildings and the faithful who had been listening to the morning prayers. Munim Khan, flush in the pride of his quick victory and the easy capture of the Sikh leader, poured scorn upon his prisoner. Gulab Singh said not a word. He stood there, smiling, his face bathed in the radiant light of calm serenity. His silence angered Munim Khan and his invectives against Banda Bahadur became stronger and more virulent. At last his anger got the better of him and he raised his hand and struck Gulab Singh so severely across the face that he drew blood. Still Gulab Singh smiled.

'Why do you smile even when you are struck?' Munim Khan asked, unable to mask his bewilderment at Gulab Singh's reaction.

'I smile because you remain ever true to your character, to the character of your emperor and all who obey his commands. You strike one who stands before you chained and helpless. You have always oppressed the weak, the ones who could not strike back.'

'And you, who were the champion of the oppressed, who often boasted that you would free them of their shackles, where stand you now? Chained and helpless, a mere step away from death. Where is all your proud boasting and vaunting now? Where are all your Sikhs, your hordes of followers? They have all abandoned you.'

'It was not I who was the champion of the oppressed. It was

my leader, and he lives a free man, free to see the day when he will strike again at you and your tyranny. And his Sikhs have not abandoned him. They have scattered far and wide to bide their time till their leader calls them again to strike another blow. Then you will face the full wrath of my leader and his followers once again.'

Munim Khan's heart was filled with dread. What he heard could not possibly be true. If it were, the consequences would be terrible to be dwelt upon. 'You lie, you scoundrel. You lie in order to save your life. For this lie I will skin you alive and give you the most horrible death.'

'I died the day I took my leader's place. It is only a dead body you see before you, you can do with it what you will.' He paused. Munim Khan could not bring himself to speak. He had promised to bring Banda Bahadur before the emperor and he had failed.

'I see that you do not wish to believe me.' Gulab Singh looked around at the assembled Mughal soldiers and courtiers. He scanned each face and then he saw two soldiers who were from his village. 'Oh, Shafiq and Rahim,' he called out to them. 'Come forward and look closely into my face and then vouch safe to the Nizam-ul Mulk that I am no Banda Bahadur Singh but only a poor imposter.' The two came reluctantly forward and looked closely into Gulab Singh's face. Then they lowered their eyes to the ground.

'Speak. Tell me what you know,' Munim Khan called out to them. His voice was a cry of anguish.

'It is true, what he says, my lord.' Rahman said, without raising his eyes. 'He is from my village, one Dina Nath, who afterwards took the name of Gulab Singh, when he became a follower of the guru.'

Great was Munim Khan's grief at being thus deceived. Tears

of helpless rage sprang to his eyes and not wishing for anyone to see him thus, he turned and, without another word, retreated to the privacy of his camp.

When Bahadur Shah heard of Banda's escape, he was enraged beyond reason. He ranted and raved: 'That dog, that pig, he promised us the head of that infidel and he has failed to fulfil his promise. We wish never to see his face again. We banish him from our sight.' In just a moment all the long years of devoted service had been forgotten. 'Oh, how could this happen. Allah has abandoned me, my Allah has abandoned me.' Like a village woman who ritualistically mourns and laments the death of a beloved, he mourned his failure to capture the Sikh leader. He tore his clothes and banged his head against the tent poles. He slapped himself and scratched his cheeks. His courtiers did all they could to restrain him but he would not be comforted. When Gul Muhammad, his faithful slave, tried to make him drink the hakim's draught, he knocked it away and bit the slave's hand. The princes held their father down on his bed and forced the draught down his throat. At last the ranting, raving and the violence abated and the old man drifted off to sleep.

It was obvious that others must do what needed to be done. Gulab Singh and the small band of survivors were taken over by Sarbrah Khan, the kotwal, and executed. Rustamdil Khan took charge of the imperial sappers and miners and dug ditches and trenches in the now deserted fort, searching for buried treasure. In three days they recovered eight lakh rupees in gold coins.

Bahadur Shah's fit passed and he recovered his mental equilibrium. Munim Khan was forgiven and allowed into the emperor's presence. But the faithful old wazir never recovered from the slight and died a few months later. The rajas of Nahan and Srinagar were ordered to capture the Sikh rebel leader and bring him to the emperor's court since they had let him pass through their kingdoms. Failing this, they would be held culpable of Banda's escape and would be punished accordingly. In spite of these orders, no trace of Banda Bahadur was found. The raja of Srinagar lived high in a forbidding mountain area, too far for the hands of the Mughal retribution to reach him. But the raja of Nahan was within reach. Hamid Khan, who was sent in pursuit, not finding the raja, brought his son, Bhup Prakash, as a captive. The prince and thirty of his leading courtiers were executed on 23 March 1711.

Heavy with the sense of failure, sick at heart, his mind now wandering more and more, the emperor realized that no purpose would be served by tarrying in this part of the Punjab anymore. He began his march to Lahore in short, slow stages to reach there on 11 August.

Chapter Seven

When Banda appeared on the outskirts of Batala, the inhabitants shut themselves in the fort and prepared to withstand the Sikh onslaught. Sheikh Ahmed with his followers marched out of the Hathi Gate to join battle with the invaders. He made a valiant stand but was defeated and killed and his followers were decimated in the face of the far greater numerical strength of the Sikhs. On getting the news, the emperor was enraged to the point of dementia.

T HEY CALLED THE PLACE SUNETI, WHICH IT WASN'T. Suneti, a small hamlet of six dwellings, was the nearest human habitation. So they used its name. It was a small plateau dominated by two ancient trees – one, a banyan with dozens of aerial roots reaching almost to the ground; the other, a massive maunsari, leaning precariously to one side, as if it were waiting for the next storm to send it crashing down. There was an abandoned temple on the northern side and a few small huts on the southern side. The roof of the temple had caved in a long time ago and there was dense shrubbery and undergrowth growing all over what had once been the sanctum sanctorum. The deity had long since been evacuated to a more frequented place of worship. The huts were in a better state but required intensive work before becoming habitable again. The one manmade thing on the plateau that time had not destroyed or damaged was the stone arch over the spring. Fresh, clear water sprang from a stone spout and splashed into a shallow basin gouged out of the rock below. The water was as clean and sweet and cold as it had been when some long ago ascetic had built the spring and the hermitage attached to it.

The sun came late to the plateau, but when it did it remained long into the evening, warming every stone, every leaf and every blade of grass. The place was situated high in the hills above

Kiratpur, hidden in a fold of the range, so long disused that even the local people had forgotten its existence. The approach road, if there had ever been one, had been lost to nature. Without the help of an expert guide it was not possible to find it, not till one had been to it a dozen times. It was here that Banda Bahadur came to.

The Sikhs were faced with a paradoxical situation. On the one hand was the sad awareness of their depleted strength. They had lost so many to death and desertion that even with their legendary valour and strong motivation they were not in a position to take on their enemies. But if the abandoning of Lohgarh was to be perceived as a strategic retreat and not as a defeat, then some offensive action was called for. The guru's brief had been to attack forces of tyranny and oppression. Banda and his Sikhs had so far concentrated only on the Mughal forces. The broader interpretation of the guru's brief would include the hill rajas who had been as guilty of exploiting and oppressing the poor and the weak as the Mughals. Banda suggested that while they waited for the build-up of their forces and for an opportune time to resume their battle with the Mughals, they should focus their attention on the hill rajas. Depleted as their forces were, they were still strong enough to deal with them.

Hukumnamahs were sent out under Banda Bahadur's seal, which enjoined upon all Sikhs to live according to the tenets of their religion and to practise the ways the gurus had preached. They emphasized the need to eschew all intoxicants and live lives of truth, purity and chastity and reiterated that only those who lived according to the Rahat of the Khalsa would find salvation. The hukumnamahs commanded all able-bodied Sikhs to arm themselves and to come forthwith to Kiratpur to support Banda in the next phase of his struggle against tyranny.[13] Soon, small jathas of armed Sikhs began to arrive in Kiratpur and the next three months saw the influx of a sufficient number of soldiers to give them a fair chance of success in the coming battles.

In the early months of the year, he found pleasure in spending the day in the open space that lay between the temple and the huts. The sunlight filtered through the leaves of the two trees and fell dappled on the wild grass, its warmth tempered by the alternating patches of shade. The soft warmth of the sun seeped into his body and relaxed his tired bones and frayed nerves, and he found himself regaining a measure of his old equanimity. There was such deep peace and silence in the world around him that he, and those with him, could not help but be touched by it. He was glad for this rest as it gave him and his followers time to come to terms with their losses, to heal wounds both of the body and of the mind.

Through these months he held conferences in his eagle's nest. He would sit on a stringed cot, listening to the opinions and advice offered by his leaders, to the discussions that sometimes became acrimonious and heated and required him to slip in a few words and tactfully diffuse the tension. The position and strength of each of the rajas was also reviewed. The raja of Sirmur, with his capital at Nahan, had always been a friend of the Sikhs and had permitted Guru Gobind Singh to set up his temporary headquarters at Paonta. Deeply influenced by the guru's teachings and under his influence he had tried to improve the lot of his subjects in many ways. Since, Bhup Prakash, the son of Raja Hari Prakash, had recently been executed for permitting Banda Bahadur to escape through Sirmur territory, the Sikh leaders were sure that in Hari Prakash they had a strong and unwavering ally.

Raja Bhim Chand of Kahlur, with his capital at Bilaspur, was regarded as the biggest enemy of the Sikhs and also had a long history of treacherous behaviour against Guru Gobind Singh. He saw in the guru's socialistic and democratic ideas, which struck at the very root of the caste system and taught that all men were equal, irrespective of the circumstances of their birth, a threat to his position and power. His power, and the power of the other like-minded rajas, stemmed from the fact that the lower castes were kept in a constant state of subjugation. They were taught to believe that it was God's will that they should be born in a lower caste and it was their destiny to be constantly abused and exploited, a destiny that they must accept as their lot. And they had accepted it for generations. Now suddenly they saw before them a casteless society, a society where the high-born and the low-born sat side by side to partake of meals. They saw a society where it was actions, not birth that earned merit. The lowest of the low-born could aspire to achieve the highest rank and position. There would be no legions of unpaid labourers to till their lands, no hosts of underpaid, underfed servants to do all their menial tasks for them, no conscripted soldiers to go out to fight battles for them as and when their whims and fancies dictated.

The raja of Mandi, Sidh Sain, though a weak and vacillating man, was cast in the same mould as Raja Bhim Chand. The Sikhs were convinced that if Bhim Chand were defeated, Sidh Sain would immediately come down on his knees. Past history showed that the other smaller rajas would follow Sidh Sain's example and sue for peace on the Sikhs terms. The only remaining raja worth reckoning with was Raja Uday Singh of Chamba. He had never shown any open hostility against the

Sikhs. If on the one hand he had held back support to the Sikhs when it was called for, he had never joined any expedition against them either, maintaining careful neutrality. Raja Uday Singh had the reputation of being a firm but fair ruler. In moments of difficulty and crisis he had shown kindness and compassion for his subjects. It was said that the poorest of the poor could seek and obtain audience with him and be sure of obtaining redress, if injustice had been meted out to him. During periods of drought, Uday Singh was known to waive the peasants taxes. Keeping all this in mind, the Sikh leadership was convinced that they could win Uday Singh's support to their cause and have him as their friend. Banda Bahadur singled out Raja Bhim Chand as his next target and by mid-February felt confident of taking him on.

As was customary, a parwana, in the nature of a show cause notice before the actual declaration of war, was sent to Bhim Chand, which as expected, was torn and thrown into the messenger's face. The reason for Bhim Chand's over-confidence and arrogance, was that ever since Banda's advent in the Punjab, he had been expecting to be attacked and had taken advantage of Banda's preoccupation with the Mughals to prepare for the attack. He had called upon the zamindars of the Jalandhar Doab to come to his aid and they, having borne the brunt of Banda's efforts to end the zamindari system, were grateful for this ally in their battle for survival. They had come to Bilaspur with large numbers of mercenaries and large quantities of arms and ammunition. The hill rajas from the smaller states also pledged support. This, coupled with his knowledge of the Sikh reversals at Sadhaura and Lohgarh had given him a sense of superiority over the Sikhs. What he had failed to take into account was the strength of Banda's hukumnamahs and the response they would evoke.

In spite of all his preparations, he could not make a stand against the Sikh attack when it came. In a matter of hours the swarms of Sikhs overran the fort and the king's forces were put to the sword. For two whole days, groups of Sikhs could be seen, moving around the town of Bilaspur, stripping the palace and houses of all that was of value and carting it away to their camp near Kiratpur. Bhim Chand disappeared into the shadows of time. He suffered from a mental disorder and was forced to abdicate in favour of his son Ajmer Chand to die an unrecorded and unnoticed death.

The complete and easy victory of the Sikhs brought fear to the heart of the other rajas. They heard stories of the ruthlessness with which all the soldiers of the defeated army had been slain and of the plunder and destruction that had been unleashed upon the capital of Kahlur. They knew that if they offered resistance they would meet the same fate and shuddered at the very thought. Far better to submit and accept whatever terms the Sikhs might offer.

As expected, the first to submit was Raja Sidh Sain of Mandi. Two days after the fall of Bilaspur, he came in person, with lavish and expensive presents and was willing to pay tribute in return for peace. Other rajas were quick to follow, at least in appearance, and tendered the much needed monetary tribute and pledged support of arms and men in his struggle against the Mughals. The only one who did not offer submission or did not send any emissary to Banda's camp, was Raja Uday Singh of Chamba.

Soon, Banda decided to set up camp a few miles from the town of Chamba. The next evening, through the darkening gloom of the evening and the haze of the cooking fires, the soldiers saw a solitary horseman riding furiously from the town towards their camp. They rose to their feet and gathered around their leader. Many of them fearing treachery, formed a protective ring around Banda Bahadur. But they need have had no fears for when the rider flung himself from his horse they saw an old man, his back bent and a venerable beard upon his chin. He took care to show that he was unarmed. Banda rose to greet him.

'I am Amin Chand, Raja Uday Singh's wazir. I must speak with your leader, the great Banda Singh Bahadur Sahib.'

'Yes,' Banda said with a softness in his voice, a reflection of his admiration for the raja who had maintained his neutrality even when all the others were falling over themselves to swear allegiance to the victor. 'What message does your king have for me?'

'He would like to know your intentions towards him, you who have come in such great force to his very doorstep.'

'Assure him, that towards him my intentions can only be honourable. I come in friendship. I ask that he permit me to visit him, alone and unarmed, as earnest of my friendship.'

'I will seek my king's advice.' The wazir saluted Banda, mounted his horse and rode back to the fort.

All the leaders were shocked at Banda's proposal as they feared the worst. But Banda stuck to his resolution. He knew that Uday Singh was fair and fearless and would never resort to treachery.

Early next morning a group of a dozen horsemen came to escort Banda into the town. And he, without even the assurance of his sword, mounted his horse and went with them. There was no fear in his heart, only the feeling that he was on the brink of something momentous. The streets were decorated with banners and bunting and all the townsfolk stood along the street and on balconies, terraces and ramparts to welcome him. The first few steps were taken in silence. Then a section of the crowd set up a tentative cheer, which was soon taken up whole-heartedly by the others. By the time he reached the king's palace, the cheer had become a deafening roar and he knew that the people of Chamba welcomed the friendship of the Sikhs as much as the Sikhs sought theirs.

The king came down the steps to meet him and put a garland of flowers around his neck, embraced him warmly and then, his arm still around his waist, led him up the steps to the open terrace. He had fixed this venue for the meeting so that all should see what transpired between the two leaders. Uday Singh had put aside his throne and the two sat side by side on identical seats.

'You bestow great honour by your presence, Banda Sahib.'

'No, your majesty, it is you who honour me. You are a king and I but a poor bondsman of my guru.'

'And what a bondsman,' Uday Singh said with a smile. 'I wish all of us were such bondsmen to our gurus for the world would be a much better place to live in.'

The visit passed in great pleasantness. There was honesty and sincerity in what the two men had to say to each other. Each moment strengthened the bond that had been established between these two so different men. By the time Banda ended his visit after the midday meal, it was as if they had been friends all their lives.

In the evening, once again through the gathering gloom and the haze of the cooking fires, the soldiers of Banda's camp perceived horsemen riding towards them from the town. As the riders came closer they saw that there was a horse-drawn carriage and a group of six horsemen. But this time there was no fear of treachery, no need to form a protective ring around their leader. They had all heard the details of Banda's visit to the raja and were happy that they had won an ally.

It was Amin Chand again who came as an emissary of the raja, bearing presents from his king for Banda and his leaders. They were beautiful things, things that had been chosen with great thought and care. But they were not gifts of excessive value, which could be construed as symbols of submission or looked upon as tribute.

Amongst the gifts was a slice of ivory four inches square, painted, with fine meticulous strokes, each the thickness of a single hair – the portrait of a beautiful girl. The portrait, like all portraits in the pahari style, was done in profile. Amin Chand held his peace, a look of pure speculation in his eyes as he watched the Sikh leader examine the portrait with great care, turning it this way and that to catch the light of the nearby lamp. At last Banda looked up and there was no mistaking the question in his eyes. Amin Chand did not wait for him to voice this question.

'This is the Princess Sushil, only daughter of the king's late brother Pratap Singh, the apple of the king's eye, dearer to him than are his own children.'

'And?'

Again the question was plain in Banda's eyes and again Amin Chand did not wait for him to give voice to it. A smile played about his lips as he spoke, 'The king would be honoured if you would accept the princess' hand in marriage.'

The suspicion of what was to come had already begun to form in Banda's mind. But now that the proposition had been stated in such bald and open terms, he could not help but be shocked. He started from his seat. But Binod put his hands on his shoulders and pushed him firmly down again. Banda looked up into his old friend's eyes in utter helplessness. Binod looked back steadily and shook his head and Banda understood that he was being asked to hold his peace.

'We are greatly honoured by this very generous and affectionate gesture. But you must understand that our leader has lived for long the life of a bairagi, a celibate who has abjured all knowledge of women. The proposal comes upon him suddenly and startles him. We ask the king for time till the morning to send him our acceptance in suitable terms.'

The old wazir smiled into Binod's face and the light from the lamp showed clearly the glint in his eyes. The old rascal was mocking them, mocking the position in which they had been placed by the proposal. But Binod could feel no anger at this mockery.

'I understand and so, I am sure, will his majesty.' He saluted Banda. 'Do I have your permission to leave?' Banda nodded his head and Amin Chand turned to leave. Then, as if remembering something that he had forgotten, he turned back again.

'One last thing. The king has also sent this Chamba roomal, a large handkerchief. It is an ancient art form, peculiar to our kingdom. The raja has done much to revive this once dying craft and now it is again popular and thriving and has come into its own. The princess embroidered this particular specimen with her own hand. We in Chamba set great store on the dexterity with which our girls ply their needles. It is through the practice of this art that they learn the virtues of patience, meticulousness and attention to detail. The girls work in groups and through the criticism of their work by the other girls they learn tolerance. They also gain the ability to laugh at themselves, which is one of the greatest gifts that nature can give us. When they run into difficulty with their work, the other girls help them out and they learn the virtue of cooperation and helpfulness and of courtesy.' He paused for breath and then went on. 'I could go on and on the whole night on this subject. But I must take your answer back to my king. Not ever having embroidered a Chamba roomal himself he has not learnt the virtue of patience and in his impatience he will berate me if I tarry. I hope the princess' gift will give you pleasure.'

Long into the night the leaders sat discussing this strange and unlikely development. Banda was adamant that he could not go into this marriage. His very nature rebelled at the thought. His celibacy was too deeply ingrained for him to be able to violate it.

'Do not look upon this as a marriage between Banda Bahadur and the princess Sushil,' Binod said. 'Royal marriages are always much more than the mating of a man and a woman. Through this offer Uday Singh is offering a seal to his friendship. From being mere friends you will become relatives, bound to each other by family ties, supporting each other in all contexts. You must remember that a refusal on your part will be seen as a rejection, the spurning of the hand of friendship. Uday Singh will be humiliated and his honour will demand revenge. You will be forced into a battle that you do not seek, against an adversary whom you both respect and admire.'

Banda was silent as the enormity of his situation at last sank in upon him. There was no escape. 'But what of the girl? I cannot give her what all girls have a right to demand of their husbands. Will this not be a rejection too, a humiliation?'

'You will give her much more than other husbands give their wives,' Binod said, putting his hand lightly on his friend's shoulder. 'And in the end it will be all right. She will find joy in what you give her and not regret what you cannot give her.'

There was a hushed silence. Time stretched. The inevitability of acceptance came upon Banda. He made one last effort to avoid it: 'The guru had enjoined on me that I must continue to be celibate.'

'The guru advised you to remain celibate because you had already been celibate for so long. It was to protect you from the possibility of your enemies being able to do you harm through the persons of your wife and children. I assure you that if the guru were here with us today he would strongly advise you to accept this proposal because through this marriage you will gain a strong ally and a faithful friend.'

Late into the night, when the others had gone, Banda sat alone staring into the flame of the lamp, not able to come to terms with this strange turn of events. Suddenly he realized that he was holding something in his hands. He looked down and saw that it was the Chamba roomal. He spread out the square of silk and studied it closely in the light of the lamp. The light was not sufficient to study the fine workmanship, so he brought a second lamp to bear light upon the roomal. It was magnificent. It portrayed a princess at her toilet, her handmaiden in attendance. The individual stitches were so fine and so closely worked that it was impossible for the naked eye to pick them out. The faces were both worked in the same stylized manner, the same limpid eyes, the same chiselled noses and the same pointed chins. And yet, as if with a touch of magic, the artist had imparted to each a distinctive uniqueness, an individuality of their own. There was in the princess' eye, as she turned to look at her handmaiden, a questioning look. What was the question that she asked? And Banda smiled as he read the question: 'Do I look pretty enough for my prince?' Then, with a start, he recognized the resemblance between the portrait painted on the square of ivory and the portrait that the princess had painted with her needle: the princess had used her needle and threads to create a self-portrait. If all that old Amin Chand had said about the art of embroidering

Chamba roomals were true, then the princess must indeed be a remarkable young woman.

The marriage was performed in the first week of March. Banda on his part had firmly rejected all forms, all trappings, which might carry a suggestion of royal splendour. He did not wear the richly embroidered silk coat that Uday Singh had sent for him and wore instead his usual everyday robe.

'It is distinctive enough,' he said firmly. He wore no kalgi, (aigrette) in his turban, none of the jewellery that had been sent for him to wear. He left his sword behind in his camp and when they were within walking distance from the walls of Chamba, he dismounted, thus compelling the rest of the marriage party to dismount too and accompany him on foot into the city. He had forbidden any musician from accompanying them and when they entered the fort, the citizens gaped at them in silent wonder. There could have been nothing more unlike a royal wedding party. If Uday Singh was disappointed, he did not show it. He was unfailing in his courtesy and, with his gentle smile, put Binod and the others at ease. He understood Banda's need to be seen as the leader of his men and not as their king.

If Banda had ensured that there was nothing kingly about his appearance, he could not escape the references that were made to him as the 'King of the Sikhs' in the various ceremonies and rituals and in the announcements connected with the wedding. In the eyes of the people of Chamba he was a king, the princess could have married no less. And if he chose to be married in the garb of a fakir it was just another instance of royal whimsicality and that was something they had long been familiar with.

Banda returned with his bride to the seclusion of Suneti. A new hut had been hastily raised to give the bridal couple some privacy. But they did not need this privacy, because Banda Bahadur had no idea what to do with his wife. He treated her with an affectionate indulgence as if it was the indulgence of a father for an only child, not the affection of a husband for a wife. Sushil was a bright, cheerful girl, who did not let her cheerful disposition be clouded by her husband's strange behaviour. The king, her uncle, had in his wisdom told her about Banda's predicament.

'Be patient, my child,' he had said, placing his hand on her head. 'It is not easy for him to accept the role of a husband. You must give him time.' She smiled at the memory of this exchange. She would give him all the time in the world, because she knew, as surely as she knew that the sun would rise on the morrow, that he would, one day, be hers.

Having won the promise of support from the rajas, Banda Bahadur was able to convince his leaders that they were ready to make a trial raid against the Mughals. He descended to the plains near Raipur and Bahrampur. At this time Bayzid Khan, the faujdar of Jammu, and his nephew Shamas Khan were in the vicinity of Raipur. They received the news of Banda's descent to the plains with total disdain. So strong was their arrogance and so poor their intelligence regarding the strength of the Sikhs, that they did not feel it worth their while to face Banda personally. They deputed one Shahbad Khan, with a force of 1,500, to hasten to Raipur and deal with this minor irritant. Uncle and nephew, with 900 horsemen to accompany them chose to hunt deer instead of facing Banda Bahadur.

'You will still be in time to join us in the hunt,' Bayzid Khan told the departing Shahbad Khan, 'after you have destroyed that pig.'

Shahbad Khan met a gory and hasty end and Bayzid Khan had to abandon his hunt and turn his full attention towards the approaching Sikhs. The Sikhs repeated the tactics of the battle of Rahon. They pretended to be overwhelmed by the sight of Shamas Khan and his army and fled from the field. Shamas Khan, fired by the thought of this easy victory, gave chase. When he was separated from the main force, the retreating Sikhs turned upon him and the other Sikh formations who had assumed positions of ambush streamed down upon the Mughal forces. The Mughal casualties in the ensuing battle were heavy. Shamas Khan was killed and Bayzid Khan was mortally wounded.

Emboldened by this success and by the total rout of the combined armies of Bayzid Khan and Shamas Khan, Banda advanced upon the town of Batala, which like Samana, was a prosperous trading town. It was also an important seat of religious learning. On learning about the approach of Banda's army the town council held an emergency meeting. The two most important citizens were Sayyad Muhammad Fazil-ud Din Qadir and Sheikh Ahmed. The former had come but recently to Batala. He was a merchant prince who had brought vast material resources with him, which he used to establish a hermitage and a college of religious learning, thus winning him great respect. Now that a crisis loomed large, his reaction showed his lack of roots in the town. He proposed that all inhabitants be evacuated to places of safety. Sheikh Ahmed, on the other hand, had been born and brought up in Batala, as had his father, grandfather and great-grandfather before him. He had a great love for the city and could not bring himself to agree to abandon it to the Sikhs without making a stand. He urged that those who loved Batala should stay and put up a fight, even to death, to try and save their beloved city. No agreement could be reached and it was decided that each faction must follow the course that it wanted to. Sayyad Qadir and his followers abandoned the town.

When Banda appeared on the outskirts of Batala, the inhabitants shut themselves in the fort and prepared to withstand the Sikh onslaught. Sheikh Ahmed with his followers marched out of the Hathi Gate to join battle with the invaders. He made a valiant stand but was defeated and killed and his followers were decimated in the face of the far greater numerical strength of the Sikhs.

On getting the news, the emperor was enraged to the point of dementia. On 24 May he ordered Rustamdil Khan to muster all the forces he could and march out against the Sikhs. 'Do not dare to return to my presence without his head,' he ordered. A week later, forgetting that Rustamdil Khan had already been sent against the Sikhs, he gave similar orders to Muhammad Amin Khan.

The Sikh forces were within striking distance of Lahore. Strong was the temptation to attack the seat of the Mughal power and destroy its presence in their beloved Punjab. But this time it was the leaders who prevailed upon Banda to hold back. All the Mughal forces were deployed within easy distance of Lahore and the emperor himself was camped in Hoshiarpur with his elite imperial guard. Even if they were able to capture the fort of Lahore in a lightning strike, they would not be able to hold on to it in the face of the onslaught of the combined Mughal forces. It would be far better to continue a policy of harassment, to trouble the Mughals with minor battles like the battle of Batala and then to withdraw to the safety of the hills. From all accounts the emperor was seriously ill and fast losing his mind. The end was near. There would be confusion in the Mughal camp after his death with his forces divided in the war of succession that was sure to follow. There was greater tactical wisdom in waiting than to attempt it now when the chips were clearly drawn against them.

Banda accepted the advice and decided to withdraw, but could not bring himself to leave without fulfilling a long-cherished desire. Ever since he had heard that poem of the mystic Bulleh Shah at the Guru's camp near Nanded, he had wished to meet him in person. Since his return to the Punjab, he had gained greater familiarity with the poet and the Qadiri Silsila, the order that he belonged to. He had heard and learnt many of his kafis. These poems found such a strong echo in his own heart and spirit that the desire and longing to meet the mystic had become very strong within him and he could not bring himself to leave the vicinity of Lahore without fulfilling this desire.

The Qadiri Sufis can be traced back to the Sufi saint, Abdul Qadiri Jilani, who lived in the eleventh and twelfth centuries in Baghdad. He is also known as Pir Dastgir and Piran-i-Pir. In India the influence of the Sufi Qadiri was felt after three centuries through the person of Muhammad Ghaus, a Sufi dervish who first settled in Bhawalpur but the influence of whose teachings spread far and wide. Perhaps because of an inherent similarity in the values that they preached, perhaps because of their approach to the universality of the human spirit and the equality of mankind, a strong sympathy was built up between the Sufis of the Qadiri tradition and the Sikhs. Thus it was that Mian Mir, a Sufi saint of the Qadiri tradition, who laid the foundation stone of Harmandir Sahib in Amritsar and it was Mian Mir, who, in spite of being a Muslim, spoke out fearlessly against Jehangir's persecution of the fifth guru, Arjun Dev.

Banda Bahadur had been drawn towards the Qadiri order because he saw in Bulleh Shah's life and spiritual practices much that he himself wished for and had tried to achieve. Bulleh Shah had always looked upon his teacher as his master and regarded himself as a bondsman held in thrall by his love for his master and when this thought found expression in his beautiful poems Banda could not but be moved as he saw much of his own relationship with his guru reflected in Bulleh Shah's verse. Many of the tenets of the Qadiri Silsila, the Sufi order, were tenets that Banda practised himself. Living a life of poverty, living within the limits of goodness and morality, learning to be content with what God had given, meditating in solitariness, singing the praises of God and of one's master, all were spiritual practices which Banda followed and shared with Bulleh Shah and all those who followed the Qadiri Silsila. No wonder then that he regarded the mystic poet as a kindred spirit and wished very much to meet him.

Bulleh Shah lived with his master, the great Sufi saint, Inayat Shah Qadiri, in the dera that the master had established just outside Lahore. Late one evening, shortly before his departure, Banda Bahadur disguised himself and made his way to the dera. The day's activity in the dargah had long since come to an end. The stream of pilgrims and supplicants had dried up and the few attendants who were still awake turned with surprise to their visitor. He was escorted to Bulleh Shah's apartment. Bulleh Shah sat cross-legged on his cot, telling his beads, as Banda stood at the doorway, overwhelmed to be at last in the presence of the great poet. Bulleh Shah sensed his presence, glanced at the doorway and then sprang to his feet. Banda was confused. He felt that there had been some mistake. He saw before him a young man in his mid-thirties while his mental picture of Bulleh Shah was of a venerable old man: the wisdom and the strength that flowed through his poems came only after long years of study and meditation.

'I am sorry to disturb you,' he said. 'There has been some mistake. I wished to meet the wise old poet and mystic, Bulleh Shah, instead I have been brought to you. Forgive me for my intrusion,' he turned to leave the apartment.

'No, wait. Please don't go.'

Banda turned back. The young man walked to the doorway with quick, short steps as his face broke into an effusive smile. Banda was at once struck by the great spiritual radiance on that beautiful young face, the light in those clear luminous eyes.

'Come, come,' the young man took Banda by the hand and led him to the cot. 'I hate to disappoint you. I am neither venerable nor wise, yet I am the man you seek: I am Bulleh Shah.' There was no mistaking the amusement in the smile that lit up his face and Banda knew that he was not the first to have made this mistake.

'You must forgive me, for breaking in so rudely upon you and disturbing your rest so late at night.'

'I know you do not do so by choice, it is your need that compels this nocturnal visit. Come, be seated.' They sat side by side on the cot and after a pause, Bulleh Shah put his hand on Banda's shoulder and spoke in a voice that was kinder and more compassionate than any he had heard since he had last heard the guru's voice: 'What is it, my son?'

Banda felt no strangeness in being thus addressed by a man who was much younger than him. He felt only a sense of security in his presence. He felt the weariness of the endless struggle sweep over him and he longed to put his head on the saint's lap and rest. But he had been asked a question and he must answer.

'I needed to be with you, even if but for a short while. I have long admired your poetry and the wisdom that it contains. It has given me the strength to do what I must do.'

The sage smiled and it was the smile of a little child. 'And what is it that you have done that makes you come to me alone, in the silence of the night like a fugitive?'

'I have led my people in rebellion against the tyranny and oppression of the Mughals.'

Understanding dawned in the poet's eyes and he pulled his hand away form Banda's shoulders. 'Banda Bahadur?' he said, and his amazement was so strong that there was a question in his tone. But it was there only for a moment and then the smile came back again: 'How can you say that my poems have given you the strength and inspiration to do what you have done? My message is one of peace, your path has been one of violence and bloodshed.'

'But our goals are the same. You seek through your poetry and your sermons to free people from the bonds of hypocrisy and the sham that society imposes upon them. You seek to help people to find their true selves so that they will finally abandon the desires that lead to the tyranny and oppression of other people. You seek an end to exploitation of all kinds. I too work towards the same end. I too strive for the freedom of the poor, and the exploited, from the bondage that they have endured for centuries.' The poet put his hand back upon Banda's shoulder.

'The means are as important as the ends. You cannot hope to achieve noble ends through means that are not altogether noble. You cannot achieve what you strive to achieve through violence. Violence will only breed more violence and give those who would be your friends and supporters, reason to fear and shun you. Already people think of you more as the enemy of the Muslims and less as the champion of the poor.'

'I came to you because I look upon you as a kindred spirit, working to achieve the same goal. There is much in our lives that is same and yet I also know that the paths that we have followed to achieve our common goal are totally different. You teach the path of patience and of love. You preach that if someone strikes us we must turn the other cheek and so win him to the path of goodness and compassion. But the people we are dealing with do not understand such patience and forbearance. They look upon it as yet another sign of weakness, as subjugation to their power. The only language they understand is the language of force, an eye for an eye and a tooth for a tooth', Banda sighed.

'You cannot change the world for the better with the power of the sword. You will frighten people into obeying you, you will cow them into submission while the sword is in your hands. You will never be able to make them believe that your path is the right path. Once the sword has fallen from your hand, they will revert to their old ways.' The poet paused to catch his breath and then carried on: 'I hold no brief for the Mughal officials. They are bloodthirsty villains, most of them; perhaps they deserve the gory destruction that you inflict on them. But even if you were to exterminate all of them there would be others to take their place. To put a permanent end to this exploitation you have to prevail upon the minds of the people, even the minds of these officials, to make them realize that what they do is evil. You have to lead them along the path of righteousness for them to abjure all evil and only then will you be able to put an end to this oppression and tyranny. I try, through my poems, to bring people to the right path in life. People read my poems and are influenced by them. Why, even you claim that they have influenced you, though it is not the kind of influence I sought to exert. I would have wished for you to be influenced by the virtues that my order, my master and I lay the greatest emphasis on, the virtues of tolerance and forgiveness. Indeed these virtues are the keystones on which the entire archway of our faith is built and without them you cannot be a man of God.' His soft voice took on urgency: 'Listen to me, abjure the path of violence. Seek the path of peace for therein lies your salvation. This killing, this bloodshed will bring you nothing but damnation and on the Day of Judgement, God will condemn you for this.'

'Tolerance and forgiveness are indeed the keystones of any faith that is noble and good. But tolerance is an acceptance of mistakes made by others; tolerance is the understanding that others have a right to their beliefs and practices. Tolerance cannot be the acceptance of deliberate acts of oppression and exploitation practiced upon those who are too weak to fight back or even to raise their voices in protest. The tolerance and acceptance of these acts makes us party to them, makes us as guilty of perpetuating them as these cruel officials. We fight for the same cause – you and I, each with the weapon that he is most familiar with – you with your pen and I with my sword. It is true that your pen has influenced the minds of many men and God-willing, in the end will reach into the minds of them who practice these acts of tyrannical barbarity and influence them to the path of righteousness. But while we wait for this to happen, countless innocent men and women will continue to pay with their lives. I cannot let this happen; I cannot wait indefinitely to bring this freedom to the suffering masses. So I must go forth with my unsheathed sword. It is true that innocent men and women and children have been killed as a consequence of my actions. I have mourned their deaths and taken the responsibility for these deaths upon my shoulders. But there is no other weapon that I am familiar with so I must fight on with the weapon that I know how best to wield. This is the only path open to me and I must follow it to its end. And if in the process my soul is to be damned to eternal damnation, so may it be.'

The poet took a taviz, a charm to bring down God's blessings on the recipient, from under his pillow, recited a prayer over it and tied it around Banda Bahadur's arm. 'I cannot condone the means you employ. But you have come to me with hope and I must give you my blessing. I admire your steadfastness of purpose. So I hope and pray that God may guide you and show you the path, which in His eyes is best suited for the fulfilment of your purpose. Through you, may the peasant and the common man find escape from his suffering.'

Having received that conditional blessing, Banda stole away into the dark as quietly as he had come.

The Mughals learnt of the Sikh plan to abandon the plains and return to the comparative safety of the eastern hills. Muhammad Amin Khan and Rustamdil Khan pooled their resources and, with remarkable speed and skill, attempted to encircle Banda's forces. However, the Sikhs had long developed strategies to avoid such traps, broke up into small groups and rode away in different directions. Once comfortably away from the immediate reach of the enemy, they regrouped and, in two separate strengths, fell upon Rustamdil's forces from opposite sides. There were large-scale massacres of the imperial forces near Parol and Kathua. Having wreaked tremendous havoc on the enemy, Banda gave orders to retreat and the Sikhs made their escape over the hills to Jammu. Rustamdil Khan, totally dejected by what he saw as a complete defeat, lost heart and defying the emperor's orders, returned to Lahore. Muhammad Amin Khan continued to camp in the foothills but with little success.

The emperor, who had arrived at Lahore, was now in a pitiable condition and ranted and raved at Rustamdil Khan, and at the Sikhs who continued to elude him.

'With immediate effect the Sikhs are no longer to be treated as dhimnis, non-believers who follow religious teachings from a holy book. They are pagans and so not to be tolerated. Send firmans to every village, to every post along the roads. These infidels are to be killed on sight, every last man, woman and child, and may God assign their souls to purgatory. Post an award of one gold mohur for every ten Sikh heads brought to me. I want the entire race exterminated from my kingdom.' But in a more lucid moment, a glimmer of practical sense shone in his mind. 'However, where for some reason the faujdar feels that a particular community of Sikhs needs to live, he may declare them still as dhimnis, but the jeziya imposed upon them should be so strong that they are reduced to a state of penury.' He had in his mind the strong and powerful lobby of Sikh merchants in Delhi, without whose monetary support a comfortable life in the court would have been virtually impossible. As a result of the emperor's orders, thousands of Sikhs were beheaded. Others fled to the safety of the hills.

By the third week of January 1712, it was clear that the end was near. The emperor would have everyone who came into his tent searched for hidden weapons. He would make Gul Muhammad taste all his food and drink. With each passing day he reduced the number of people who could have access to him, till finally there were only a handful of people who were allowed to visit him and that too only for a few minutes at a time.

One night the baying of a dog awakened the emperor. While he lay awake, listening to the sound, he summoned Rustamdil, now restored to favour, and Gul Muhammad. 'Listen, listen,' he said, his voice little more than a whisper, his finger to his lips to suggest that they should be silent. They listened but all that they heard was the baying of a dog and were perplexed by the emperor's anxiety.

'Do you not hear?'

'Hear what, Your Majesty?'

'That awful, awful sound?'

'I hear only the baying of a dog,' Rustamdil said, the confusion showing on his face.

'That's all that I too hear, Your Majesty,' Gul Muhammad said.

A triumphant gleam came into the emperor's eyes and he wagged his finger at them: 'So you too have been deceived. It is not a dog – it is Banda Bahadur who has taken the form of a dog and bays at the moon to haunt us.'

There was silence and the baying of the dog came to them loud and clear in the stillness of the night. He went up to Rustamdil and clutched his arm. 'Help us, help us. Help us to be rid of him. He will not let us eat. He will not let us sleep. You must kill him once and for all.'

The dog was killed but after a few days another dog began

to bay at the moon and to bring some measure of peace to the troubled emperor, orders were given for the killing of all dogs in Lahore and its vicinity. Day after day groups of soldiers went around the city and killed all the dogs they could find. Soon it was reported to the emperor that all dogs, the incarnations of the Sikh devil, had been killed. No Banda Bahadur would come to haunt him now.

That evening the emperor heard the braying of a donkey. 'Listen,' he said, his voice the barest of whispers, his eyes rounded with terror. 'The Sikh is clever. He knows you will kill him if he takes the form of a dog. So he comes to hound me now in the form of a donkey.'

So, groups of soldiers went around slaughtering all the donkeys. Even with the killing of the donkeys the emperor knew no peace for on the fifth day he was awakened once again by the baying of a dog.

'He's back, he's back,' he cried out, his cry a cry of the deepest torment. 'We will never be rid of this plague. He will torment us to our dying day.' He buried his head in his pillow and wept and would not be comforted. Gul Muhammad brought him his draught and having drunk of it, the tormented soul at last found some measure of peace.

A fakir appeared at the camp one day and went from tent to tent begging for alms. The emperor saw him through the open flap of his tent: 'Who is that man in saffron clothes?'

'He is but a bairagi, Your Majesty,' Gul Muhammad said reassuringly. 'A mendicant who is begging food from our soldiers.'

'A mendicant! Don't underestimate him. Banda Bahadur was once a bairagi. This is one of his followers, sent to do us harm.' No amount of reassurance would shake this conviction. The only course left for Rustamdil was to expel all fakirs, yogis and bairagis from Lahore.

The end came soon after. The emperor died on the night of 27-28 February, still hallucinating about Banda coming to wreak vengeance upon him and upon the Mughal leaders.

On hearing the news of the emperor's death, Muhammad Amin Khan abandoned his hunt for Banda Bahadur and rushed back to Lahore to be at the centre of the power struggle that was to follow. A war of succession did ensue. Jahandar Shah emerged victorious after the defeat and death of his three brothers, and ascended the throne on 29 March 1712. It was an uneasy throne that he came to. A faction of his nobles supported the claim of Farukh Siyar, the son of the emperor's brother Azim-us Shah, to the throne. Matters were made worse by the fact that Jahandar Shah was a weak king who allowed his paramour, Lal Kunwar, to replace all the important officials of the court with members of her family which resulted in a great deal of dissatisfaction and the pro-Farukh Siyar group gained strength. Finally Jahandar Shah was overthrown and executed on 11 February 1713 and Farukh Siyar ascended the throne.

Banda took full advantage of the confusion in the Mughal court and with surprising speed and agility moved his forces back to Sadhaura, which he recaptured along with Lohgarh soon after. A new fort was built at Sadhaura and the battlements of Lohgarh were repaired and strengthened, which became the capital of the Sikhs and was to remain so for almost two years.

One of the first things that Farukh Siyar did on ascending the throne was to resume the war against the Sikhs in right earnest. In the period following his death, Bahadur Shah's orders that all Sikhs be considered as pagans and be exterminated, had gradually fallen into disuse. Many Sikhs had returned to the cities and towns where they once again led useful and productive lives. Farukh Siyar issued fresh orders that all Sikhs were to be killed. In an attempt to please the new emperor and so win favour with him, his officials carried out his orders with ruthless ferocity and efficiency. Thousands of Sikhs were killed; their heads strung together and hung on the gates of the towns. Those who survived abandoned the towns and once again sought the safety of the hills or of remote villages.

Farukh Siyar appointed Samad Khan as the governor of Lahore and his son Zakariya Khan as the faujdar of Jammu. At their investure ceremonies, they were both clearly given to understand that they had been appointed with the sole purpose of ensuring the destruction of Banda Bahadur. Should they fail or falter in their task they would be recalled to Delhi, stripped of their ranks and titles and punished and humiliated.

The combined forces of father and son reached Sadhaura, where the forces of Ahmed Khan joined them. Banda Bahadur decided to make a stand both at Lohgarh and Sadhaura. The Sikh army was divided into two defending forces. Banda hoped that the Mughal army too would be divided into two and the two sieges would be carried out simultaneously. But Samad Khan, very wisely, decided to deal with the two garrisons one at a time. He threw in his entire strength against the fort of Sadhaura and encircled it. The Sikhs had been so sure of their ability to break through the Mughal cordon and forage for food that they had not bothered seriously about piling up a sufficient stock of food supplies. When they did attempt to cut their way through, they found that the cordon was so tightly and thickly drawn that there was no breaking through. Banda Bahadur, entrenched in Lohgarh, realized the predicament of his followers in Sadhaura. He did, at regular intervals, send reinforcements of three or four divisions to provide relief to the beleaguered Sikhs.

The ring around Sadhaura was made tighter and the siege was complete. It was only a matter of days before the food supplies ran out and the Sikhs were forced to eat their horses and camels. At last all sources of nourishment were exhausted. On 4 October 1713 the surviving Sikhs made a rush on the besieging forces and were able to cut their way through and escape towards Lohgarh.

Samad Khan regrouped his forces and hurried towards Lohgarh without delay. The Sikhs realized that it would be futile to attempt a stand against a force so obviously superior. While the Mughal army was busy setting up camp, digging trenches, throwing up earthworks and scouting for water, the Sikhs abandoned Lohgarh and escaped into the hills. The Mughals realized that the Sikhs had fled but did not give pursuit. They knew from past experience that this could well be a ruse to lure them into an ambush. By the time the Mughals realized that the Sikhs had indeed abandoned Lohgarh, their quarry had escaped too far for them to be able to give chase. His capital was again to fall into a state of neglect and disuse while Banda was to spend the next two years on the banks of the Chenab, near Jammu.

Chapter Eight

'I came to the Punjab with the guru's command that I must fight the agents of tyranny and oppression and I fought them with sincerity and determination and all the weapons that I could muster. For a while it seemed that I had made a difference. My enemy was in a state of disarray, the poor, the exploited, seemed freed from the old shackles and bonds that had held them down. The landless peasants, who had given their sweat and blood to till the fields of the landlords and still gone hungry, now at last had land that was their own.'

It was a restful place. Banda had camped here, though a mere two days, on an earlier sojurn too, but its beauty had come to his mind repeatedly and had often haunted him in his dreams. Now that he had needed to set up camp in this area, he came straight back to it like a homing pigeon. There was an aura of magic about it. Twenty miles north of Jammu the Chenab took a definite turn towards Akhnoor and here it lost all the characteristics of its long passage through the hills and became a river of the plains. Gone was the turbulence and passion of its youth and in its place was the soft mellow music of maturity, of a stream that had come to terms with itself and with life. Gone were the craggy rocks and cliffs of its upper reaches and in their place were gently rolling slopes and meadows. The vegetation along its banks had also changed. Though there was still the occasional wild pear and a rare pine, the trees were those of the plains: the toon, the shisham and the sal. At this point in its journey, two miles from the village of Bhabbar, the river made a loop around a low-lying plateau, with some magnificent old trees, bringing back to Banda's mind memories of the two beautiful trees at Suneti.

It was early evening by the time the camp was set up. Some time remained before the evening prayers and Banda made his way to the edge of the plateau and looked across the fast flowing waters. The sun, bright and orange, hung low over the hills that fringed the right bank of the river, and its glowing light seemed to cover the waters with a shimmering golden sheet. Banda heard the myriads of birds chirping as they returned to their nests. It was so different from his ashram on the banks of the Godavari and yet so much the same. It would be a good place to dwell in, to do what the river had been able to do – to come to terms with himself and with his life. There was a sudden gust of wind and because of the nearness of the water, it was colder than it would otherwise have been. He felt a sudden chill and drew his robe tighter about his person. It was time for the evening prayers and he turned and walked back towards his camp.

After the prayers he went to address the congregation which, in the vastness of the plateau, looked pitifully small. He knew his strength had been sadly depleted, but in the gathering gloom he felt a deep sadness as he realized how small it was. It was this shrunken state of his following that became the theme of his discourse: 'This camp is different from our other camps. Earlier, whenever we set up camp, it was with the certain knowledge that it is a temporary one. And we lived in each camp, always on the alert for the first opportunity to go forth to harass our enemies. However, for the first time we are setting up camp with the knowledge that it will be a fairly permanent one, with the knowledge that we will not sally forth for at least a year.'

He paused for breath and in that pause he heard the collective sigh of dismay that went up from the group of young warriors who stood amassed to the left. He smiled to himself. These youngsters had a romantic notion of war. To them, war was an opportunity to win laurels and cover themselves with glory. War was little more than a chance to become heroes, the stuff of legends and folk songs. They had looked upon this break from war as just another pause to mend their wounded bodies and marshal their forces. They were impatient to get back to their enemies. And here was their leader telling them that it would be a year before they could take up their swords again. Banda turned towards these young warriors.

'Look around you,' he said, his voice soft in its sadness. 'Our numbers are so small that there is little chance of swelling them with fresh recruits, at least not in a hurry. The camp followers who used to support us in battle in the hope of sharing in the loot and plunder have melted away because they see no chance of any gain. The zamindars, who had at first supported us against the cruel Mughal governors, have turned against us because they realize that we are committed to taking their surplus land away and giving it to the landless. The poor Muslim peasant, groaning against his exploitation was the backbone of our force in the early days of our struggle. Now he does not dare to support us. The mullahs have declared jihad against us and even the oppressed Muslims do not dare to disobey the fatwa calling for their support. Their sympathies are with us but they do not dare to risk the damnation of their souls. As for our own Sikhs, you are well aware of the royal firman, which has now declared all Sikhs as infidels. Mughal officials, eager to win favour with the new emperor, have slaughtered thousands of our brethren. Those who live are in deep hiding, too afraid to be seen because they will be killed on sight. Yet, do not despair, if it is the Guru's will, our time will come. But, it will not come soon and it would be best that we wait for it here.'

The settlement came up quickly. The structures had an air of permanence. The focal point of the settlement was a gurdwara, in front of which was a large, paved terrace with a huge banyan tree at one end of it and from this terrace a flight of stone steps led down to the river. Climbing these steps after bathing in the river, Banda was reminded of the ghat at his ashram near

Nanded and of that fateful evening when he had come back and found his guru waiting for him. So much had happened between then and now, so much had changed within him that the meeting seemed to have taken place a long time ago, if not in another life, in another world. It was difficult to believe that it had been just four years ago.

The days of peace stretched on and though Banda and his leaders insisted on a fair amount of military drill and training to keep their soldiers fit and ready, the need for earning a living soon established precedence over preparing for a distant war. It was no surprise that the settlement took on the ambience of a dera rather than of a military cantonment. Most of Banda's followers had been careful with their share of war booty, husbanding their wealth, spending only when it was absolutely necessary. Now, when the need to earn a livelihood pressed upon them, they turned again with ease to their professions of the pre-war days. Those who had been farmers invested their money in buying or leasing pieces of land, on farm tools and on seed and manure. Those who had been shopkeepers and merchants invested money in buying goods and with these set up shop once again. Those who were craftsmen and artisans: the carpenters, the potters, the blacksmiths and the cobblers, bought tools of their trade and set up workshops. Those who were entertainers: the jugglers, the magicians and the minstrels made forays into neighbouring habitations to display their skills. They all worked hard and prospered. Banda and a few like him, had no way of earning a livelihood, and now with a wife and son to support this lack weighed heavily upon him. It was his wife Sushil who gave him the answer.

She came to him, as she always did, at the end of the day after having put their son Ajay to bed. He moved over and made place for her beside him. Though, she snuggled up against him and put her head upon his chest, he remained unaffected by her nearness and she knew that his mind was troubled. 'What is it that weighs upon your thoughts?'

'Nothing,' he said.

She was silent for a while and then said: 'You are a wise man, my lord, and in your wisdom you must know that troubles are doubled if they are borne alone, but halved if they are shared.'

Hearing her voice, soft and gentle, he smiled, remembering that she often spoke with the homilies of a grandmother. He marvelled at her perceptiveness. 'Tell me what is on your mind. I may not be of any help but you will feel the better [for] the telling.'

'Go to sleep,' he said, patting her lightly on the head.

'I can't go to sleep while you lie awake with some great worry on your mind. I am your wife, the mother of your son, and co-sharer of your fortune. Yet you treat me the way an indulgent father would treat his only child. You want to protect me, to insulate me from your worries. But I will not be treated in this manner any more. I am strong both through my birth and by virtue of my marriage. I can cope with all the troubles and misfortunes that may befall us. Tell me what is on your mind.'

'You are a persistent woman and I should have known better than to try and conceal anything from you. I am concerned about the fact that we are now no longer on the battlefield and have settled down to a life of extended, if temporary, peace. Others have gone back to the professions they followed before they joined my ranks but I cannot go back to the life I knew, a bairagi, content to live on the charity of others because I am no longer a bairagi. I am a householder, with a wife and a child and the responsibility of providing for their needs rests upon my shoulders. I do not know how to perform this new role.'

Sushil traced patterns with her finger upon his chest and when she spoke her tone was light and playful: 'Perhaps I should take Ajay with me and go back to Chamba. That would permit you to resume the life of a bairagi.'

He grasped her hand tightly and replied: 'No. I don't think I can now live without you.'

She laughed at this: 'Be truthful. It is not me you would not be able to live without. It is our son who would leave a vacuum in your life.'

'I speak the truth. I will miss him too — but more than him I will miss you.'

'Then hold me close while I am with you and try to sleep. Sorrow and trouble always seem greater than they are in the stillness of the night. Daylight always restores to us our sense of proportion and shows us that what weighs on our minds is not as heavy as we thought it to be. You will see, when daylight returns, this trouble too will seem small and we will easily find a solution to it.'

He held her close. She was right. His worry did seem lighter and soon he drifted off to sleep.

Sushil lay awake, marvelling as she so often had done in the last two years, at the naivety of her husband. He was a leader of men, a renowned general and a brave warrior. He was a man who understood other men and this enabled him always to choose the right man for the right job. Yet, in his personal life he was as naive as a newborn baby. She, who had lived in the centre of court life and had experienced at first hand the grim reality of court intrigue, had learnt quite early in life to look beyond words and gestures and deeds, quite into the hearts of men. Because of this skill she had known for quite some time now what troubled her lord. Her questioning was a ploy to get him to admit his worries so that she could administer to them. She had already set in motion a scheme of things, which would provide her husband with a means of livelihood. Through the good offices of a cousin at the court of Jammu, she exchanged her jewellery for the ownership of a hundred kilas of land, close to their camp. A few days after this conversation she gave him the title deed for the land.

'You should have told me you were going to do this,' he admonished her.

'And have you refuse to let me part with my jewellery?'

'Yes.'

'Why? You who have been a bairagi even after becoming a warrior, shown no attachment to wealth and material belongings, would have me hold on to a few useless baubles? Baubles that I would never wear?' she paused for a moment and then swept on. 'See what this land will mean to you. You have worried how you will provide for my son and me. You need not worry any more. You will also be able to provide employment and a livelihood to a few who, like us, have no resources to set themselves up in life again. The income from this land will be more than what we need and you will be able to give to the poor and the needy as well.'

After a shaky start, he took readily to his new life as a farmer, and with the help of four young men, was able to make a success of his farm.

A daily routine was soon established. There was a session of kirtan, communal singing of hymns and prayers in the morning, held at the first light of day which his followers took turns in leading. He himself did so on important religious occasions like Baisakhi and the birthdays and the days of martyrdom of the ten gurus. Two days a week time was allotted for military exercises. Other than this his followers were free to pursue their professions and attend to the demands of their households and their families. Though it wasn't spelt out in certain terms, attendance at the evening prayers was mandatory. The inhabitants of the neighbouring villages of Bhabbar, Kanjli, Mansuh and Seri, heard of these meetings and came to attend them. They came first out of curiosity, in ones and twos and were soon impressed by the simplicity of this religion, by the richness of the gurbani and by the beauty of the kirtan. They approached the leader and sought his help and advice. At first he avoided meeting these supplicants, directing them to Binod or one of his deputies. Then the demands for personal meetings became too strong to resist and he began to meet people. He still did not offer any advice. He merely directed the supplicants to relevant passages of the Guru Granth with a gentle but firm reminder that it was the holy book that they should now regard as their guru and not any living being, not even him. But as time went on he found himself sometimes face to face with such immense tragedy or pain that the sufferers would not be consoled by such solace. They sought his blessings, and moved by their plight, he could not contain himself and offered words of comfort and advice. Reports of this healing spread beyond the neighbouring villages and the number of supplicants increased. Once again, he came to be regarded as a wise and holy man. His fame spread far and wide and through it there was a fresh wave of sympathy for his cause.

The two years respite from war gave him a chance to be what he had failed to be in the first two years of his marriage: a good husband and a good father. His step into matrimony had been a reluctant one and for months after his wedding he had not been able to overcome the feeling that he had betrayed his long-standing beliefs and values, that there had been a recession in his growth as a man, in the evolution of his spiritual being. Because of this he tended to avoid coming to Sushil. He did not come to her even at the time of her childbirth, which had been a difficult one. The two midwives who had been in attendance had despaired of bringing the labour to a successful conclusion. There was a moment when they had felt that they would lose both the baby and the mother. Frantic messages had been sent to Banda but he had come only when the baby had been delivered. Of course, he had stayed by his wife's bedside while the midwives pronounced that her life was in danger, but once the danger had passed he had gone away again. She was troubled by this but consoled herself with the knowledge that their relationship had moved ahead a few steps. She had waited patiently for an opportunity to win him over.

One evening, after they had both finished their chores for the day, she said: 'I have the feeling that you have been a long time on this earth, many lifetimes spun into one, and that you dwell in private places that I have not even dreamed about. Because of this, though you are always gentle with me, you frighten me.'

He smiled, conscious that he was a little embarrassed by her new found ease and said: 'Don't ever be frightened of me. You are a strong woman as you have proved again and again, and also a woman of great perception. You must have read the deep turmoil in my heart and mind over these last two years. At a time in their lives when young men are still finding joy in games and trivial pastimes, I had chosen the life of a bairagi. Long years of discipline and self-denial had made deep impressions on my personality. Celibacy had become a part of me and I had by choice eschewed the company of women. As a result I still don't know how to cope with my role as a husband and a father. This is what you have perceived as the private places of my mind, as secrets held from accumulations of many lives. There are really no such secrets or private places, only thoughts and feelings that I have found myself unable to voice. But you need only ask and I will try to find the words.'

The first harvest had been a good one. Banda had more time on his hands now and spent most of it with Sushil and Ajay. There should have been a greater intimacy, a growing together of the family, yet this was not to be. The vital spark was still missing. Banda was cheerful and talked a great deal. He laughed when laughter was called for, but Sushil had to admit that something was still missing. One evening while they sat together on the terrace, Sushil noticed him to be in a pensive mood. She touched his hand. He gave a start, looked at her and smiled, a smile of embarrassment, the smile of a boy caught at something he should not have been doing. 'Your new vocation seems to become you, my lord,' she said, her voice light, and deliberately free from the anxiety that had risen within her heart.

'A bit too much, I am afraid!' he said patting his stomach, which, to her eyes, was as flat and firm as it had always been.

'And is that what makes you so thoughtful and takes you away from me?' she asked.

He looked away for a moment and then looked back, fixed her with a steady gaze but took his time to reply, as if he wanted to be certain of the words he would speak: 'Doubts about my mission assail me and fill my mind with dark foreboding.' His words came slowly at first, one at a time, with long pauses between them. But then as he spoke, they gathered fluency and strength and poured out of him. And through it all she sat listening patiently, not prompting when he paused for an undue length of time, expressing neither dissent nor agreement while he spoke: 'At first these doubts came fleetingly, like small soft whispers of fleecy white cloud that drift across the azure blue of the winter sky, not frightening, not threatening, merely accentuating the blue with their contrasting white. But since the fall of Lohgarh they have quickly gathered strength, like dark monsoon clouds which are ominous with their threat of a storm. They produce a sombre mood in my mind and I question the past and despair for the future. A certainty begins to grow upon me that I have failed in my mission, betrayed the trust that my guru reposed in me.' He paused. As it stretched on she sensed that he had more to say and held her peace.

'I came to the Punjab with the guru's command that I must fight the agents of tyranny and oppression and I fought them with sincerity and determination and all the weapons that I could muster. For a while it seemed that I had made a difference. My enemy was in a state of disarray, the poor, the exploited, seemed freed from the old shackles and bonds that had held them down. The landless peasants, who had given their sweat and blood to till the fields of the landlords and still gone hungry, now at last had land that was their own. They strove and laboured for themselves and not for others. They had found their place in the sun and everyone at last, was free and equal. But time took all this away. The tide of battle turned against me. The Mughal officials with their cruel, ruthless laws, rule again and the sadistic zamindars once again control the lives of the common people. The poor are again oppressed and exploited. If anything, the lot of the common man has become worse. Look at the Sikhs, my own people. As a consequence of what I attempted to do, they are now the victims of bloodthirsty revenge. There is a royal firman that offers rewards for the severed heads of the Sikhs. No Sikh, who ventures forth in the morning, is sure that he will return safely in the evening. The few, who survive, like us, live in hiding, like thieves, far away from their homes. Or else, like the Sikh merchants of Delhi, they are exempted from the scope of the firman, but are burdened by a crippling tax, which makes it virtually impossible for them to keep body and soul together.

'Even though we had Muslim rulers, ours was essentially a secular society. The common folk lived together in complete amity and a sense of brotherhood prevailed amongst the Hindus, Muslims and the Sikhs. As a consequence of my efforts, the secular fabric of our society has been destroyed. The Muslim shuns the non-Muslim and the non-Muslim looks upon the Muslim with suspicion, hostility and distrust. Gone is the easy camraderie that existed before and I must bear the responsibility for the destruction of something that was beautiful beyond words.'

He paused again and saw that she was looking intently at him and had a mischievous sparkle in her eyes. 'And if, when the guru laid his command on your shoulder, you had known that this would be the result, would you have refused that command?'

'No,' he answered without a moment's hesitation. 'I could not have done that. I am but my guru's slave, and no matter what the consequences, whatever the fruit of my endeavours, it would have been impossible for me to refuse his command. I could only accept whatever behest he laid upon me and spare no effort in carrying it out.'

She touched him lightly on the cheek. The mischief was gone from her eyes and in its place there was now a look of deep tenderness. 'That is all that is given to us to control – the strength and vigour of our efforts. The fruit that our efforts will bear lies beyond us and beyond all our efforts. Remember what the Bhagvad Gita tells us: "In the secret places of the human soul, God dwells but He is unrecognized by it so long as the soul does not acquire the redeeming knowledge. We acquire this knowledge by serving God with our whole heart and soul, without hope of reward or fear of punishment, with total indifference and detachment to success or failure. We are not called upon to solve the meaning of life but to find out the deed demanded of us and to perform this deed with total disregard for the fruit of the action."'

Banda was amused by the irony of the situation. He had lived the life of a bairagi, spent long hours over the years in the study of the sacred texts of the Hindus, including the Bhagvad Gita. She, a Rajput princess, had been born and brought up in the lap of luxury and splendour. Her study had been the study of court etiquette and protocol, of managing households and the servants. She had learnt to excel at the embroidering of Chamba roomals and in the designing of clothes and jewellery. She had learnt how to retain her place in the royal favour against the manipulations of the other royal ladies. Her study of the scriptures, if it did at all take place, was not expected to be anything other than cursory. Yet here she was, the princess, quoting from the Gita to the bairagi.

'You do not need to worry about the degree of your success because success is based on many factors and the honesty and intensity of your efforts is merely one of these factors. What should occupy your thoughts is concern about the truth, the clarity and the single-mindedness of your efforts. If you have to look back, and indulge in introspection then you must focus on the nature of your effort and on nothing else.'

He pondered over this for a while and then shook his head: 'No. There was nothing wanting in my effort. I did the best that was possible for me to do with the means that were available to me.'

'That is the most that we mortals can hope to do and you should be grateful that this was given to you to do. As far as the schism between the Muslim and the non-Muslim is concerned, it would not have come if the fatwa for jihad against the Sikhs had not been given out. The mullahs called upon all Muslims to join in the holy war against the infidel. It was they who gave the struggle a communal colour. It was natural that the Hindus and Sikhs should follow suit and also call it a religious war. There was nothing you could have done to stop the process once the mullahs had set it in motion.'

A few weeks later, late in the evening Sushil sensed, rather than saw, that the pensive mood had come to haunt Banda again. She did not attempt to draw him out and after a while he spoke of it of his own accord: 'There seems to be a feeling that I alone can lead the Sikhs in our struggle. The Mughals believe that if I am exterminated the revolution against them will fizzle out and my leaders too seem to subscribe to this view. On more than one occasion they have ruled that I must be evacuated from the scene of battle to a place of safety. It is their way of ensuring that no matter what the outcome of the battle, the Sikhs will continue to have a rallying point, thus ensuring the continuity of our war.'

He fell silent and she waited patiently for him to continue. 'I have always believed that no man is indispensable. I have seen how bravely my soldiers have fought, seen the initiative and daring many of my leaders displayed in the heat of battle, which convinces me that anyone of them could take my place as the leader of our people. But, I can understand how this misconception about my indispensability has come about. Both my followers and my enemies have given me an image that is much larger than life and because of this my leaders hold themselves back. They defer to me on matters where they could well take their own decisions. Even when they do take decisions on their own they look over their shoulders to see if I approve. It is said that nothing grows in the shade of a giant tree. Perhaps this is what has happened to the Sikhs. My image has been made so large that no true leader can develop in its shadow.'

Sushil cast her mind on what her husband had said. It was true. The men she knew – Binod Singh, Raj Singh, Fateh Singh, Gaj Singh and many others – were great men in their own right. But when compared to Banda their stature seemed strangely diminished and it was difficult to visualize them in Banda's place.

'I am the leader and I must own responsibility for the failure of the Sikhs to throw up an obvious successor. Perhaps it is time for me to step down, to take my place in the serried ranks of the common soldiers and designate one of the others to lead, who I am sure, if given complete responsibility, will rise to prove that the Sikhs are not dependent on just one man.'

'The leadership is not yours to give, my lord,' she said. 'You talk of it as if it were a jagir, a landholding or a crown that you could accede to someone else and renege on the promise you made to your guru.'

As Ajay whimpered in his sleep, she turned and patted his back till he slept again. 'You know that there can be no going back for you. Even if you were to deliberately step back and appoint a leader in your place, people would still look upon you as their leader and defer to you in all matters of import. No, my dear, there is no escape for you. Leader you are and leader you will remain till you die or are incapacitated. You have done all you can to prepare the others for leadership. You have assigned responsibilities to them and encouraged them to take the lead. Have no fear. It is as you said, no man is indispensable and when the time comes for one of them to take over, he will prove to be a worthy leader.'

Banda had from the beginning of his campaign, won great respect and admiration from his followers. He had brought complete sincerity and dedication to his cause. In battle as in peace, he believed that personal example was better than precept. He always led from the front and never expected his followers to do what he did not. But there was something lacking in his relationship with his followers. He was cold and aloof. So, while his followers admired and respected him and gave him their loyalty very few, if any, could say that they loved him. This was true even of all the other leaders of the Panth, the community. He led a simple, spartan life and had no desire for material possessions, for rich clothing and food. His needs were few and there was always a surplus that he immediately gave away. But in his giving too he was cold and impersonal, as if he did not really care for the difference that his giving made to the recipient. His role was to give and if he did not give to one individual he would be giving to another. Thus, though he won the gratitude of those who were the objects of his generosity, he was never able to endear himself to them. Perhaps, it was the result of the carefully cultivated and preserved detachment, which had been a precondition of his life as a bairagi. Now, on the banks of the Chenab, in the calm and peaceful atmosphere of the dera, Sushil gently and carefully drew him back into the world of human relationships. To some extent he learnt to care for others. There was a warmth that came gradually to his dealings with men and won for him, at last, something akin to love from his people.

One day, well into the second year of their sojourn near Bhabbar, Banda surprised the sparkle of unshed tears in Sushil's eyes. They had been indulging in their favourite pastime, watching little Ajay at play. At first Banda felt that they were tears of happiness and pride that had come unbidden to his wife's eyes. But when she turned her head away to hide them from him, he knew there was some other reason. He reached out and took hold of her hand: 'What is it?' he asked.

She shook her head and without looking at him, with her hand still in his, smiled – a small sad smile – and said: 'I found myself wishing for our Ajay to have a sibling. It is not right for a child to grow up alone without a brother or sister.'

'You know that cannot be. Your trouble at Ajay's birth precludes the possibility of your having another child. Both the midwives were categorical in their opinion. If God had willed otherwise, we would have had a second child by now.'

'I know,' she said. 'But I cannot help the wishing.' He moved closer to her and put his arm around her shoulder.

'It is God's will, our destiny, and we must accept it with a smile and bow before it. Be grateful for what has been vouchsafed to us. We sit here and watch Ajay at play and our hearts brim over with joy. It is much that has been given to us and there is nothing to be gained in pointless regrets and wishes that lie beyond fulfilment.'

As in the case of the land she had already worked out in her mind how her wish could be fulfilled. Custom and convention both decreed that Banda could take a second wife and it was this that she would have him do. 'It is my destiny that I should not have another child, not yours.'

He understood what she was trying to suggest and looked at her with horror. His hand fell away from her shoulder and he started to his feet. 'I forbid you to ever mention this subject again.' He turned and strode away.

In the days and weeks to come Sushil was persistent. She would come back to the subject again and again, first in subtle and gentle ways and then more directly and bluntly. She would not let a day pass without reference to the subject till he began to feel hounded by her persistence. Finally, she refused to eat and threatened to starve herself to death. Her condition deteriorated till the hakim and vaid feared for her life. Finally, her will prevailed. Banda married Sahib Kaur, daughter of Sri Chand, a Khatri of Wazirabad.

The period of peace gave Banda an opportunity to play the part of a father to his son. He spent a great deal of time with the little boy and found pleasure in bathing him, changing his clothes and feeding him. He was clumsy and awkward at first and the boy made it clear that he preferred his mother to do these chores for him, but at Sushil's gentle prodding, Banda persisted, and Ajay found himself warming to his father. Banda invented new games for Ajay to play and told him stories. Soon Ajay could not bear to let his father out of sight. Unlike other little children, the boy would wake at the crack of dawn and insist on going with his father to the fields. At first Banda would carry the boy on his shoulders, but then Ajay insisted that he wanted to carry a plough. Raja Ram, the carpenter, fashioned a miniature plough for the little boy and it became a ritual for residents of the dera to watch the little boy carrying the plough on his shoulder and following his father with an air of complete earnestness.

Banda made little paper boats for the boy and father and son would then go to the lowest step and launch their boats on the water. Then they would run up the steps and along the ridge of the riverbank to see their boats racing along the surface of the water.

The months after the autumn harvest were idyllic. Banda spent a great deal of time with his wives and Ajay. One morning, early in February, Banda stood on a little plateau a few miles upstream from the dera, trying to teach Ajay to fly a kite. It was difficult for him at first, because he had not flown a kite for over thirty years. Gradually the forgotten skills of his boyhood returned. As the kite soared higher Banda let Ajay hold the twine. The little boy's heart swelled with pride in the knowledge that his kite was flying higher than all the other kites. Sushil and Sahib Kaur sat on the edge of the plateau, their hearts filled with the quiet domestic bliss of this togetherness, of the beautiful vision of the blue sky studded with kites of different colours and shapes and sizes, the din and the grief of the battlefield all forgotten.

Suddenly Sushil put her hand to her heart and gasped for breath. Sahib Kaur turned to her with concern, a concern that changed into alarm when she saw the tears streaming down Sushil's cheeks.

'What is it, sister, that troubles you?' But Sushil shook her head and smiled weakly through her tears. 'Let me get help,' Sahib Kaur said. But Sushil reached out and caught her hand in a vicelike grip.

'No. No. I am all right. It has passed. It was the perfection of this day that touched me. It is so beautiful, more beautiful because we know it is so fragile. The pain of knowing that it could not last swept over me and I could not cope with it. It has passed now. It has been a perfect day and we must be grateful for it. We must draw strength from it to face what we know is sure to come.'

It was an idyllic period in Banda's life and he had everything that a man could wish for. His two wives lived in perfect peace and harmony. Though he would never be the husband and father that other men were he had at least brought to these roles a depth that he had not thought that he was capable of bringing. All doubts and questionings had been stilled and he was sure once again that there was nothing earthly that could disturb this stillness, not defeat nor death nor the loss of loved ones. The lightness had returned to his step. He was ready to face the future with all its consequences.

His absence from the political scene did not mean that the Mughals had not encountered any opposition. Early in this period of hibernation, in April 1714, news came to the settlement of Sardar Jagat Singh's victory over the Pathans of Kiri Pathan, in the parganah of Khanuwan. These Pathans had carried out the emperor's orders against the Sikhs with such ruthless vigour that the surviving Sikhs decided to punish them. They rallied under the leadership of Sardar Jagat Singh and on 27 March, fell upon the village and entered the fortress. All resistance was soon overcome, the Pathans were killed in large numbers and the Sikhs captured rich booty. Banda had found great joy in these tidings as Jagat Singh had proved that the Sikhs were not dependent upon Banda Bahadur alone to lead their struggle against the Mughals.

In August, Banda received reports of a Sikh attack on the town of Ropar. A body of 7,000 Sikhs had crossed the Sutlej from the right bank and mounted a fierce attack upon the town. Then reinforcements under Khwaja Mukaram, deputy governor of Sirhind had arrived and the Sikh attack had been repulsed, but not before the defenders had suffered heavy casualities.

This was a curt reminder to the Mughals that in spite of all their efforts to exterminate the Sikhs it had not made a dent in their resolve. Restlessness swept over the dera and there were many who believed that the time had come for them to marshal their forces and return to the Punjab to resume their war against the Mughals. The leaders decided to bide their time a little longer. They began to enlist fresh recruits in their ranks and procure arms and ammunition. The training, which had never really ceased, was now taken up as top priority and the dera took on the look of an army establishment.

'Are we ready?' Binod had asked in a private meeting with Banda.

'As ready as we will ever be. We have gained a fair number of new recruits in our ranks and procured large quantities of arms and ammunition. Reports come to us that our brethren in the Punjab are now ready to make another attempt to dislodge the Mughals. We may not have the strength that we need, but we will not get it by tarrying here. If we linger here in inactivity any longer, our war and our cause will both be forgotten. I do not serve the guru's cause by living this quiet humdrum life in this peaceful place. I must return to doing what I seem to be best at, fighting the Mughals. This is my last campaign. I can feel it in my bones. I do not ask Wahe Guru for victory. All I ask is that our conduct in this campaign, no matter what its outcome, be an inspiration for generations of Sikhs who come after us.

It was decided to leave the old and the infirm, the women and the children in the dera. Sushil refused to stay back.

'My life is with you my lord, and I must live it with you.'

'You will not be safe in the places where I will be going.'

'My safety is in your safety and if you would go into unsafe places I would be unsafe even here in the dera. Far better to be unsafe with you than be safe without you.'

'Your place is here in the dera, to look after the people who are left behind. While the men expect me to lead them into battle, the women expect you to be here to look after their welfare.'

'Sahib Kaur, my sister, is heavy with child and cannot travel with us. She will be here, your wife, to look after the welfare of those who remain behind.'

There was much that Banda, Binod, Sahib Kaur and others said and did to dissuade Sushil from her resolve, but she remained adamant. Thus, when the Sikh army, led by Banda Bahadur Singh marched from the dera towards Kalanaur, Sushil and Ajay Singh rode in its midst.

Chapter Nine

The executioner then turned his attention to Banda... his limbs too were hacked off piece by piece and he was kept alive for as long as possible. If Banda felt any pain he did not show it and sat through the gruesome ordeal unmoved. When at last the executioner raised his sword to hack off his head, Banda called in a loud clear voice: 'Bole Soh Nihal,' while the other Sikhs gave the response: 'Sat Sri Akal.' The executioner, his sword raised high, hesitated to bring it down. Then as Sarbrah Khan administered a sharp rebuke, it went swishing through the air, flashing in the morning sun.

It was a tough, sinewy army, an army that was stronger than any other he had commanded. It was small in number as Banda had shed off the mercenaries and booty seekers. His soldiers were now all highly motivated men. While, almost half the army was made up of veterans, the survivors from Banda's earlier battles, the other half was of fresh recruits who had joined Banda's forces at the dera. They were men who had been influenced by Banda's discourses during the prayer meetings, men who had been helped by Banda's advice, men who had come to admire his nature and his simple lifestyle. They were men who were new converts and like all new converts deeply committed to the cause. The months of intensive training had helped them assimilate into Banda's army and make friends with their comrades-in-arms, the veterans. The two types of soldiers were organized in mixed units so that there would be a happy blend of experience and youthful enthusiasm, vigour and dynamism, a determination to brook no resistance to its onslaught.

The army marched straight to its first target, the town of Kalanaur. So sudden and swift was their approach that the faujdar, Suhrab Khan had little time to prepare. The mullahs gave their customary call of jihad and Suhrab Khan was able to muster a band of religious zealots to offer resistance to the Sikh army and also recruited a large number of mercenaries whom he lured with the promise of more than double a soldier's normal salary. He turned to the zamindars too and called upon them for the levies they had committed themselves to send to the faujdar in times of war. By the time Suhrab Khan rode out to meet Banda he had a large number of men under his command, but these men were an undisciplined crowd, with little or no skill in war. The Sikhs bore down upon them with the fury and intensity of a hurricane and cut them to pieces. Suhrab Khan and most of his commanders fled from the field. Kalanaur fell with little resistance and the inhabitants sued for peace.

This victory was marked by a singular absence of bloodshed and vandalism. The civilian population was left in peace – there was no brutal killing, rape, looting or destruction.

Banda called for a meeting of the elders of the parganah where all the officials were stripped of their rank and position and deserving candidates from among both the citizens of the town and his army were appointed to these positions. All zamindaris were abolished. The huge landholdings were divided into small lots and distributed to the landless peasants who had been tilling this land for generations. Banda left a small, well provisioned garrison and moved swiftly to his next target, the prosperous town of Batala.

The faujdar of Batala, Muhammad Dayam, rode out to meet Banda at the head of a well-trained, disciplined army. The odds were evenly matched and, as was to be expected, the encounter that ensued was fierce. For six weary hours the battle raged as the two armies fought on equal terms. Then, by slow degrees, the Sikh army pushed the Mughal soldiers back. Many of the nobility, who commanded their own small detachments, fell and their troops were left leaderless, confused and disheartened. Muhammad Dayam lost heart and fled. This was the signal for the Mughal retreat. The surviving commanders abandoned the battlefield and the Sikhs occupied Batala and its neighbourhood.

Because of the strong resistance that their army had put up, the inhabitants of Batala feared that they would all be put to the sword and their town would be razed to the ground. As a result, most of them fled from their homes with all that they could carry. Those who had friends and relatives in nearby towns and villages sought sanctuary with them. Others fled to Lahore and some even to the hills of Chamba. But Banda belied their fears with his conduct. His occupation of Batala was characterized by magnanimity. Though taxes were imposed and indemnity demanded and taken, there was no spilling of civilian blood, no loot and plunder.

Surprisingly, Samad Khan, the governor of Lahore, did not react to Banda's decisive victories at Kalanaur and Batala. Perhaps, he was not sure of his own ability to confront Banda's army, because he took great care not to utter any word, make no move that would bring him into conflict with the Sikhs. For all intents and purposes it was as if for Samad Khan, Banda and his army did not exist, as if they had no presence in the Punjab and the two battles had never taken place. Almost deliberately, Samad Khan ignored the Sikhs and turned his attention elsewhere – the Bhatti Rajputs who had settled around the forests of Lakkhi, south of Lahore and had risen in revolt against the Mughals fomenting unrest among the local population. Samad Khan chose this moment to march against the Rajputs and to crush their revolt. Perhaps this was an excuse to avoid a confrontation with Banda; or perhaps it was a way of demonstrating his strength and a warning to Banda to stay away from Lahore. Whatever the cause, it earned him a sharp reprimand from the emperor, who wrote a letter dated 20 March 1715. The emperor said that the Bhatti zamindars could wait, the Sikhs couldn't. The emperor pointed out that the Sikhs had already won two quick decisive victories and one more victory would inspire the entire population of the Punjab to rise against the Mughals.

The emperor stated that Samad Khan must engage the Sikhs in battle and contain their growing strength. The emperor also informed Samad Khan that he had already written separately to Qamruddin Khan, Afrasaid Khan, Muzaffar Khan, Udet Singh Bundela and Gopal Singh Bhaduriya, telling them to set out immediately with their armies for Lahore. He said he had also issued firmans to all the faujdars and jagirdars ordering them to bring their soldiers to Lahore and place them at Samad Khan's command.

The emperor emphasized that there must be no doubt about the outcome of the battle – there must be no trace left of the abominable Sikhs. He warned Samad Khan that failure on this account would bring down the emperor's wrath on his head and the consequences would be terrible for him and for all the other commanders.

The tone of the emperor's orders to the others must have been equally firm and peremptory for by the time Samad Khan returned to Lahore, a considerable force of imperial soldiers under various leaders was already camped on the plains around the fort. In the succeeding days more reinforcements continued to pour in.

Banda's spy network, though depleted in numbers during the years of peace, was still strong and reliable enough to provide him with all essential information. He had the details of the emperor's orders even before they had reached the generals. In view of the great preparations being made by the Mughals, the defence that the Sikhs put up would have to be of extraordinary strength. After a quick reconnaissance of the area, Banda Bahadur and Binod Singh decided that their first line of defence would be at the village of Kot Mirza Jan, situated between Kalanaur and Batala. The second line of defence would be at the village of Gurdas Nangal, four miles to the west of the town of Gurdaspur.

Banda ordered his engineers to construct a mud fortification at Kot Mirza Jan. Work on this fortification was started in right earnest and the walls came up with the speed of lightning. Things were made easier for the Sikhs at Gurdas Nangal as a strong fort-like enclosure already existed there. This enclosure, which belonged to Bhai Duni Chand and was situated just outside the village of Gurdas Nangal, had massive walls around it, thick enough to withstand any artillery fire for a considerable length of time.

The Sikhs realized the importance of accumulating sufficient food and ammunition in the fort to withstand a long siege. They knew that they had little time at their disposal. Hence, small bands of Sikhs were dispatched to scourge the countryside and lay their hands on all the food, and arms and ammunition that they could find.

For a while it seemed the Sikhs would be able to complete the fort at Kot Mirza Jan before the advance of the Mughal forces but ultimately when the enemy did advance Banda knew that the fortifications were not ready to serve their purpose. The Mughals attacked in full force and the Sikhs were forced to abandon the incomplete fort and retreat into the countryside. Here Banda's men made a stand at every thicket that gave them cover from the enemy fire and at each stand they inflicted heavy damage on the enemy. But the thickets were not really suitable places of defence for more than an hour or two. Each time the Mughal onslaught became fierce the Sikhs had to retreat. At last they were within sight of Bhai Duni Chand's fort and the Sikhs retreated across the moat into the safety of those walls.

When Samad Khan and his forces arrived at Gurdas Nangal, some of Banda Bahadur's men were still out scouring the countryside for fresh recruits, food and arms and ammunition. Samad Khan threw a rough cordon around the walls and when these Sikhs attempted to return to the fort they ran into the Mughal ambush and were killed with extreme cruelty.

A small delegation of Sikh horsemen was able to break through the cordon and enter the fort. Great was the joy of those within to discover that this was a delegation from the dera. They brought tidings of great joy: Sahib Kaur had given birth to a son. The Sikhs gathered around Banda in great exultation and congratulated him on this news. 'There must be a celebration,' Sushil said and called upon the handful of other women to help her. That evening, for one last time, there was feasting and joyous laughter and song among the Sikhs and all thoughts of the impending battle were brushed aside. The enemy soldiers listened to the sounds of merry making within the walls and marvelled at the spirit of the Sikhs who could be moved to such gaiety even on the eve of battle.

Late in the night when the festivities were over, Sushil sought out Labh Singh, the leader of the delegation from the dera. 'You have gladdened my heart, brother, with your news, more than this heart has ever been gladdened before.' Labh Singh blushed, not knowing how to respond to this expression of gratitude. 'I know that you have risked your life to join my husband in this final battle. Yet, I must ask you to risk your life once more.' Labh Singh, like all the other Sikhs at the dera, had come to look upon this wisp of a girl as the embodiment of maternal love. With her caring and her compassion she had won their love and their respect. They were men who would do anything for her and feel honoured to be thus called upon.

'Your wish is my command even to the giving up of my life.'

'Then ride back to the dera. Take this as a token of my blessing for the child.' She drew off the solitary gold bangle that she wore on her wrist and gave it to Labh Singh. 'Tell my sister that we are well and to take good care of the child. Tell her to name our son Ranjit Singh. May he always be victorious in war, in the war against evil.'

Labh Singh hesitated. He had come to fight alongside his leader and he was now being asked to abandon the battle even before it had started. He knew that by the time he returned from the dera the noose around the fort would be drawn so tight that he would not be able to enter it again. Sushil understood his hesitation. 'The service you will perform for your leader by going back to the dera will be far greater than what you will be able to do for him by staying here. Ranjit and his mother will need guidance and protection and there is none at the dera to give them this in sufficient measure. You must go back and shoulder this responsibility.'

Labh Singh could not deny the wisdom of these words. He sought out Banda, told him what Sushil had asked him to do and obtained his leader's endorsement and blessing. In the dead of night he stole out of the fort and rode out to the hills of Jammu once more.

The next day Binod brought home to Banda the urgent need for Sushil and the other women to make their escape from the fort: 'The enemy hems us in from all sides. But Labh Singh's escape has shown us that the cordon is still not too tight. We must take immediate advantage of this and send our women to a place of safety. The cruel death that the Mughals will subject us to holds no fear for us. We are ready to face this with courage and cheerfulness. What we will not be able to bear is the dishonour that will be meted out to our womenfolk. The prospect of this dishonour will haunt us all through the impending battle and will shift our focus and undermine our resolve and determination. If we are to fight with single-mindedness we must send our women from this place.'

Banda could not help but smile at the irony of his situation. This was just the kind of eventuality that his guru had foreseen when he had advised him to remain celibate and he had ignored the guru's advice and allowed himself to be persuaded into marriage. What Binod said was true. Ever since they had come into the safety of these walls, he had agonized over the fate that would befall his wife and child should the Mughals be successful in their siege of the fort. The women and children would have to leave. So arrangements were made to try and smuggle them out of the fort in ones and twos under cover of darkness and escort them to some place that would provide them greater safety. But when this plan was communicated to Sushil she refused.

'It is already too late for us to make an attempt to escape, my lord. Bhai Labh Singh was able to escape because he was a man and, in the dark, it was easy for him to be mistaken for one of the Mughal soldiers. We as women would never be able to escape detection. If it is our honour that you seek to protect, then it were best protected here in the fort. If we ride out, the chances are that we will ride straight into the hands of the enemy and you know what our fate will be, especially when they realize that they have your wife and child in their custody. Your resolve will be weakened and there will be no determination left in your fight. Like you we too have accepted the certainty of death and when the time comes we will face it with the same courage and cheerfulness as the men. If we have to die, then let us face our death here, alongside our menfolk.'

The other women nodded their heads in agreement. Sushil

looked at her husband and a playful smile came upon her lips: 'You forget, my lord, that I am a Rajput princess. Without you there can be no life for me, not here nor in any other place. If destiny should so command, it will be far better for me to commit Sati, here on your funeral pyre, than to immolate myself in an uncertain land among strangers.'

The other women too were staunch in their refusal to leave the fort and the plan to evacuate the women and children had to be abandoned.

The siege started in right earnest. Samad Khan and Zakariya Khan, at the head of several thousand troops, made many attempts to storm the fort. But each time the Sikhs let loose such a barrage of arrows and gunfire that the Mughals were forced to fallback after sustaining grave losses. After half-a-dozen attempts, Samad Khan realized that he was paying too heavy a price for a victory that now seemed uncertain. He abandoned his plans to storm the citadel. Instead, he decided to tighten the cordon around the walls, stop all movement in and out of the fort and wait till the Sikhs had exhausted their supplies of food and ammunition. He took charge of the blockade on one side and divided the responsibility for the other three sides between his son and two of his generals. The Mughal tents were set up close together in a square formation along the sides of the fort. Trenches were dug in front of the tents and the artillery launched its fire from them. It took over 30,000 men to mount this blockade. The Sikhs were not intimidated, either by the superior numbers of the enemy or by the close blockade that had been mounted against them. They rained a heavy and almost ceaseless fire of arrows and shots on the enemy camp. When they did hold their fire it was to permit bands of Sikhs to sally forth right into the Mughal trenches and kill the enemy soldiers in hundreds in hand-to-hand fights.

Clearly this could not continue. If the Mughals did not take steps to counter these harassing attacks by the Sikhs, their force would soon be decimated. The Mughal soldiers saw their friends and colleagues falling around them in large numbers, which began to take its toll and the morale of the Mughal forces had reached an all-time low. The soldiery could not understand why they had taken up what appeared to them to be a defensive position and exposed them to such heavy casualities. They felt that with their superior strength they should have made an all-out attack on the fort and taken it in a quick assault no matter how heavy the price in human life. It would have been far better than suffering heavy casualties every day with no gains to show for this sacrifice.

A fresh strategy had to be adopted. In the days that followed, the cordon was quickly tightened till the Mughals were just a musket shot away from the fort. To obtain protection against the Sikh fire, they threw up earthworks in front of their tents. Each earthwork was about twenty feet long which was gradually extended on each side till they formed one continuous wall around the fort.

Banda and his followers soon realized that while the walls of the fort had ensured their safety by effectively keeping the enemy out, the second wall that had been thrown up by the Mughals had made them virtual prisoners in the fort. Even in the face of this development the Sikhs remained undaunted. Bhai Binod Singh sallied out of the fort again and again at the head of a small group of intrepid Sikh warriors, sweeping all obstacles away and showing a ferocity and vigour that belied his age. He planned his raids with meticulous precision, always retaining in them the element of surprise by riding out when the Mughal soldiers least expected him to do so, when they had tired of waiting for his attack. He rode straight into the enemy's camp, snatched whatever he could lay his hands on and rode swiftly back to the fort. What he took was of little intrinsic value, but each of these raids served to boost the morale of the Sikhs and to show the Mughal force that, no matter how tight the cordon that had been thrown around the fort, nothing could dampen the bold and indomitable spirit of Banda Bahadur and his followers.

The Mughals, alarmed by Binod's marauding sorties, felt that these inroads into their camp were of an exploratory nature, designed to find the weak links in the blockade. Some also felt that these were diversionary tactics to draw attention away from Banda Bahadur and help him escape, as had been done when Banda had escaped from Lohgarh. Samad Khan was petrified at the possibility of Banda's escape as there was too much at stake for him personally to even consider this eventuality. A council of war was called and after much discussion it was decided that a palisade should be built around the fort, a third encirclement to contain the Sikhs.

A large task force consisting of axe men, carpenters, masons, labourers and camel drivers was pressed into service. A great number of trees felled, reduced to logs and thick planks and carried to the site. Vast quantities of loose earth were brought in. A circle of logs and planks was raised around the enclosure while the earth was piled and pressed into the space between the joints to create a strong stockade. All through the construction the Sikhs kept up heavy firing on the workers and a large number of the labour force was killed. But numbers were what the Mughals had in ample measure and the work continued till the stockade was complete. The blockade of the fort was now so strong that it was inconceivable that Banda would ever be able to break through.

In the fort, their brave and valiant stand notwithstanding, the siege now into its eighth month, began to take its toll. In spite of the careful management that Binod had exercised from the very beginning, what had appeared to be a sufficient stock of food had begun to run out. Their ammunition stores too had reached an alarmingly low level and it was now clear that it was only a matter of days before the end.

Bhai Binod Singh called for an assembly of the Khalsa and Banda was glad that his old friend was at last taking the initiative: 'Remember the siege of Lohgarh, brothers. Our most prized possession then was the life of our leader and we took all steps to preserve it. His life still remains our most prized possession and we must again take steps to preserve it. I have made the necessary arrangements. In the early hours of the morning we must make an all-out raid on the flank commanded by Samad Khan. This will be a diversionary attack and while the Mughal forces are engaged in containing this attack, Bhai Banda Bahadur Singh, Mata Sushil and Ajay Singh, will make their way to that part of the earthworks commanded by Suhrab Khan. His deputy has been bribed and will let the three of them through.'

Before any of the others could react to this proposal, Banda rose to his feet: 'There is wisdom in recognizing that moment in battle when the tide is finally turning against you and retreating. This is a strategy that the guru taught us and a strategy that we have used effectively. But he also taught us that retreat is wise only when there is hope of a fresh grouping, when there is a chance of another battle, another chance to defeat the enemy. When no hope is visible then we must give the battle everything that we have and die the death of martyrs. Look around you at our pitiful numbers. What hope is there of a fresh grouping even if we do break through the enemy lines. Would you make a coward of me by making me attempt an escape only to save my life and the lives of my wife and child?'

'Then you will have us admit that we have lost our cause?'

'Our cause is a just cause, the cause of righteousness and as such, it can never be lost. Even when we are dead and gone, there will be others who will rise to take it up and wage the war that the guru has enjoined us to wage.'

'But till such time the guru's message must be kept alive and the best person to ensure this is you.'

There was silence and Banda, scanning the handful of faces before him, saw relief writ large upon them, relief that their leader was at last being persuaded to leave the fort. They could now be sure that the struggle would continue even after they were gone. When Banda, at last, did speak, his voice was so soft that the others had to strain their ears to catch the words.

'Let me ask you a question, Bhai Binod Singh. Which to your mind are the two events in our history which have provided us, with the greatest motivation to struggle against the tyranny and oppression of the Mughals?'

The question drew a smile to Binod's lips: 'I thought your question was going to be more difficult than that. Even a child could answer you. The events you speak of are the martyrdom of Guru Arjan Dev and Guru Tegh Bahadur.'

'Exactly. It is always a sacrifice that motivates most strongly. The time has come for someone to make the supreme sacrifice, a sacrifice that will galvanize and mobilize Sikhs to the cause for generations to come and strengthen their resolve to fight against the oppressors.'

Binod understood the turn the discussion was taking and was frustrated by it. He saw the chance of saving Banda's life slip from his hands. His frustration led to anger and the desire to hurt Banda for being so obdurate, which led him to speak words he would regret for the rest of his life: 'You seek to be remembered and spoken of in the same breath as the two great gurus.'

Banda had not been consumed by such anger ever before as he was now with the insinuation that these words contained: 'How dare you make this accusation?' his hand going to his sword.

The others stood watching, too amazed by the course of events to be able to react. It was Kahan Singh, Binod's son, who took the matter in hand by stepping between the two friends. 'Forgive me if I speak out of turn. You are both older than I am and more experienced. You must both see that this is too important a matter to be entrusted to the outcome of a sword fight. Refer it to the Khalsa and bide by its decision.'

'Yes, my son, you speak with great wisdom. Let the Khalsa decide and we will bide by its decision. There is need for two courses of action, each as important as the other. And there is need for two men. One will have to go out to ensure that the guru's message is carried forward and the other will have to remain behind to make the supreme sacrifice. Let the Khalsa decide which man will perform which action.'

The leaders went into a huddle, but it did not take them long to come to a decision. It was decided that Bhai Binod Singh should make good his escape from the fort and ensure that the struggle did not die. Bhai Banda Singh Bahadur was to remain in the fort till the very end.

The hours ticked away and Banda sat in his apartment in solitary silence, waiting for his friend to come to him. The day grew into night and in the darkness Banda heard the rustle of a garment and his heart surged with joy. But it was only Sushil come to light a lamp and to bring him his evening meal. She knew the pain in Banda's heart and did not wish to intrude upon it. Banda drank some water but had no desire for food. He sat on, looking at the flickering light of the lamp, letting the hours slip quietly away. At last he heard the sound of the neighing and galloping of horses, the distant sounds of gunshots and the cries of pain. Then all was still again.

When the first light of day came into the room, Sushil came to him. 'Bhai Binod Singh has got away,' she said. Banda Bahadur lay down on his pallet, closed his eyes and tried to sleep.

The stocks of food at last ran out.

> The besiegers kept so watchful a guard that not a blade of grass, not a grain of corn, could find its way to the fort, and the magazine within being at last emptied of their contents as the blockade drew to a length, a famine commenced its

ravage against the besieged, who fell at eating anything that came their way. Asses, horses and even oxen became food and what is incredible, cows were devoured. Nevertheless such was the animosity of those wild beasts that not one of them would talk of surrender. But everything within even to the most loathsome, having already been turned into food, and this having produced bloody flux, that swept them by shoals.[14]

In spite of all this, the infernal Sikh chief and his men, withstood all the military force that the great Mughal Empire could muster against them for eight long months.[15]

Eight thousand died in those few short months. Firewood to cremate the dead had long since run out and bodies of men and animals lay putrefying in the sun, filling the air with an obnoxious smell. The smell of decay hung heavy over the fort and drifted out to the Mughal forces bringing with it the clear and definite signal that the end was near. But the Mughals still hesitated to launch an all-out attack against the defenders. In fact, so strong was their desire to avoid an open battle even at this late stage that they had called upon some of their well-known sappers to dig tunnels that would give them access to strategic locations in the fort. Qamaruddin, son of Amin Khan, used a tunnel to capture a bastion while Zakariya Khan gained possession of a gate.

On 16 December, Samad Khan sent a small group of men commanded by his son Zakariya Khan to the gates of the fort. They sought audience with Banda Bahadur. Samad Khan's message was clear and simple. If Banda and his followers surrendered, the governor would intercede with the emperor on their behalf and obtain a pardon for them. They could then go to a place of their choosing and live the rest of their lives in peace. If the Sikhs persisted in holding out, their end would be an end too terrible to describe in words. They had till the morning to make up their minds.

Banda had no faith in this offer. He knew that as soon as they surrendered they would be made examples of and subjected to the most horrible and gruesome deaths. For himself he would have welcomed this because the more gory his death the more it would inspire anger and a desire of revenge amongst the Sikh youth. The story of his end would be told and retold, and with each retelling an ever-larger number of young men would be motivated to take up arms against the Mughals. But then he looked at Sushil, and Ajay in her lap, gently tapping his head and crooning a soft lullaby to lull him to sleep. If he surrendered, the Mughals would take Sushil prisoner, subject her to such a terrible dishonour that death, when it came, would be a sweet blessing. Ajay would be circumcised and paraded for the entire world to see – the son of the Sikh leader now converted to Islam. He could not choose a course that would inflict such indignities on his wife and child. He would spurn the governor's offer. He would ride out one last time to face the enemy and do battle till they were killed to the last man. He knew that Sushil would kill herself rather than be captured by the Mughals and would take Ajay with her. They would all three be regarded as martyrs and songs would be composed about them, songs that would be so popular that they would be sung at all festive occasions and listened to with awe and wonder by generations to come.

Sushil came to him in the night and lay down besides him. She caressed his forehead and muttered the name of God under her breath. He clasped her hand and held it to his heart.

'Do you pray, Sushil? What is it that you pray for?'

'I pray that God will give you the strength to take the decision that is in the best interests of the Panth. I pray that you will not let your judgement be clouded or your resolve weakened by your love for me. No matter how cruel the end that may befall your son and me, you must still decide to do what you know is best for the community and for the fulfilment of the behest that was given to you by the guru.'

He smiled in the dark. She, who had once said that he dwelt in private places that she could not reach, could look into his very soul. She had seen the compromise that he had been ready to make. His death in battle would be sung about, would be a source of pride to all who heard these songs. His death in Mughal captivity, gruesome as it was bound to be, would provoke anger and pain and a desire for revenge. If the fire that he had fanned were to be kept alive, a gory and bloody end would serve better than a swift and painless death in battle. He had known this but his love for his wife and son had made him decide on the easier end. How right the guru had been, without his wife and child he would have had no hesitation in surrendering. He must not hesitate even with them – this is what she was trying to tell him. He would go out in the morning with all the survivors and surrender to the enemy.

'What will become of Ajay?' he asked.

'Whatever is in God's will. You must accept it as you have always accepted it and bow before it.'

A burden lifted from his shoulders. He found again the still centre of his being that he had once known so well and with this finding came a deep peace. He drew her close and cuddled thus in each other's arms, they were given their last moments of togetherness.

A weak winter sun broke through the mist that hung close over Gurdas Nangal the next morning and those that were left of the garrison stirred again. There was no sound of gunfire. The Mughals held their fire as they waited for Banda's response to Samad Khan's offer. The Sikhs had no ammunition left. Banda assembled those who could still walk, a pitiful group of skeletons, all that was left of the once proud army that had fought so fiercely against the Mughals at Kalanaur just eight months ago. He told them of his decision to surrender. A look of surprise flashed in the eyes of some of them but they made no protest, voiced no opinion and meekly followed Banda when he ordered the gates to be thrown open and stumbled towards the enemy lines. The Mughals stared in awe at the pathetic remnants of what had once been a proud and invincible army. Then, when no more Sikhs came through the gates, the Mughal soldiers gave a cry and fell upon the survivors. Banda and 200 of the more prominent Sikhs, including Sushil and Ajay, were taken prisoner. The rest were put to the sword.

Banda was chained and locked inside an iron cage, which was mounted on an elephant. As abundant precaution an official rode on the elephant to ensure there was no attempt to escape. At the first suspicion of trickery, he was to plunge his dagger into Banda's heart.

The prisoners were brought to Lahore. They were halted outside the gates of the city and formed up into a triumphal procession. At the head were drummers and bandsmen. There were row upon row of Mughal soldiers carrying the heads of Sikhs upon their spears. Then came Banda in his iron cage. Behind him were the other Sikh prisoners, chained and mounted on the most sorry looking asses and camels that the Mughals could find.

Finally, came all the amirs, faujdars and rajahs who had taken part in the siege, dressed in full regalia, their men marching behind them. The streets of Lahore were thronged with thousands of people, all turned out to see the sorcerer who had for so long evaded defeat and capture at the hands of the mighty Mughals. There were people lining the sides of the Shahi Sarak, so close to the procession there was danger of their being trampled upon. There were people massed on the rooftops, craning their heads and bodies to catch a glimpse of the terrible monster as the procession passed below them. There were hundreds of spectators clinging to the trees and leaning so far forward there was every danger of their falling into the melee and being done to death. There was an air of rejoicing and festivity amongst the onlookers. They had heard a hundred stories of his bloodthirstiness and cruelty and they were relieved that he had been captured and would at last meet his nemesis. There was laughter, cheering and even hooting as he passed. Insults were hurled at him and some even threw old shoes and rotten vegetables at the elephant as he lumbered past.

Then Banda mustered all this strength and cried: *'Bole Soh Nihal'*, and the captive Sikhs found their strength too and answered in a chorus that resonated through the evening air: *'Sat Sri Aka!'*

The crowd fell silent and those who were closest to the passing captives drew quickly back. In this silence Banda began the recitation of the evening prayer and the others joined him. None of them looked to the left or the right – their eyes were fixed on the road ahead of them. The crowd now held its breath in awe, afraid that this show of fortitude was a precursor to the display of some terrible supernatural feat, perhaps to the escape of Banda himself.

The procession reached the governor's palace where Samad Khan waited to see his prisoners taken to the dungeons. The Mughal leaders were all invited to a celebration in the palace and the soldiers went to their billets in the cantonment area. The crowd dispersed.

Samad Khan sought permission from the emperor to escort his prestigious prisoner. The emperor, fearing a reaction to Banda Bahadur's arrest, advised him to stay in his province to take care of any eventuality that may arise and to send his prisoner under the charge of his son Zakariya Khan. Zakariya, eager to gain favour with the emperor, looked at his 200 emaciated prisoners and felt that they were not good enough to make a proper show before the emperor. He gave orders to the faujdar and the choudhris, to scour the countryside and bring him more presentable specimen of the Sikhs to take to Delhi. These officials were, in their turn, eager to curry favour with the governor's son and vied with each other to capture more and more Sikhs. Thousands of innocent Sikhs and Hindus who wore long hair and beards were rounded up and brought to Lahore. Eight hundred of these were manacled and made to join the other prisoners who were being taken to Delhi. The rest were slaughtered ruthlessly, their heads accumulated as war trophies.

Banda and the train of prisoners were marched to Delhi under the most degrading circumstances and subjected to every conceivable humiliation that their captors could think of. As the procession moved out of Lahore, it passed close to the Qadiri Dera. At its gate stood a man in his mid-thirties, in flowing blue robes and a flowing beard already flecked with white. It was obvious that he was a holy man of some eminence because people stepped away from him as they passed and bowed to him. Those who knew him told the others who he was in whispered asides. Banda glanced towards him and recognised Bulleh Shah. He tried to raise his hand to his forehead in greeting but because of the shackles he could not lift it. Bulleh Shah smiled at him and stepped out into the middle of the street. The mahout brought his elephant to a halt. The official riding with Banda saw the saint and called out a greeting.

'I would wish to speak to your prisoner,' Bulleh Shah said in answer to the greeting.

'If it is his soul that you seek to save, O holy one, you will be wasting your breath. He is guilty of such evil deeds that nothing can save his soul now,' the official called back and all those who were within hearing distance laughed at this remark. The official looked around, pleased at the reaction his remark had produced. 'But I respect you too much not to accede to your request. Please feel free to speak to the prisoner. Only don't take too long, the emperor waits impatiently for this arrival in Delhi and we would not like to keep him waiting any longer than is necessary.'

Bulleh Shah stepped forward as the mahout lowered the elephant to his knees so that the saint could address the prisoner without having to raise his voice.

'I see that my blessings and my taviz have done you little good. God did not show you the way in which you could best achieve success and fulfil your mission.'

'Why do you say that?'

'If it had been otherwise you would have been heading this procession in triumph, not be dragged, caged like an animal, to a terrible and ignominious death.'

'It is only my body that is caged. My spirit soars above in triumph.'

The sage smiled and for a moment it seemed that the interview was over. But he did not turn away to signal the end. Banda still held his eye and the officials waited with growing impatience.

'What have you achieved that makes you so sure that your spirit triumphs?'

It was Banda's turn to smile now. 'I have ensured that no more will the crown sit easily on the Mughal emperor's head. Simple village lads when they find the yoke of tyranny and oppression weigh too heavily upon them will know that they too can draw their swords, like I did, and lead an uprising against their oppressors.'

Bulleh Shah nodded his head to indicate that this was well said. And yet he would not let Banda go.

'Are you not afraid of death?' he asked.

'Are you?' Banda asked in turn.

Bulleh Shah's face broke into a radiant smile. 'Though I do not pretend to your wisdom and your holiness, I know that we are alike in many ways. One such way is that we are both unafraid of death. Death is inevitable and if it must come then it does not matter when and how it comes.'

'Yes, there is much about us that is the same. Perhaps this will ensure that we will find ourselves in the same place after death. Wait for me there, there is still much that I would like to talk to you about.'

'I will wait,' Banda said as he turned his face away from Bulleh Shah to indicate to his captors that the meeting was over and that they could now proceed on their journey.

The spectacle of Lahore was repeated at every town they passed through where the local population turned out in thousands to jeer and shout at the captive Sikhs. However, it was Sirhind which saw the worst treatment meted out to the prisoners. Obscenities were shouted and filth and offal was poured upon them from the balconies of homes. However, the Sikhs remained calm all the time singing hymns in praise of God. As the procession passed out of Sirhind it was held up due to an altercation on the road between some people. As the elephant stood still Banda was compelled to look into a pair of eyes, which were focused unblinkingly upon his face. The man had an open beard, generously streaked with grey. He was dark complexioned, with a prominent scar high on his right cheek wearing his turban in the Pathan fashion. He looked fixedly at Banda and his wide-open eyes seemed to ask a question. There was something vaguely familiar about that face though Banda could have sworn that he had never seen it before. There was also something familiar about the question in those eyes, which brought it almost to the point of recognition. Then the altercation that had halted their progress was sorted out and the procession moved on. The face continued to haunt Banda even after he had passed it. Recognition came to him in a flash a few moments later. It was his old friend and colleague Bhai Binod Singh, in disguise, risking his life to catch one last glimpse of his leader. Painfully, Banda turned his head as far back as his iron collar and chains would permit, but there was no sign of Binod. He had been swallowed up in the crowd.

On 27 February 1716, the procession entered Delhi.

There was hardly anyone in the city who had not come out to see the tamasha. Such a crowd in the bazaars and lanes had been rarely seen. And the Musalman could not contain themselves for joy. But those unfortunate Sikhs who had been reduced to this last extremity were quite happy and contented with their fate; not the slightest sign of dejection or humility was seen on their faces. In fact, most of them, as they passed along on their camels, seemed happy and cheerful, joyfully singing the sacred hymns of their scriptures. And if anyone from amongst those in the lanes and bazaars called out to them that their own excesses had reduced them to that condition, they quickly retorted saying that it had been so willed by the Almighty. And if anyone said: 'Now you will be killed.' They shouted: 'Kill us, when were we afraid of death'. [16]

Without any sign of dejection or shame they rode on, calm and cheerful, even anxious to die the death of Martyrs.[17]

The procession halted at the fort. Orders were passed that Sushil and Ajay be taken to the harem. Sushil stood rooted to the ground, loath to part from her lord, till Darbar Khan, wazir of the harem, tugged gently at her sleeve. She led Ajay by the hand and walked quickly from the courtyard, stopping once to look back at her husband. There was no sadness in that look, no regret, no awareness of the impending tragedy. She looked only as if she sought to fix forever the image of his face upon her mind. Then she shrugged her shoulders and turned and followed her captor. Banda Bahadur, Raj Singh, Fateh Singh and the other leaders were held captive in Tripolia.

The emperor had heard of the cheerful behaviour of the Sikhs in the face of the taunts and humiliation that had been heaped upon them, of their singing of religious songs and reciting of prayers as they were being paraded through town after town. He had heard of their undaunted courage in the face of certain and horrible death, which to an extent, had turned the sweet taste of victory into the bitter gall of failure in his mouth. His moral ascendancy would only be re-established if he could persuade even one Sikh prisoner to renounce his faith. He promised rich rewards to any of the jailors who made every effort to fulfil their emperor's wish. They used threats, cajolery and the promise of rich rewards, but all to no avail. The Sikhs would not renounce their faith.

The massacre began on 5 March 1716. Each morning Sarbrah Khan, the kotwal, led the prisoners to the place of execution. Small groups were selected from amongst them and herded to one side where they were subjected to the sight of the sharpening of the executioners swords by a group of blacksmiths. Then they were led to the execution blocks where Sarbrah Khan addressed each one in turn and the address was invariably the same: 'You have one last chance to make your peace with Allah and enter the portals of paradise. Renounce your mistaken belief in the false teachings of the Sikh gurus and the emperor, in his infinite compassion, will spare your life.'

From each Sikh he received the same answer: a triumphant smile and a negative shake of the head. Each went to his death with the name of God upon his lips, while those who waited their turn for execution recited prayers and sang hymns. The populace marvelled at the calm acceptance and the cheerfulness while facing death. Those who had come to jeer fell silent and whispered words of wondering praise.

All observers, Indian and European, unite in remarking on the wonderful patience and resolution with which these men met their fate. Their attachment and devotion to their leader were wonderful to behold. They had no fear of death, and they called the executioner Mukta, or the Deliverer.[18]

After a week this daily ritual of slaughter was called to a halt. 'We must give them time to consider the horror that awaits them,' the kotwal advised the emperor. 'At the moment, in the ecstasy of faith, they welcome death. But if they are left prisoners for a sufficient length of time they will consider the horrible fate that has befallen their fellow Sikhs. They will have time to think of their loved ones, their parents, their wives, their children and their friends. They will feel the pain of parting and there is every chance that the weaker ones among them will break, Your Majesty, and you will perhaps get what you want: a Sikh who apostatises from his faith and embraces Islam.'

The kotwal did not voice his personal reason for wanting a pause in the mass executions. He had after the first day, seen the look of revulsion that had come into the faces of many amongst the spectators. By the fourth day he had noticed how they no longer jeered or hurled abuses at the Sikhs. A hushed silence had descended upon them and some of them even had a look of admiration in their eyes for the way in which the Sikhs went so bravely to their deaths. The turnout at the executions, in spite of the compulsory attendance that had been forced upon the citizens of the district, had fallen sharply. This last morning it had been possible to count the number of people present. The public executions were no longer serving their purpose and the kotwal was afraid that their continuation might set in motion a secret wave of sympathy for the Sikhs.

The emperor paid heed to the kotwal's advice and a temporary halt was called to the executions. Sarbrah Khan visited the prisoners in their cells and once again tried through blandishment and threats to get some of the Sikhs to do what the emperor wished. Amin Khan would sometimes accompany him. They would stop at the cell where Banda was held in solitary confinement and saw the leader of the Sikhs, always at prayer or telling the beads of his rosary, with a radiant glow on his face. Normally, they would exchange a wondering glance, shrug their shoulders and move on, but one day they were at his cell when Banda had just finished his prayers. He opened his eyes, looked at them and smiled in greeting.

'Oh tell us, leader of the Sikhs, you have murdered thousands of Muslims, denied many of them the eternal peace that comes from decent burial. How come you still have such a tranquil and untroubled mind?' Amin Khan asked.

'When I killed, I did so for the cause that the guru asked me to champion: the true and just cause of fighting to free the people from oppression. I have fought not for any personal gain or reward. I fought for justice and for the right of the common people and in this fight there can be no room for remorse or regret. There can only be a deep and abiding sense of peace, a peace that comes only with knowing that one has tried to do one's duty.'

'If you were championing the cause of the oppressed, then why are you yourself being punished? You are in prison, waiting to meet a horrible end. Surely, if your cause was just, you would not have merited such punishment.'

'I deserve such punishment as much as those I sought to punish for I have strayed from the path shown to me by my guru. I permitted my people to look upon me as a guru and to elevate me to the rank of a king and invest me with the trappings of royalty. I permitted myself to be persuaded into marriage against the guru's advice, disobeying whom is amongst the deadliest of sins and for this I deserve all punishment. Whatever

Sirhind Fort

The battle of Sirhind is considered to be the first major battle fought and won by the Sikhs against the Mughal Empire.

Gurdwara at Chhat

Children playing around the tunnel that was connected underground to the Jama Masjid of Banur (7 km from Chhat).

The mound (*theh*) of Gurdas Nangal, where Banda Singh Bahadur fought his last battle against the Mughals (in 1715).

Martyrdom: End of a Mission
Gurdwara Shahidi Asthaan Baba Banda Singh Bahadur is situated in the Mehrauli area of Delhi near the Qutab Minar. Here Baba Banda Singh Bahadur, his four-year-old son, Ajay Singh, along with forty Sikhs were tortured to death by the Mughals.

punishment you may award me will be far milder than the punishment that I deserve.'

'If you carry such a burden of guilt, such an awareness of your unworthiness, how is it that your mind remains untroubled, that you have such stillness within you, such a calmness of spirit?'

'When a man accepts his sins with all humility, admits in his heart that he is guilty and seeks forgiveness, he is redeemed. His mind is strong again and he is ready to face the future with peace and tranquillity.'

Amin Khan and Sarbrah Khan hurried to the emperor and reported the conversation to him. Once again the emperor felt the strong sharp pain of defeat stir within him: 'Kill him. Kill him in so horrible and painful a manner that you are able to penetrate this shield of calmness and cause him some degree of disquiet. Make his end so terrible that no one will dare again to claim that he is a Sikh.'

On 19 June 1716, Banda and the surviving Sikhs were taken to the tomb of the late emperor Bahadur Shah where Banda was made to pay obeisance and then seated for execution. Ajay Singh was brought forth and seated in front of him. Banda smiled at his son but made no effort to reach out to him. Sarbrah Khan was troubled by the smile and wished the whole business to be over. He signalled to the executioner, who came forward and hacked Ajay to pieces, limb by limb. Banda sat still, the smile still on his lips, unmoved by the boy's cry of pain or his call to

his father for help. The boy's heart was drawn from his body and thrust into Banda's mouth. Still he sat in silence, unmoved.

The executioner then turned his attention to Banda. Like Ajay's, his limbs too were hacked off piece by piece and he was kept alive for as long as possible. If Banda felt any pain he did not show it and sat through the gruesome ordeal unmoved. When at last the executioner raised his sword to hack off his head, Banda called in a loud clear voice: *'Bole Soh Nihal,'* while the other Sikhs gave the response: *'Sat Sri Akal.'* The executioner, his sword raised high, hesitated to bring it down. Then as Sarbrah Khan administered a sharp rebuke, it went swishing through the air, flashing in the morning sun.

The emperor heard the gruesome details of Banda's end, clapped his hands and taking a bag of gold from a tray at his side tossed it to Sarbrah Khan: 'Congratulate the executioner on a job well done and give him this for his pains. Now we shall have peace at last. The cursed man has been killed and there will be no one to lead the Sikhs, if any dare to call themselves Sikhs. His spirit will never again return to plague us.'

Epilogue

Then he turned again to the emperor: 'You have sought to destroy Banda Bahadur and you have sought to do so with brutal cruelty. But you have destroyed only his body; you have not been able to extinguish the flame that he lit.... You have destroyed his physical frame but with this destruction you have fanned the flame that he lit and made it burn ever stronger. You have given him immortality because now his spirit will live forever.'

He was a humble nineteen-year-old peasant from a nameless village in the dusty plains of the Punjab. He was the only son who had lost his father while still a boy. His mother doted on him and looked forward to the day when she would have grandchildren, a dozen of them, playing at her feet. So she got him a bride, a beautiful, cheerful young girl.

A few days after the marriage Zakariya Khan gave his notorious order for the rounding up of all Sikhs and the, boy was one among those captured. As a young boy he had seen and understood the brutalities practiced by the Mughal officials on the common people. His blood had boiled and he had longed to rise up against them. But his mother's pleas had restrained him.

Then Banda Bahadur had arrived in the Punjab and won his famous victories. Stories of these victories had been told and retold a hundred times and the boy had found his spirit being fired at each telling. He had yearned, above all, to march out and join Banda's forces. But his mother's tearful entreaties had once again held him back.

'I am getting on in years,' she said. 'If you go away there will be no one to look after me and when I die it will be left to strangers to light my funeral pyre.'

Now chained and manacled he was at last being led to join Banda's Sikhs. The mother tried to intervene and stop her son from being led away. But the soldiers pushed her aside. He was brought to Lahore and locked up with the other Sikh prisoners. He saw their cheerfulness in the face of suffering, their fortitude in the face of impending death. They had a strong sense of camraderie and made every effort to make him feel that he was not alone. Gradually he found himself warming to them, being fired again by their spirit and learnt to live with his own sorrow. He too went around with a smile on his lips and a joke for every occasion.

Often he could not help feeling that he was an impostor. Many of those around him had risked their lives, abandoned their homes and families and fought with Banda in the cause of freedom. In spite of his own strong feelings on the subject, he had allowed his mother to persuade him to stay at home. He had done nothing that entitled him to be amongst them, to deserve the status of a martyr. But soon he learnt to accept this too. He began to walk with their proud erect bearing; he practised their extreme patience, which refused to be provoked by the taunts and jeers of the spectators. He too found joy in all the community activities that they were still able to practise.

The procession reached Delhi and the youth saw the Sikhs being led one by one to their death culminating in the gruesome death of Banda Bahadur. He saw their unflinching acceptance of death, their equanimity and their unwavering faith and he was proud to be in their company, to be one of them.

With a determination born of despair, his mother had followed him to Delhi. She established contact with Diwan Ratan Chand, who had influence in the court, and was able to present a petition to the emperor. She begged the king to spare the life of her only son. She said that he had been captured by mistake, that he was not a Sikh. The emperor sensed an opportunity of at last getting what he had wished for. Here at last was a chance of getting a public apostasy by a Sikh. The woman was summoned to the royal presence and presented her case: 'I am a poor widow, Your Majesty, and my son is all I have to support me in my old age. He has been married but recently and I cannot yet hope for grandsons. His end will be the end of my husband's name. He is being punished for no fault of his. He is a simple law-abiding boy and has never had anything to do with Banda Bahadur and his men. Why, he has not even been baptised, he has not taken amrit, nectar, and is not a true Sikh.' She threw herself at the emperor's feet. 'I beg you, Your Majesty, spare the life of my son. By so doing you will save my life and the life of his wife, for without him we will surely die.'

The emperor pondered over the woman's words, reached down and raised her to her feet. 'It shall be as you desire. We will spare his life. All we ask is that he should declare that he is not a Sikh.'

The woman smiled through her tears. She was certain that, as always before, her son would do what she asked him to do. His life would be saved. 'That I am sure he will do, Your Majesty.'

The young man was brought to the court. 'This woman claims to be your mother. She also claims that you are not a Sikh – that you have been brought here by mistake. She has begged for your life and in deference to her age and her need of you, your life will be spared if you will but confirm that you are not a Sikh.'

The mother came close to her son and looked into his eyes: 'Say you are not a Sikh, my son. You have not taken amrit and in saying this you will not be telling a lie. Look closely at your mother, look at my miserable condition. Look at your bride,' she dragged the girl forward from where she had been standing in the press of the courtiers. 'See. See. Look closely at her. Since your arrest she has not eaten, has known no sleep. Her eyes are red and swollen with weeping. She has spent each moment of the day and night praying for your deliverance and this deliverance is now in your hands. Just say what the emperor wants you to say, say you are not a Sikh.'

The young man looked first at his wife and then at his mother. Then he turned to the emperor: 'It is true, that it is my mother that stands before you, begging for my life. But it is not true that I am not a Sikh and you must forgive my mother for claiming this for it is a mother's misguided love anxious to save her son's life that makes her lie. I am a Sikh though I have not yet been confirmed through baptism. If there had been any doubt in my mind it would have been stilled these last few months.'

His mother moved closer to plead with him yet once again. But he held up his hand with such firmness that the words died on her lips. 'What use is a life given to you in charity, like alms to a beggar? Far better to die with dignity.' Then he turned again to the emperor: 'You have sought to destroy Banda Bahadur and you have sought to do so with brutal cruelty. But you have destroyed only his body; you have not been able to extinguish the flame that he lit. There are many amongst us, both Hindu and Sikh, who did not have the good fortune to fight by his side. Yet we have been with him in captivity these last few months and learnt to respect and admire him and to wish with all our hearts that we had been an active part of his war against you. We saw the manner of his death, his patience and strength in the face of your weak barbarism, and we vowed that if *we* had not been able to live like him we would at least die like him. And when you have killed us there will be a thousand more who will think and feel like us and be willing to die like us. You have destroyed his physical frame but with this destruction you have fanned the flame that he lit and made it burn ever stronger. You have given him immortality because now his spirit will live forever.'

The young man looked towards his wife and mother and then without waiting to be dismissed by the emperor, walked from the court to his death.

NOTES AND REFERENCES

1. J. R. Puri and T. R. Shangare, *Bulleh Shah*, p. 231. Quoted from Nazir Ahmad, *Kalam-i-Bulleh Shah*.*
2. Khushwant Singh, *Hymns of the Gurus*.
3. William Irvine, *Later Mughals*, Vol. I, pp. 298-99.
4. Fauja Singh (ed.), *Sirhind through the Ages*, p. 46. Quoted from Salamat Rai, *Tarikh-i-Sudan*.
5. Fauja Singh (ed.) *Sirhind through the Ages*. Quoted from Khafi Khan et al, *Muntakhab-ul Lubab*.
6. Surjit Singh Gandhi, *Sikhs in the Eighteenth Century*, p. 31. Quoted from Khafi Khan et al, *Muntakhab-ul Lubab*.
7. Ibid., p. 32. Quoted from Muhammad Qasim, *Ibrat Namah 1720*.
8. Harbans Kaur Sagoo, *Banda Singh Bahadur and Sikh Sovereignty*, p. 159.
9. Ibid., p. 144.
10. Khushwant Singh, *History of the Sikhs*, Vol. I, p. 107.
11. Ganda Singh, *Life of Banda Singh Bahadur*. Quoted from Qazi Nur Muhammad, *Jangnamah*.

*For publication details, please see Further Reading.

12. William Irvine, *Later Mughals*, Vol. II.
13. Paraphrase of the Hukamnamah, dated 26 December 1710, sent to the Khalsa of Jaunpur, (now in Uttar Pradesh).
14. Ganda Singh, *Life of Banda Singh Bahadur*. Quoted from Ghulam Hussan Khan, *Siyar-ul Mukhterin*.
15. Surjit Singh Gandhi, *Sikhs in the Eighteenth Century*. Quoted from Kamvar Khan, 'Tazkirat-us-Salatin-Charghatiya'.
16. Ganda Singh, *Life of Banda Singh Bahadur*. Quoted from Mirza Muhammad Harisi, *Ibrat Namah* 1720.
17. H. Wilson, 'Massacre of the Sikhs in Delhi in 1716' in Ganda Singh (ed.), *Early European Accounts of the Sikhs*.
18. William Irvine, *Later Mughals*, Vol. II.

FURTHER READINGS

Bhagat Singh, *A History of the Sikh Misals*, Punjabi University, Patiala, 1993.

Gopal Singh, *A History of the Sikh People*, World Sikh University Press, New Delhi, 1979.

Khushwant Singh, *A History of the Sikhs*, Vol. II, Oxford University Press, London, 1963. Indian edition published by Oxford University Press, New Delhi, 1999.

Raj Pal Singh, *Banda Bahadur and His Times*, Harman Publishing House, Delhi, 1999.

Gurdev S. Deol, *Banda Bahadur*, New Academic Publishing, Jalandhar, 1972.

Sant Singh Sekhon, *Banda Bahadur*, B. R. Publishing Corporation, Delhi, 1985.

Piara Singh Dalta, *Banda Singh Bahadur*, National Book Shop, Delhi, 2006.

Harbans Kaur Sagoo, *Banda Singh Bahadur and Sikh Sovereignty*, Deep and Deep Publications, New Delhi, 2002.

Sohan Singh, Bhai Narain Singh and Lahore Giani, *Banda the Brave* or *The Life and Exploits of Banda Bahadur*, Punjabi Novelist Co., Lahore, 1915.

J. R. Puri and T. R. Shangare, *Bulleh Shah*, Radha Soami Satsang, Beas, Amritsar, 1986.

Hari Ram Gupta, *History of the Sikhs*, Vol. II, Munshiram Manoharlal Publishers, New Delhi, 1978.

William Irvine, *Later Mughals*, Luzac, London, 1922.

Ganda Singh, *Life of Banda Singh Bahadur*, Khalsa College, Amritsar, 1935.

John Surman and Edward Stephenson, 'Massacre of the Sikhs at Delhi in 1716', in Ganda Singh (ed.), *Early European Accounts of the Sikhs*, Today & Tomorrow's Printers and Publishers, New Delhi, 1974.

Gian Singh Giani, *Sri Guru Panth Prakash* (reprint), Bhasha Vibhag, Patiala, 1970.

Ratan Singh Bhangu, *Prachin Panth Prakash*, (Punjabi), Khalsa Samachar, Amritsar, 1939.

Fauja Singh (ed.), *Sirhind through the Ages*, Punjabi University, Patiala, 1972.

Bhagat Singh, *Sikh Polity in the 18th and 19th Centuries Delhi*, Oriental Publishers, New Delhi, 1978.

J. S. Grewal and Indu Banga (eds.) *The Khalsa over 300 years*, Indian History Congress, Tulika Books, Delhi, 1999.

Bhai Jodh Singh, *Some Studies in Sikhism*, Lahore Book Shop, Ludhiana, 1953.

Harbans Singh (ed.) *The Encyclopaedia of Sikhism*, Punjabi University, Patiala, 1992.

Harbans Singh, *The Heritage of the Sikhs*, 1985, Manohar Publications, New Delhi, 1983.

W. L. M. Gregor, *The History of the Sikhs*, Allabahad, 1846. Reprinted by the Department of Languages, Punjabi University, Patiala, 1970.

Mohammad Akbar, *Punjab under the Mughal Raj*, Vanguard Books, Lahore, 1985.

Surjit Singh Gandhi, *Sikhs in the Eighteenth Century*, Singh Brothers, Amritsar, 1999.

Khushwant Singh, *Hymns of the Gurus*, Penguin/Viking, New Delhi, 2003.

Glossary

Amil – revenue officer.

Amir – honorific title for someone of wealth and exalted social standing, recognized as such by the king.

Amrit – nectar, essential ingredient of Sikh baptism ritual.

Bairagi – a man with religious leanings who has renounced the world and spends his time travelling from one place of pilgrimage to another.

Bakshi – military officer incharge of disbursement of salaries to soldiers.

Bakshish – alms, reward.

Bandai Khalsa – followers of Banda Bahadur.

Banjaras – gypsies who lead a nomadic life.

Chamar – the lowest caste who were deployed in the most menial of tasks.

Chichra – thorny bushes.

Dargah – a Muslim place of pilgrimage, usually the tomb of a saint.

Dasvand – the one-tenth of one's income that the Sikh religion enjoins on one to give away as charity.

Degh – cauldron, symbol not only of community living as symbolized by the langar, but also of charity symbolized by the feeding of the poor.

Dera – the abode of a holy man, which would include a place of worship, residences for his disciples and often a stretch of agricultural land which grateful followers have gifted to him.

Dewan – chief adviser.

Dhimnis – Muslim term for non-believers who follow the religious teachings from a holy book.

Fakir – mendicant.
Fatwa – the hukamnamah of the Muslims.
Faujdar – the army commander of a province.
Firman – royal order.

Gazis – holy warriors who answer the call for jihad.
Ghat – hill, small mountain.
Gurbani – the text of the Guru Granth Sahib.
Guru – teacher, specially of spiritual and religious subjects.

Haveli – a palatial house.
Hukumnamahs – orders regarding both temporal and spiritual matters, which carry a sanctity about them because they have emanated either from the guru or at the behest of religious leaders.

Jagir – large landholding bestowed by the king for services rendered.

Jagirdars – large landholders who usually got their land from the ruler in recognition of services rendered.

Jahanpanah – king of the world-honorific term of address favoured for kings.

Japji Sahib – the morning prayer composed by Nanak Dev, the first guru of the Sikhs.

Jathas – groups: term is used for pilgrims as well as for soldiers.

Jeziya – tax levied by Muslim kings on non-Muslim subjects.

Jihad – holy war between believers and non-believers of the Muslim faith. The cry of jihad is raised when the faith is perceived to be in danger.

Kafir – infidel.

Kalgi – aigrette.

Khaima – tent, pavilion.

Khalsa – the pure, who lived life according to the percepts laid down by Gobind Singh, the tenth guru.

Khool – stream.

Kila – measurement of land, usually over one acre; varies from place to place.

Kirtan – the communal singing of hymns.

Kos – medieval unit of measurement equivalent to a distance of almost two kilometres.

Kotwal – senior police official – station house officer.

Lagaan – the revenue tax paid on agricultural income.

Glossary

Langar – community kitchen.

Majhaili – resident of Majha, the area between the Beas and the Ravi rivers.

Marasis – professional singers, story tellers.

Maryada – tenets and principles of life that give to a religion or belief its distinctiveness.

Moksha – freedom from the cycle of birth and death.

Mullahs – Muslim priests.

Nagara – drum, used to beat the call to battle.

Panj Piarey – the first five to be baptized as Khalsa by Guru Gobind Singh in Anandpur Sahib. The guru considered them as powerful leaders of the community and they could take decisions in all matters.

Panth – community.

Pargana – district.

Parwana – message.

Rehras Sahib – the evening prayer of the Sikhs, includes hymns by Nanak the first guru, Arjan Dev the fifth guru, and Gobind Singh the tenth guru.

Rishi – a holy man who has renounced the world and lives in a holy place, usually in a remote hill area where he spends his time in meditation and in the study of holy books.

Roomal – square piece of cloth, like a big handkerchief.

Sadhus – holy men who have renounced the world and spend their time in an ashram: they usually belong to a particular sect or order.

Sahibzada – of the rank of a prince.

Sajda – genuflection: lowering of the head and raising fingers of the right hand to the forehead as a mark of respect.

Salwar – loose trouser worn by women.

Sangat – congregation.

Sardars – leaders.

Serai – an inn.

Shabad – hymn.

Shaitan – devil.

Sherbet – a sweet, cooling drink.

Shikari – hunter.

Silsila – order, like the Christian brotherhoods.

Suba – province.

Subedar – governor of a province.

Swami – a religious leader who has a good knowledge of Hindu religious texts and is able to preach from them to his followers.

Tat Khalsa – the pure Khalsa. (This schism occurred after Banda Bahadur's death when some of his followers began to look upon him as a guru.)

Tavas – flat iron gridle on which chapattis are made.

Taviz – charm to bring down God's blessings on the recipient – usually given by a holy man.

Tegh – sword, symbol of a war fought in the cause of justice.

Vaid – doctor who practices the ayurvedic system of medicine.

Vaishnavite – worshipper of Vishnu, strict vegetarian, abhors the killing of animals.

Wazir – chief minister.

Yogi – one who has detached himself from material things, practises yoga.

Zamindars – agriculturists with substantial land holdings.

INDEX

Ahmed, Sheikh, 203, 219
Ahuluwalia, Jassa Singh, 128
Ajay, 241, 242, 246, 251, 253-255, 258, 272, 277-279, 285, 289
Akbar, 108
Akhnoor, 237
Amarnath, Swami, 36
Amber, 174
Ambeta, 133
Amil, 139, 303
Amir/s, 70-74, 76, 77, 109, 280, 303
Amrit, 21, 48, 295, 303
Anandpur, 28, 145, 306
Asaf-ud Daulah, 64
Aurangzeb, 108, 109, 179
Azim-us Shah, 231

Bahadur, Banda Singh (Lachman Dev/Madho Das), 6, 13-24, 42-43, 48-51, 53, 55, 57-69, 71-72, 74-90, 98-101, 105, 108, 110-119, 121-130, 133-171, 176-177, 180, 182, 185-186, 194, 199-203, 206-209, 210-233, 237-240, 245-246, 249-269, 271-295

artistes and, 157-160
as a family man and a farmer, 237-256
as a wrestler, 13, 29
as an able military leader, 134-136
battle victories of, 85-169
battle with the Mughals, 173
birth of a Sikh State and, 145-148
childhood of, 22-34
coins in the name of, 152, 154-157
education of, 29
elimination of dacoits by, 61-63
establishment of the Khalsa Raj by, 15
haunting abilities of, 24-33
initiation as Swami Madho Das, 35-47
knowledge of holy books and scriptures by, 13, 35
learning the art of hypnosis and telepathy and meditation by, 13, 36

INDEX

managing the newly formed Sikh state by, 144-157
marriage of, 217, 254
martyrdom of, 289-290
meeting with Bulleh Shah by, 221-227
Muslims in the army of, 140
poems written by Rabindranath Tagore in tribute of, 6-7
Punjab and, 65-81
regrouping the army by, 261-262
setting his ashram at Panchvati by, 37
songs in praise of, 159-160
spy network of, 264
the last fight with the Mughals, 261-290
vows of celibacy by, 36
yogic practices by, 37
Bahadur, Guru Tegh, 72, 75, 274
Bahadur, Shah Alam, 156
Bairagi, 160, 214, 230-231, 242, 243, 245, 249, 252, 303
Baksh, Kam, 173, 174
Bakshi, 193, 303
Bakshish, 21, 48, 303
Bakshi-ul Mumalik, 194
Bandai Khalsa, 303
Barha, 180, 185
Batala, 203, 219-221, 262, 263, 265
Beg, Bashal, 73, 75
Beg, Shashal, 75

Behut, 133
Bhaduriya, Gopal Singh, 264
Bhagu, Bhai, 67
Bhangu, Rattan Singh, 15, 17
Bhatti Rajputs, 263
Bhatti zamindars, 263
Bundela, Raja Chatarsal, 175, 195
Bundela, Raja Udet Singh, 175, 194

Chamar, 80, 303
Chamba roomals, 213-217, 249
Chand, Amin, 211, 213, 214, 216
Chand, Bhai Bidhi, 79
Chand, Bhai Duni, 265
Chand, Diwan Ratan, 294
Chand, Raja Bhim, 208-210
Chand, Sri, 254
Chappar Chiri, battle of, 15, 16, 120, 121
Chichra, 186, 303
Chishti, Khwaja Moinuddin, 175
Chopra, Ashok, 19
Chopra, Pushpinder Singh, 19
Coins
   Shah Alam Bahadur, 154, 156
   Banda Bahadur, 152-153, 158
Cole, Dr, 46

Das, Bhai Ram, 79
Das, Madho (*see under* Banda Singh Bahadur)
Dasvand, 61, 304
Delhi, 55, 59, 61, 64, 65, 70, 91, 107-109, 125, 133-135, 137,

310

INDEX

161, 168, 173-174, 178-180, 184, 228, 232, 248, 281, 282, 284, 294
Dev, Arjun, 59, 222, 273
Dev, Bhai Nam, 79
Dev, Lachman (*see under* Banda Singh Bahadur)
Dev, Ram, 28, 29
Dhillon, Kanwar Singh, 19
Dhimnis, 228, 304
Diwan, Hafiz Khan, 174
Dronacharya, Guru, 26
Dutt, Pundit Dev, 29

Fatwa/s, 114, 239, 250, 304

Ganj-i-Illam dargah, 91
Gazis, 114, 119, 304
Ghaus, Muhammad, 221
Ghudani, 128
Ghuram, 64, 85
Gurbani, 126, 244, 304
Gurdas Nangal, 264-266, 279
Gyasuddin, 119

Hamid, Shah Abdul, 91
Hansi, 137
Harkara, Bhagwati Das, 140
Harmandir Sahib, 126, 154, 222
Hiuen Tsang, 107
Hindus, 53, 67, 91, 108, 112, 140, 180, 185, 190, 191, 248-250, 281
Hukumnamahs, 45, 46, 66, 69, 155, 206, 209, 304

Inder, Bhim, 20
Irvine, William, 15, 17

Jalalabad, 64, 166, 167, 185
Jalaluddin, Sayyad, 71-76
Jalandhar, 64, 166-168, 185, 188, 209
Jathas, 105, 112, 123, 206, 305
Jehangir, 108, 202
Jeziya, 92, 138-140, 228, 305
Jihad, 17, 114, 119, 136, 239, 250, 261, 304, 305
Jilani, Abdul Qadiri, 221
Jodhpur, 173, 175

Kadam-ud Din, 88-90
Kafir, 91, 114, 305
Kaithal, 63, 64, 138
Kamal, 64
Kapoori, 64, 85, 88-90, 113, 128, 162
Kaur, Anoop, 129, 130, 149
Kaur, Sada, 129, 147
Kaur, Sahib, 254-255, 258, 266
Kaur, Sushil, 17, 215, 218, 241-242, 245-246, 250-251, 253-255, 257-258, 266-268, 272, 275, 277, 279
Khalsa, 14, 48, 58, 134, 154, 155, 206, 272, 274, 275, 297, 305-307
Khan, Afrasaid, 264
Khan, Ahmed, 232
Khan, Asad, 174, 175, 180
Khan, Bayzid, 188, 218, 219

Khan, Darbar, 285
Khan, Dindar, 162-164, 167
Khan, Gul, 45
Khan, Hamid, 202
Khan, Jalal, 166
Khan, Jamshed, 45
Khan, Kafi, 17
Khan, Khizir, 111
Khan, Mahabat, 186, 188, 194
Khan, Muhammad Amin, 185, 220, 227, 228, 231, 276, 289
Khan, Munim, 173, 175, 179-183, 188, 190, 195-196, 199, 200, 202
Khan, Muzaffar, 264
Khan, Nashtar, 111
Khan, Osman, 90-92, 94, 96, 98-102
Khan, Qamruddin, 264, 276
Khan, Rustamdil, 189, 201, 220, 227, 228, 231
Khan, Salim, 29, 30, 117
Khan, Samad, 109, 232, 233, 263, 264, 269, 271, 272, 276, 279, 281
Khan, Sarbrah, 201, 259, 286, 287, 289, 290
Khan, Sayyad Wajib-ud Din, 185, 186
Khan, Shahbad, 218, 219
Khan, Shamas, 185, 188, 218, 219
Khan, Suhrab, 261, 262, 272
Khan, Wali Muhammad, 111
Khan, Wazir, 15, 17, 67-69, 109-110, 112-114, 119-121, 123, 125-126, 136, 178, 194

Khan, Yaqub, 188
Khan, Zakariya, 232, 269, 276, 281, 293
Kiratpur, 66, 204, 206, 210
Kot Mirza Jan, 264, 265
Kotwal, Hassan Raza, 174
Kunwar, Lal, 231

Lagaan, 140, 305
Lahore, 64, 70, 107, 109, 135, 137, 154, 167, 179, 202, 220, 221, 222, 228, 231, 232, 263, 264, 279, 280, 281, 284, 293
Langar, 80, 155, 164, 165, 304, 306
Lodi, Bahlol, 107
Lohgarh, 131, 145-147, 151, 153, 155, 157, 160, 161, 165-166, 187, 189-193, 196-197, 206, 209, 231-233, 247, 271, 272

Machhiwara, 133, 167
Majha region, 167
Majhaili Sikhs, 66, 110, 111, 306
Malcolm, Lt. Col. M., 11,
Malerkotla, 65, 110, 111, 128, 129
Mewati, Firoz Khan, 183-187, 189
Mir, Mian, 222
Mir-i Miran, 107
Moradabad, 185
Mughal/s, 6, 7, 14, 15, 29, 39, 43-45, 46, 48, 53, 55, 56, 63, 65, 68-70, 73, 78, 83, 87, 100, 101, 108, 109, 110, 118, 123, 125, 133, 135, 136, 137, 140, 142, 144, 147, 151, 153, 154, 161,

166, 167, 168, 174, 178, 186, 186-194, 196-198, 199, 200, 202, 206, 209, 210, 218-221, 224, 225, 227, 231, 232, 233, 239, 247, 250, 256, 257, 262-273, 276-281, 283, 293
Muhammad, Darwesh, 174
Muhammad, Gul, 178, 179, 182, 201, 229, 230
Muhammad, Jan, 140
Mukaram, Khwaja, 256
Mukhlispur, 29, 30, 117-119, 141, 144, 145
Muslims, 53, 67, 108, 112, 114, 125-127, 136, 138, 140, 162-164, 168, 174, 176, 177, 180, 181, 190, 191, 225, 239, 248, 250, 288, 304
non, 92, 94, 95, 99, 109, 131, 138, 146, 176
Mustafabad, 85, 184

Nand, Nitya, 38
Nanded, 15, 37, 53, 55, 67, 68, 133, 138, 221, 240
Nath, Dina, 200
Nizamuddin, Sayyad, 91

Panipat, 64
Panj Piarey, 306
Pathans, 45, 91, 111, 256
Pir Dastgir, 221
Piran-i-Pir, 221
Prakash, Bhup, 202, 207
Prakash, Raja Hari, 207, 208

Prasad, Swami Janki, 33, 36
Punjab, 11, 39, 42, 45-47, 53, 58, 60, 61, 64-69, 72, 78, 81, 99, 105, 107-110, 112, 114, 133, 139, 140, 144, 154, 162, 165, 166, 168, 174, 175, 178-180, 182-186, 190, 202, 209, 220, 22, 235, 247, 257, 263, 264, 293

Qadir, Sayyad Muhammad Fazil-ud Din, 219, 220
Qadiri Silsila, 221-222
Qadiri, Inayat Shah, 222
Qasim, Muhammad, 15
Qutab-ul Aqtab dargah, 91

Rafik-us Sham, 194
Rahim, 200
Rahon, 166, 167, 168, 219
Rai, Hakumat, 92, 98, 102
Rai, Jaswant, 91-96, 98
Rai, Ram, 92, 96-98, 102
Raikot, 128, 133
Raj, Mulk, 24, 32
Rajputs, 133, 173-178, 181, 249, 263, 269
Rakhana, Hafiz Sultan, 108
Ram, Raja, 254
Rehras Sahib, 306
Ropar, 105, 110-112, 256

Sadhaura, 26, 29, 64, 85, 86, 90, 92, 94, 95, 98, 99, 113, 121, 128, 133, 140, 176, 184, 186-188, 209, 231, 232

Sagoo, Harbans Kaur, 14, 20
Saharanpur, 64, 133
Sain, Sidh, 208, 210
Sajda, 307
Samana, 64, 69-71, 73-76, 78-80, 85, 121, 128, 137, 138, 176, 184, 185, 219
Samanand family, 69
Sayyads, 70, 102
Shafiq, 200
Shah Jehan, 108, 180
Shah, Azim, 195, 231
Shah, Badar-ud Din (Sayyad Budhu Shah), 102
Shah, Bahadur, 11, 46, 64, 65, 68, 123, 137, 165, 168, 174-176, 178, 179, 180, 181, 182, 185, 188, 189, 190, 191, 193, 194, 196, 201, 202, 231, 289
Shah, Bulleh, 17, 42, 43, 221-223, 282, 283, 297, 299
Shah, Inayat, 42
Shah, Jahan, 195
Shah, Jahandar, 231
Shahbad, 85, 184
Shamsuddin, 71-73
Sikhs, 11, 14, 15, 17, 38, 39, 46-49, 53, 57-60, 63, 65-69, 71, 72, 75, 78, 80, 99, 100-102, 110-113, 119, 121, 122-124, 126, 128, 13, 137, 140, 144, 147, 150, 151, 153-155, 163-168, 174-178, 180, 181, 185-191, 195-200, 203, 206-210, 212, 217-220, 222, 228, 229, 231-233, 239, 248, 250, 251, 256, 257, 259, 262-266, 269-271, 274, 277, 279-281, 284-288, 290, 293, 294
Singh, Ajay, 173, 179, 258, 272, 289
Singh, Ali, 67, 68, 113, 122, 124
Singh, Baj, 17, 138, 188
Singh, Bhai Binod, 43, 45, 46, 48, 58, 76, 113, 127, 134, 135, 186, 187, 191, 192, 251, 264, 270, 272, 273, 275, 284
Singh, Bhai Daya, 46, 48, 60, 146
Singh, Bhai Kahan, 48, 274
Singh, Bhai Karan, 79
Singh, Bhai Prem, 145, 150
Singh, Bhai Raj, 48, 123, 251, 285
Singh, Bhai Ram, 48, 66, 79, 138, 186
Singh, Bhai, 126
Singh, Chuhar, 67
Singh, Dharam, 67, 122
Singh, Dindar (Dinar Khan), 164
Singh, Dr Ganda, 14, 15, 20
Singh, Dr Sukhdiyal, 15
Singh, Fateh, 17, 67, 71, 74, 75, 78, 79, 121, 124, 138, 251, 285
Singh, Gaj, 192, 251
Singh, Gulab, 193, 198-201
Singh, Gurbaksh, 21, 48
Singh, Guru Gobind, 13, 14, 17, 42, 46, 56, 69, 73, 75, 102, 109, 113, 151, 154, 155, 159, 178, 207, 208
Singh, Harinder, 13

Singh, Jagat, 256
Singh, Jai, 173, 179
Singh, Kahan, 274
Singh, Karam, 67, 121, 122
Singh, Labh, 266-268
Singh, Mali, 67, 68, 113
Singh, Malkiat, 19
Singh, Mir Nasir (Mir Nasir-ud Din), 164
Singh, Pratap, 213
Singh, Raja Amar, 174
Singh, Raja Man, 109
Singh, Raja Uday, 208-212, 215, 217
Singh, Randhir, 61-63
Singh, Ranjit, 267
Singh, Sant, 60, 85
Singh, Saran, 152
Singh, Sham, 124
Singh, Sohan, 15
Singh, Subha, 188
Singh, Trilok, 66
Singh, Zorawar, 75
Singha, Bhai, 126
Sirhind, 14, 17, 64, 67-69, 105, 107-110, 112, 113, 119, 121, 123, 124, 127, 128, 135, 137, 138, 140, 144, 146, 153, 157, 163, 167, 178, 185, 187, 188, 192, 257, 284, 292
Sirhindi, Sheikh Ahmed, 108

Siyar, Farukh, 231, 232
Sood community, 108, 109, 127, 163
Sood, Dev Dutt, 127
Suchanand, 113, 114, 125, 126
Sunam, 64
Suneti, 205, 218, 237
Swami, 307

Tagore, Rabindranath, 6
Tahir, Muhammad, 174
Tat Khalsa, 307
Thanesar, 85, 137, 186, 187, 188
Thaskar, 85
Tughlaq, Firoz, 107

Udaipur, 174
Ullah, Aman, 89

Vaishnavite, 13, 38, 39, 308

Wahab, Shah Abdul, 91

Yasin, Muhammad, 179

Zaman, Khan, 194
Zamindari system, 43, 79, 114, 138, 139, 209, 262
Zamindars, 113, 114, 138-140, 180, 209, 247, 262, 308